Eighth Edition

PMP® EXAM

Practice Test and Study Guide

ESI International   Arlington, VA

ESI
INTERNATIONAL
an **informa** business

J. LeRoy Ward, PMP, PgMP
Ginger Levin, DPA, PMP, PgMP

Published by

ESI International
901 North Glebe Road, Suite 200
Arlington, Virginia 22203

Parts of *A Guide to the Project Management Body of Knowledge*, 2008, are reprinted with permission of the Project Management Institute, Inc., Four Campus Boulevard, Newtown Square, Pennsylvania 19073-3299 U.S.A., a worldwide organization advancing the state of the art in project management.

"CAPM" is a certification mark of the Project Management Institute, Inc., which is registered in the United States and other nations.

"PgMP" is a certification mark of the Project Management Institute, Inc., which is registered in the United States and other nations.

"PMBOK" is a trademark of the Project Management Institute, Inc., which is registered in the United States and other nations.

"PMI" is a service and trademark of the Project Management Institute, Inc., which is registered in the United States and other nations.

"PMP" is a certification mark of the Project Management Institute, Inc., which is registered in the United States and other nations.

First Edition 1997
Second Edition 1998
Third Edition February 2001
Fourth Edition October 2001
Fifth Edition July 2003
Sixth Edition June 2005
Seventh Edition June 2006
Eighth Edition April 2009

Printed in the United States of America

ISBN 978-1-890367-52-7

CONTENTS

PREFACE

ESI International has been helping people to prepare for the project management professional (PMP®)[*] certification exam since early 1991. During the last 18 years, it has become quite clear that most prospective exam takers (ourselves included when we studied for the exam many years ago) ask two questions when they decide to earn PMP® certification: "What topics are covered on the exam?" and "What are the questions like?" Not surprisingly, some of the most sought-after study aids are practice tests, which are helpful in two ways: first, taking practice tests increases your knowledge of the kinds of questions, phrases, terminology, and sentence construction that you will encounter on the "real" exam; and second, taking practice tests provides an opportunity for highly concentrated study by exposing you to a breadth of project management content generally not found in a single reference source.

We initiated the development of this specialty publication with only one simple goal in mind: to help you study for, and pass, the PMP® certification exam. Because the Project Management Institute (PMI®)[**] does not sell "past" exams to prospective certification candidates for study purposes, the best anyone can do is to develop practice test questions that are as representative of the real questions as possible. And that is exactly what we have done.

ESI has an enviable cadre of instructors and consultants who not only know project management but also have taken the exam themselves and regularly teach others how to prepare for it. We decided to draw on this group of respected, knowledgeable professionals to help develop this publication.

The result of our collective effort is the *PMP® Exam: Practice Test and Study Guide*. This eighth edition—like the preceding seven—contains study hints, a list of exam topics, and 40 multiple-choice questions for each of the nine knowledge areas presented in *A Guide to the Project Management Body of Knowledge Fourth Edition*, better known as the *PMBOK® Guide*,[***] as well as 40 questions in the area of Professional and Social Responsibility, for a grand total of 400.

---

[*] "PMP" is a certification mark of the Project Management Institute, Inc., which is registered in the United States and other nations.
[**] "PMI" is a service and trademark of the Project Management Institute, Inc., which is registered in the United States and other nations.
[***] "PMBOK" is a trademark of the Project Management Institute, Inc., which is registered in the United States and other nations.

And as in previous editions, this edition includes a plainly written rationale for each correct answer, along with a supporting reference list. Our reference list alone took many weeks to compile. If you had nothing but the list of exam topics and the references, you would be well on your way to passing the exam.

You will find a reference to one or more of the five process groups, Initiating, Planning, Executing, Monitoring and Controlling, or Closing—plus the Professional and Social Responsibility domain—at the end of each rationale. Those references are important because they give you an understanding of the types of exam questions that fall within each of these six major project management performance domains.

This eighth edition includes many scenario-based questions, which comprise approximately 50 percent of the questions found on the PMP® exam. It omits many of the purely definitional questions; PMI® has gradually eliminated these types of questions from the exam.

We have included questions specifically related to the *PMBOK® Guide*'s nine knowledge areas and the various inputs, tools and techniques, and outputs described in the processes and subprocesses of those areas. Additionally, we have reduced the length of many of our questions, especially in the Professional and Social Responsibility section, to more accurately represent the real exam. Finally, in response to a number of requests we have included a completely original, 200-question practice test; none of these questions are found in the other sections of this book.

We have retained the helpful Study Matrix in this edition as well. The matrix is included as an appendix. The matrix, which is based on PMI®'s *Role Delineation Study,* will help you to use the 200-question exam to its full advantage. The matrix provides a way for you to assess your strengths and weaknesses in each performance domain and to identify areas that require further study.

A special note to those who speak English as a second language (ESL): Our experience in teaching project management programs around the world has shown that most of our ESL clients understand English well enough to pass the PMP® exam *as long as they know the content*. Nevertheless, in an effort to avoid adding to your frustration before taking the exam, we have painstakingly reviewed each question and answer in the practice test to ensure that we did not use words, terms, or phrases that could be confusing to those who are not fluent in English.

Although the language issue may concern you, and rightfully so, the only difference between you and those who speak English as their first language is the amount of time it takes to complete the exam. We know of only one person who did not have enough time, and that individual was able to complete all but two questions. We would suggest, therefore, that if you can grasp the content expressed in this publication, a few colloquialisms or ambiguous terms on the real exam will not ultimately determine whether you pass or fail: Your subject matter knowledge will do that!

Earning the PMP® certification is a prestigious accomplishment. But studying for it need not be difficult if you use the tools available. You may want to include our companion piece, *PMP® Exam Challenge!,* in your study plan if you have not already done so. In an easy flash-card format, it too provides many opportunities to become thoroughly familiar and comfortable with the project management body of knowledge. We would also like to recommend our CD audio set entitled "The Portable PMP® Prep: Conversations on Passing the PMP® Exam 4th Edition" if you are fluent in American English.

Good luck on the exam!

J. LeRoy Ward   Ginger Levin
Oak Hill, Virginia   Lighthouse Point, Florida

ABOUT THE AUTHORS

J. LeRoy Ward, Executive Vice President, is responsible for ESI's worldwide product offerings and international partnerships. Complementing a 17-year career with four U.S. federal agencies, Mr. Ward has delivered project management programs to clients around the world.

Mr. Ward has authored numerous articles and publications including *Dictionary of Project Management Terms*; with Ginger Levin, *PMP® Exam Challenge!*; with Carl Pritchard, *The Portable PMP® Prep: Conversations on Passing the PMP® Exam*, a nine-disc CD audio set; and with multiple authors, *ProjectFRAMEWORK®: A Project Management Maturity Model*. A dynamic and popular speaker, Mr. Ward frequently presents on program and project management and related topics at professional association meetings and conferences worldwide.

Mr. Ward holds bachelor of science and master of science degrees from Southern Connecticut State University and a master's of science degree in technology management *with distinction* from American University. He is a member of numerous professional associations, including the International Project Management Association, the American Society of Training and Development, and PMI®. He is certified by PMI® as a PMP® (No. 431) and a Program Management Professional (PgMP®)*, one of the first to earn the designation.

Dr. Ginger Levin is a senior consultant and educator in program and project management with more than 35 years of experience in the public and private sectors. Her specialty areas include project management, business development, maturity assessments, metrics, organizational change, knowledge management, and the project management office. She is a lecturer for the University of Wisconsin-Platteville in its master's degree program in project management and is its project management program specialist.

She is the coauthor of *Project Portfolio Management; Metrics for Project Management; Essential People Skills for Project Managers; Achieving Project*

---

* "PgMP" is a certification mark of the Project Management Institute, Inc., which is registered in the United States and other nations.

Management Success Using Virtual Teams; The Advanced Project Management Office: A Comprehensive Look at Function and Implementation; People Skills for Project Managers; Business Development Capability Maturity Model; and ESI International's *PMP® Challenge!*

Dr. Levin is a member of PMI® and is a frequent speaker at PMI® Congresses and Chapters and the International Project Management Association. She received her Certified Associate in Project Management (CAPM®)** in November 2003, PMP® certification in December 2005, PgMP® certification in June 2007, and the Organizational Project Management Maturity Model (*OPM3*) Product Suite certification as an assessor and consultant in 2006.

She received her doctorate from The George Washington University in public administration, where she also received the Outstanding Dissertation Award for her research on large organizations, her master of science in business administration from The George Washington University, and a bachelor of business administration from Wake Forest University.

** "CAPM" is a certification mark of the Project Management Institute, Inc., which is registered in the United States and other nations.

About ESI

ESI International delivers continuous learning programs that help technical and specialized professionals to better manage their programs, projects, contracts, requirements, and vendor relationships. Our high-quality training and professional services include more than 100 cross-functional courses as well as assessments and coaching services. Along with our academic partner, The George Washington University, ESI awards industry-recognized certificates, including Master's Certificates in Program Management, Project Management, Information Technology Project Management, and Government Contracting, as well as Professional Certificates in Business Analysis and Business Skills.

Our extensive global infrastructure, proven operational excellence, and results-oriented philosophy allow our corporate and government clients to develop their employees' skills, consistently implement strategic plans, and increase the effectiveness of their internal systems and processes. Since 1981, ESI has served more than 900,000 professionals and 1,000 clients worldwide.

Call toll free at 1 (888) ESI-8884 for a course catalog, or visit our Web site at www.esi-intl.com for more information.

ACKNOWLEDGMENTS

We are always amazed at the number of people it takes to get a publication out the door, and we would be remiss in not acknowledging the dedicated efforts of our colleagues who helped prepare what we consider to be a most important publication for PMP® exam takers.

Our special thanks to **Julie Grafstrom**, Editor, for her skillful and highly professional effort under an extraordinarily tight time frame, as well as for managing the entire project, and to **Jonathan Hurtarte**, Graphic Designer, for his cover design. Special thanks are extended to **Myron Taylor,** Editor-in-Chief, who manages all of ESI's product development projects.

We also would like to thank our friends and colleagues, who, through the years, have participated in this publication. They include **Rick Bilbro, Paul Chaney, Mike Farr, Leonard Krapcha, Bill Pursch, Ben Sellers, Ron Whitehead, Mary Saxton, Jeanne Trapani, Rosalie Lacorazza, Nicole Peters, Kim Briggs,** and **Carl Pritchard.** Their contributions to the various editions of this publication were critical to the success of this current edition, and we once again thank them for their help and encouragement.

Finally, we would like to thank **Joe Czarnecki,** PMP and senior consultant. Joe did a superb job updating many of our references and rationales, rewriting numerous questions to coincide with the latest edition of the *PMBOK® Guide*, and adding a host of new questions to challenge your knowledge and skills. His involvement has made this publication all the better.

INTRODUCTION

The PMP® exam contains 200 questions, of which 25 questions will not be included in the pass/fail determination. These "pretest" items, as PMI® calls them, will be randomly placed throughout the exam to gather statistical information on their performance to determine their use for future exams. Accordingly, to pass the PMP® exam, candidates must answer a minimum of 106 of the 175 scored questions, or roughly 61 percent.[*] Of the 175 scored questions, 11 percent relate to Initiating, 23 percent relate to Planning, 27 percent relate to Executing, 21 percent relate to Monitoring and Controlling, 9 percent relate to Closing, and 9 percent relate to Professional and Social Responsibility. We have followed a similar distribution in our practice test so that it is representative of the PMP® exam.[**]

To use the study guide effectively, work on one section at a time. It does not matter which you choose first. Start by reading the study hints. They provide useful background on the content of the PMP® exam and identify the emphasis placed on various topics. Familiarize yourself with the major topics listed. Then answer the 40 practice questions, recording your answers on the sheet provided. Finally, compare your answers with those in the answer key. The rationales provided should clarify any misconceptions you may have had, and the process group designations will give you an understanding of the types of questions you might see on the exam that relate to those process groups. For further study and clarification, you may want to consult the bibliographic reference.

After you have finished answering the questions that follow each section, it is time to take the completely rewritten and original, 200-question practice test. Note your answers on the sheet provided, compare your answers to the answer key, and use the Study Matrix in the Appendix to determine what areas you need to study further.

---

[*] Remember, the 106 questions you need to get correct must be from the 175 scored questions. Simply getting 106 questions correct does not mean a passing grade if one or more of these come from the 25 pretest questions. Our suggestion, therefore, is to try to get at least 131 correct when you take the exam. When taking the 200-question exam in this book, we suggest you try to get 160 correct.

[**] The distribution has been applied to all 200 questions in our practice test in this Guide.

To make the most of this book, use it regularly. Take and retake the practice test. Photocopy the answer sheet in order to have a clean one each time you retake the test. Convene a study group to compare your answers with those of your colleagues. This method of study is a powerful one. You will learn more from your colleagues than you ever thought possible! Make sure you have a solid understanding of the exam topics that are provided in each section. Consult our extensive bibliography, or other sources you have found useful, for further independent study. And, most important, create a study plan and stick to it. Your chances of success are raised dramatically when you dedicate yourself to your goal.

ACRONYMS

AC	actual cost
AD	activity duration
ADM	arrow diagramming method
BAC	budget at completion
CAPM®	Certified Associate in Project Management
CEO	chief executive officer
CPI	cost performance index
CPM	critical path method
CV	cost variance
EAC	estimate at completion
EMV	expected monetary value
ERP	enterprise resource planning
ETC	estimate to complete
EV	earned value
EVM	earned value management
GAAP	Generally Accepted Accounting Principles
GERT	graphical evaluation and review technique
IFB	invitation for bid
ISO	International Organization for Standardization
JIT	just-in-time
LCC	life-cycle cost
MBO	management by objectives
MRP	material requirements planning
OBS	organizational breakdown structure
PDM	precedence diagramming method
PERT	program evaluation and review technique
PgMP®	Program Management Professional
PMBOK® Guide	*A Guide to the Project Management Body of Knowledge*
PMI®	Project Management Institute
PMIS	project management information system
PMO	program management office
PMP®	Project Management Professional

PRC	project review committee
PV	planned value
RFP	request for proposal
ROI	return on investment
SD	standard deviation
SPC	statistical process control
SPI	schedule performance index
SV	schedule variance
SWOT	strengths-weaknesses-opportunities-threats
TCPI	to-complete performance index
VAC	variance at completion
WBS	work breakdown structure

PROJECT INTEGRATION MANAGEMENT

Study Hints

The Project Integration Management questions on the PMP® certification exam address critical project management functions that ensure coordination of the various elements of the project. As the *PMBOK® Guide* explains, the processes focus on integration activities designed to ensure project success; therefore, integration characteristics involve unification, consolidation, and articulation as well as integrative activities. Project Integration Management involves making trade-offs among competing objectives to meet or exceed stakeholder needs and expectations and addresses project initiation with the development of a project charter, project plan development, project plan execution, monitoring and controlling the project work, integrated change control, and closing the project. These six processes not only interact with one another but also interact with processes in the other eight knowledge areas. It is important to note PMI®'s view that integration occurs in other areas as well. For example, project scope and product scope need to be integrated, project work needs to be integrated with other ongoing work of the organization, and deliverables from various technical specialties need integration.

The Project Integration Management questions are relatively straightforward. Most people find them to be fairly easy. But because they cover so much material, including all five process groups, you do need to study them carefully to become familiar with PMI®'s terminology and perspectives. *PMBOK® Guide* Figure 4-1 provides an overview of the structure of Project Integration Management. Know this chart thoroughly.

Following is a list of the major Project Integration Management topics. Use it to help focus your study efforts on the areas most likely to appear on the exam.

Major Topics

Project, program, and portfolio definitions

Project management definition

Project life cycle

Project management office

Project process groups

- Initiating
- Planning
- Executing
- Monitoring and Controlling
- Closing

Business case

Project statement of work

Develop project charter

Enterprise environmental factors

Organizational process assets

Stakeholders

Project management information system (PMIS)

Earned value technique

Expert judgment

Project management plan

Direct and manage project execution

Corrective and preventive action

Deliverables

Work performance information

Major Topics (continued)

Interpersonal skills

- Team building
- Decision making
- Leadership
- Communicating
- Negotiating and conflict management
- Problem solving
- Influencing
- Motivation
- Political and cultural awareness

Standards and regulations

Monitor and control project work

Performance reports

Forecasts

Integrated change control

Change requests

Change control meetings

Change control procedures

Change management plan

Configuration management plan

Configuration management system

- Objectives
- Steps to follow

Close project

Administrative closure procedure

Product, service, or result transition

Lessons learned

Practice Questions

INSTRUCTIONS: Note the most suitable answer for each multiple-choice question in the appropriate space on the answer sheet.

1. You work for a software development company that has followed the waterfall development model for more than 20 years. Lately, a number of customers have complained that your company is taking too long to complete its projects. You attended a class on agile development methods and believe that if the company used the agile approach, it could provide products to clients in a shorter time period. However, it would be a major culture change to switch from the waterfall methodology to the agile approach and to train staff members in this new approach. You mentioned this idea to the director of the PMO, and although she liked the idea, she would need approval from the company's portfolio review board to move forward with it. She suggested that you document this idea in a—

   a. Business need
   b. Product scope description
   c. Project charter
   d. Business case

2. You are managing a large project with 20 key internal stakeholders, 8 contractors, and 6 team leaders. You must devote attention to effective integrated change control. This means you are concerned primarily with—

   a. Reviewing, approving, and controlling changes
   b. Maintaining baseline integrity, integrating product and project scope, and coordinating change across knowledge areas
   c. Integrating deliverables from different functional specialties on the project
   d. Establishing a change control board that oversees the overall project changes

3. Management wants your project to yield high-value results at a low cost. Your internal client wants all the features identified regardless of the cost. When working with stakeholders, you should—

   a. Group stakeholders into categories for easy identification
   b. Proactively curtail stakeholder activities that might affect the project adversely
   c. Be sensitive to the fact that stakeholders often have very different objectives and that this makes stakeholder management difficult
   d. Recognize that roles and responsibilities may overlap

4. You are evaluating two projects and your management has asked you to determine the return on sales (ROS). Project A has projected revenues of $3.5 million; the total costs for this project are $3.3 million. Project B has projected revenues of $105 million; the costs are estimated to be $98 million. Based on the ROS, what can you conclude about these two projects?

   a. Project B has a 7.1 ROS, which is higher than that of Project A.
   b. Project A has a 6.1 ROS, which is more favorable than that of Project B.
   c. Project B has a 9.3 ROS, which is more favorable than that of Project A.
   d. Project A has a 5.7 ROS, which is more favorable than that of Project B.

5. You are leading a team to establish a project selection and prioritization method. The team is considering many different management concerns, including financial return, market share, and public perception. The most important criteria for building a project selection model is—

   a. Capability
   b. Realism
   c. Ease of use
   d. Cost

6. When you established the change control board for your avionics project, you established specific procedures to govern its operation. The procedures require all approved changes to be reflected in the—

   a. Performance measurement baseline
   b. Change management plan
   c. Quality assurance plan
   d. Project management plan

7. You are beginning a new project staffed with a virtual team located across five countries. To help avoid conflict in work priorities among your team members and their functional managers, you ask the project sponsor to prepare a—

   a. Memo to team members informing them that they work for you now
   b. Project charter
   c. Memo to the functional managers informing them that you have authority to direct their employees
   d. Human resource management plan

8. The purpose of economic value added (EVA) is to—

    a. Determine the opportunity costs associated with the project
    b. Determine a non–time-dependent measure of profit or return
    c. Assess the net operating profit after taxes
    d. Evaluate the return on capital percent versus the cost of capital percent

9. Your company is embarking on a project to completely eliminate defects in its products. You are the project manager for this project, and you have just finished the concept phase. The deliverable for this phase is the—

    a. Project plan
    b. Statement of work
    c. Project charter
    d. Resource spreadsheet

10. Certain types of communications styles are more effective in different phases of the project life cycle. For example, during the closing phase of the project, ideally, the project manager should use a(n)—

    a. Abstract/sequential style
    b. Concrete/random style
    c. Concrete/sequential style
    d. Abstract/random style

11. Your organization is characterized by hierarchical organizational structures with rigid rules and policies and strict supervisory controls. Individual team members are not expected to engage in problem solving or use creative approaches to plan and execute work; management does that. Your organization is characterized by which one of the following theories?

    a. Ouchi's Theory
    b. McGregor's Theory X
    c. Maslow's self-esteem level
    d. Vroom's Expectancy Theory

12. You are a member of your company's project selection committee. It meets quarterly to determine what new projects to undertake. A key factor used in making these decisions is the—

    a. Product description
    b. Key performance indicators
    c. Strategic plan
    d. Project success factors

13. You work for a telecommunications company, and when developing a project management plan for a new project, you found that you must tailor some company processes because the product is so different than those products typically produced by your company. To tailor these processes, you will follow—

  a. Specific guidelines and criteria
  b. Standardized guidelines
  c. Historical information contained in the company's lessons-learned knowledge base
  d. Files from previous projects

14. You are implementing a project management methodology for your company that requires you to establish a change control board. Which one of the following statements best describes a change control board?

  a. Recommended for use on all (large and small) projects
  b. Used to review, evaluate, approve, delay, or reject changes to the project
  c. Managed by the project manager, who also serves as its secretary
  d. Composed of key project team members

15. An automated tool, a configuration management system, an information collection and distribution system, and web interfaces to other online automated systems are examples of—

  a. Organizational process assets
  b. Project management information systems
  c. Project management planning approaches
  d. Tools and techniques for project plan development

16. You realize that leadership without management or management without leadership probably will produce poor project results. Which one of the following key responsibilities best represents project leadership?

  a. Developing a vision and strategy, and motivating people to achieve them
  b. Getting things done through other people
  c. Using charismatic power to motivate others even if they don't like the work
  d. Using all types of power, as appropriate, as motivational tools

17. You have been directed to establish a change control system for your company, but must convince your colleagues to use it. To be effective, the change control system must include—

    a. Procedures that define how project documents may be changed
    b. Specific change requests expected on the project and plans to respond to each one
    c. Performance reports that forecast project changes
    d. A description of the functional and physical characteristics of an item or system

18. According to Herzberg's Motivator-Hygiene Theory, when achievement; recognition; responsibility; and advancement, or promotion, are not present, employees will—

    a. Become alienated with the organization and leave
    b. Lack motivation but will not be dissatisfied with their work
    c. Lack motivation and become dissatisfied with their work
    d. Become dissatisfied only if they do not receive salary increases

19. You are a member of a project selection committee using the discounted cash-flow approach. Using this approach, the project is acceptable if the—

    a. Sum of the net present value of all estimated cash flow during the life of the project equals the profit
    b. Net present value of the inflow is greater than the net present value of the outflow by a specified amount or percentage
    c. Gross present value of all future expected cash flow divided by the initial cash investment is greater than one
    d. Payback period occurs by the second year of the project

20. You are project manager for a systems integration effort and need to procure the hardware components from external sources. Your subcontracts administrator has told you to prepare a product description, which is referenced in a—

    a. Project statement of work
    b. Contract scope statement
    c. Request for proposal
    d. Contract

21. Because your project is slated to last five years, you believe rolling wave planning is appropriate. It provides information about the work to be done—

    a. Throughout all project phases
    b. For successful completion of the current project phase
    c. For successful completion of the current and subsequent project phases
    d. In the next project phase

22. You want to minimize the impact of changes on your project, yet you want to ensure that change is managed when and if it occurs. This can be done through each of the following ways EXCEPT—

    a. Rejecting requested changes
    b. Approving changes and incorporating them into a revised baseline
    c. Documenting the complete impact of requested changes
    d. Ensuring that project scope changes are reflected in changes to product scope

23. You are managing a project to introduce a new product to the marketplace that is expected to have a very long life. In this situation, the concept of being *temporary*, which is part of the definition of a project,—

    a. Does not apply because the project will have a lasting result
    b. Does not apply to the product to be created
    c. Recognizes that the project team will outlive the actual project
    d. Does not apply because the project will not be short in duration

24. According to the expectancy theory of motivation—

    a. Poor performance is the natural outcome of poor training
    b. Managers should not expect too much of workers
    c. Motivation to act is linked to an outcome that is expected to have value
    d. Managers should expect that employees who are paid more will work harder

25. All the following are project baselines that are generally part of the project management plan EXCEPT—

    a. Technical
    b. Scope
    c. Time
    d. Cost

26. You are responsible for a project management training curriculum that is offered throughout the organization. In this situation, your intangible deliverables are—

    a. Employees who can apply the training effectively
    b. Training materials for each course
    c. Certificates of completion for everyone who completes the program
    d. The training curriculum as advertised in your catalog

27. Project governance is important on any project and especially on those projects that are complex and long in duration. Assume that you are the project manager for the development of an ultra-definition TV set that will replace existing high-definition TVs. There is a mandate that all TVs be ultra-definition sets in five years. Your company felt a governance board would be useful in this important project. Therefore, as part of your project management plan, you should include—

    a. Processes for the operation of the board
    b. A list of the board members and their levels of authority and responsibility
    c. Key management reviews for content, extent, and timing
    d. The actions the project manager can take on his or her own without involvement from the board

28. Ideally, a project manager should be selected and assigned at which point in the project life cycle?

    a. During the initiating processes
    b. During the project planning process
    c. At the end of the concept phase of the project life cycle
    d. Prior to the beginning of the development phase of the project life cycle

29. Closing a project phase should not be delayed until project completion because—

    a. Useful information may be lost
    b. The project manager may be reassigned
    c. Project team members may be reassigned by that time
    d. Sellers are anxious for payments

30. The most appropriate management style to use to encourage your staff to pool its knowledge about project issues to make the best decisions possible is—

    a. Laissez-faire
    b. Democratic
    c. Autocratic
    d. Directive

31. Project management processes describe project work, while product-oriented management processes specify the project's product. Therefore, a project management process and a product-oriented management process—

    a. Overlap and interact throughout the project
    b. Are defined by the project life cycle
    c. Are concerned with describing and organizing project work
    d. Are similar for each application area

32. The close project or phase process addresses actions and activities concerning all of the following EXCEPT—

    a. Completion or exit criteria for the project or phase has been met
    b. Stakeholder approval that the project has meet their requirements
    c. Review of the project and/or phase information for potential future use
    d. Documentation that completed deliverables have been accepted ✓

33. You are a personnel management specialist recently assigned to a project team working on a team-based reward and recognition system. The other team members also work in the human resources department. The project charter should be issued by—

    a. The project manager
    b. The client
    c. A sponsor external to the project
    d. A member of the PMO who has jurisdiction over human resources

34. Your project is proceeding according to schedule. You have just learned that a new regulatory requirement will cause a change in one of the project's performance specifications. To ensure that this change is incorporated into the project plan, you should—

    a. Call a meeting of the change control board
    b. Change the WBS, project schedule, and project plan to reflect the new requirement
    c. Prepare a change request
    d. Immediately inform all affected stakeholders of the new approach to take on the project

35. The level of Maslow's theory of motivation characterized by responsibility, a sense of accomplishment, and a sense of competence is called—

    a. Self-actualization
    b. Social
    c. Esteem
    d. Physiological

36. Change is inevitable in the project environment. It therefore is important to learn to identify, analyze, and overcome resistance to change and to become effective change agents. One tool to help in this process is force field analysis. It was developed by—

    a. Chris Argyris
    b. Kurt Lewin
    c. Warren Bennis
    d. Larry Greiner

37. Oftentimes when a project is terminated, senior managers will replace the project manager with an individual who is skilled at closing out projects. If this is done, the first step for the termination manager should be to—

    a. Notify all relevant stakeholders of the termination
    b. Complete the lessons learned report
    c. Conduct an immediate review of the work packages
    d. Review the status of all contracts

38. On your project you want to avoid bureaucracy, so you adopt an informal approach to change control. The main problem with this approach is—

    a. There is no "paper trail" of change activity
    b. Regular disagreements between the project manager and the functional manager
    c. There are misunderstandings regarding what was agreed to
    d. Lack of sound cost estimating to assess the change's impact

39. Projects are supposed to succeed, not fail. However, termination is an option to consider when all but which one of the following conditions exist?

    a. The customer's strategy has changed.
    b. There are new stakeholders.
    c. Competition may make the project results obsolete.
    d. The original purposes for the project have changed.

40. All projects involve some extent of change, because they involve work that is unique in some fashion. Therefore, it is important that a project management plan includes a—

    a. Description of the change request process
    b. Configuration management plan
    c. Methodology for preventive action to avoid the need for excessive changes
    d. A work authorization system

Answer Sheet

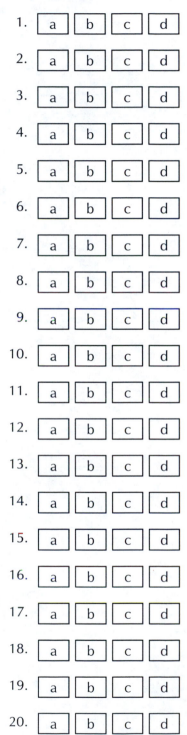

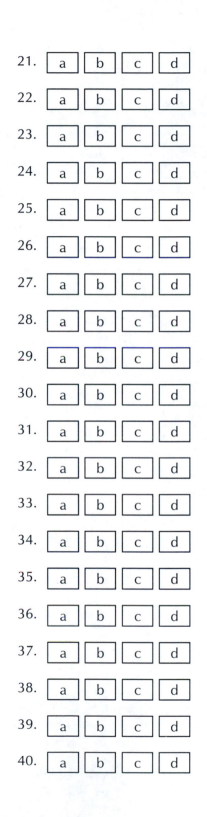

1. a b c d
2. a b c d
3. a b c d
4. a b c d
5. a b c d
6. a b c d
7. a b c d
8. a b c d
9. a b c d
10. a b c d
11. a b c d
12. a b c d
13. a b c d
14. a b c d
15. a b c d
16. a b c d
17. a b c d
18. a b c d
19. a b c d
20. a b c d

21. a b c d
22. a b c d
23. a b c d
24. a b c d
25. a b c d
26. a b c d
27. a b c d
28. a b c d
29. a b c d
30. a b c d
31. a b c d
32. a b c d
33. a b c d
34. a b c d
35. a b c d
36. a b c d
37. a b c d
38. a b c d
39. a b c d
40. a b c d

Answer Key

1. d. Business case

The business case is used to provide the necessary information to determine whether or not a project is worth its investment. It is used to justify the project and typically contains a cost-benefit analysis. [Initiating]

PMI®, *PMBOK® Guide*, 2008, 75

2. a. Reviewing, approving, and controlling changes

Performing integrated change control consists of coordinating and managing changes across the project. Activities that occur within the context of perform integrated change control include: verify scope, control scope, control schedule, control costs, perform quality control, monitor and control risks, and administer procurements. [Monitoring and Controlling]

PMI®, *PMBOK® Guide*, 2008, 93–96

3. c. Be sensitive to the fact that stakeholders often have very different objectives and that this makes stakeholder management difficult

A project stakeholder is an individual or organization who is actively involved in the project or whose interests may be affected, either positively or negatively, as a result of project execution or successful project completion. Stakeholders also may exert influence on the project and its results. Managing stakeholder expectations is difficult because stakeholders often have different, conflicting objectives. [Monitoring and Controlling]

PMI®, *PMBOK® Guide*, 2008, 23–24

4. a. Project B has a 7.1 ROS, which is higher than that of Project A.

ROS = [(revenues/costs) − 1] x 100 and is a non–time-dependent measure of profit or return as a percentage of a project's total cost. A negative return on sales indicates a loss. ROS is a ratio that expresses how much net income a company earns from each dollar of revenue. In this situation, Project B has a 7.1 ROS, while Project A has a 6.1 ROS. [Initiating]

Cohen and Graham 2001, 223

5. b. Realism

The model should reflect the objectives of the company and its managers; consider the realities of the organization's limitations on facilities, capital, and personnel; and include factors for risk—the technical risks of performance, cost, and time and the market risk of customer rejection. [Initiating]

Meredith and Mantel 2009, 41

6. d. Project management plan

The project management plan must be updated continually to reflect project modifications, and those changes must be communicated to appropriate stakeholders in a timely manner. [Monitoring and Controlling]

PMI®, *PMBOK® Guide*, 2008, 93

7. b. Project charter

Although the project charter cannot stop conflicts from arising, it can provide a framework to help resolve them, because it describes the project manager's authority to apply organizational resources to project activities. [Initiating]

Meredith and Mantel 2009, 168; PMI®, *PMBOK® Guide*, 2008, 77–78

8. d. Evaluate the return on capital percent versus the cost of capital percent

EVA quantifies the value a company provides to its investors and seeks to determine if a company is creating or destroying value to its shareholders. It is calculated by subtracting the expected return, (represented by the capital charge), from the actual return that a company generates, (represented by net operating profit after taxes). [Initiating]

Cohen and Graham 2001, 217

9. c. Project charter

This document signifies official sanction by top management and starts the planning or development phase. The project charter formally recognizes the existence of the project and provides the project manager with the authority to apply organizational resources to project activities. [Initiating]

PMI®, *PMBOK® Guide*, 2008, 77–78

10. c. Concrete/sequential style

When closing a project, the project team is concerned with transferring the product and information to the users. The concrete/sequential style is recommended because the focus is on logical organization, evaluating alternatives, and fixing problems without losing sight of details and administrative issues [Closing]

Verma 1996, 49–51

11. b. McGregor's Theory X

McGregor observed two types of managers and classified them by their perceptions of workers. Theory X managers thought that workers were lazy, needed to be watched and supervised closely, and were irresponsible. Theory Y managers thought that, given the correct conditions, workers could be trusted to seek responsibility and work hard at their jobs. [Executing]

McGregor 1960, 33–35; Verma 1996, 70–71

12. c. Strategic plan

All projects should be supportive of the strategic goals as stated in the organization's strategic plan. The strategic plan is an input in the initiating process before a project is authorized, and its charter is prepared. [Initiating]

PMI®, *PMBOK® Guide*, 2008, 75

13. a. Specific guidelines and criteria

Project management plan templates are an organizational process asset to consider as the project plan is developed. They include guidelines and criteria to tailor the organization's set of standard processes to satisfy the specific needs of the project.

PMI®, *PMBOK® Guide*, 2008, 80

14. b. Used to review, evaluate, approve, delay, or reject changes to the project

The change control board's powers and responsibilities should be well defined and agreed upon by key stakeholders. On some projects, multiple change control boards may exist with different areas of responsibility. [Monitoring and Controlling]

PMI®, *PMBOK® Guide*, 2008, 94

15. b. Project management information systems

Enterprise environmental factors influence the development of the project management plan. The project management information system is an example of an enterprise environmental factors that may be helpful.

PMI®, *PMBOK® Guide*, 2008, 80

16. a   Developing a vision and strategy, and motivating people to achieve them

Leadership involves developing a vision of the future and strategies to achieve that vision, positioning people to carry out the vision, and helping people energize themselves to overcome any barriers to change. [Executing]

PMI®, *PMBOK® Guide*, 2008, 240, 409–413

17. a. Procedures that define how project documents may be changed

A change control system is a collection of formal, documented procedures that define the process used to control change and approve project documents. It includes the paperwork, tracking systems, and approval levels necessary to authorize changes. It also provides guidance on when changes can be approved without formal review. [Monitoring and Controlling]

PMI®, *PMBOK® Guide*, 2008, 80 and 96

18. c. Lack motivation and become dissatisfied with their work

Herzberg advanced the theory that hygiene factors, such as the poor attitude of a supervisor, lead to dissatisfaction but not usually to decreased motivation. When motivators, such as responsibility and recognition, are lacking, they lead to job dissatisfaction, but when such motivators are present, they tend to motivate a person in the performance of his or her work. [Executing]

Verma 1996, 64–65

19. b. Net present value of the inflow is greater than the net present value of the outflow by a specified amount or percentage

The discounted cash-flow approach—or the present value method—determines the net present value of all cash flow by discounting it by the required rate of return. The impact of inflation also may be considered. Early in the life of a project, net cash flow is likely to be negative, because the major outflow is the initial investment in the project. When the project is successful, cash flow will become positive. [Initiating]

Meredith and Mantel 2009, 47

20. a. Project statement of work

The project statement of work describes in a narrative form the products or services that the project will deliver. It references the product scope description as well as the business needs and the strategic plan. [Initiating]

PMI®, *PMBOK® Guide*, 2008, 75

21. c. For successful completion of the current and subsequent project phases

Rolling wave planning provides progressive detailing of the work to be accomplished throughout the life of the project, indicating that planning and documentation are iterative and ongoing processes. [Planning]

PMI®, *PMBOK® Guide*, 2008, 46 and 439

22. d. Ensuring that project scope changes are reflected in changes to product scope

Integrated change control requires maintaining the integrity of baselines by releasing only approved changes into project products or services. It also ensures that changes to product scope are reflected in the project scope definition. This is done by coordinating changes across the entire project. [Monitoring and Controlling]

PMI®, *PMBOK® Guide*, 2008, 93

23. b. Does not apply to the product to be created

A project is completed when its objectives have been achieved or when they are recognized as being unachievable and the project is terminated. In this case, the end will occur when the product is finished. Thus, the concept of *temporary* applies to the project life cycle—not the product life cycle. [Planning]

PMI®, *PMBOK® Guide*, 2008, 5

24. c. Motivation to act is linked to an outcome that is expected to have value

The strength of a tendency to act in a certain way depends on both the strength of an expectation that this act will be followed by a given outcome and the value of that outcome. [Executing]

Vroom 1995, 20; Verma 1996, 73

25. a. Technical

Scope, time, and cost are examples of project baselines to be part of the project management plan.

PMI®, *PMBOK® Guide*, 2008, 82

26. a. Employees who can apply the training effectively

Most deliverables are tangible, such as buildings or roads; but intangible deliverables also can be provided. Information on work performance is collected during project execution and becomes an input to the performance reporting process for the project. [Executing]

PMI®, *PMBOK® Guide*, 2008, 83

27. c. Key management reviews for content, extent, and timing

Various items are recommended to be part of the project management plan. One is to determine the key management reviews that will be held for content, extent, and timing to facilitate how open issues and pending decisions will be addressed.

PMI®, *PMBOK® Guide*, 2008, 82

28. a. During the initiating processes

When the project manager is selected and assigned to the project during initiation, several of the usual start-up tasks for a project are simplified. In addition, becoming involved with project activities from the beginning helps the project manager to understand where the project fits within the organization in terms of its priority relative to other projects and the ongoing work of the organization. [Initiating]

Meredith and Mantel 2009, 107; PMI®, *PMBOK® Guide*, 2008, 73

29. a. Useful information may be lost

Closure includes collecting project records, ensuring that the records accurately reflect final specifications, analyzing project or phase success and effectiveness, and archiving such information for future use. Each phase of the project should be properly closed while important project information is still available. [Closing]

PMI®, *PMBOK® Guide*, 2008, 64

30. b. Democratic

A democratic management style provides maximum participation for the development of creative solutions in the group. Watch out, however, for the "tyranny of the majority," where voting can drown a creative voice. This style would not be effective in an emergency situation where fast action is required. [Executing]

Frame 2003, 30

31. a. Overlap and interact throughout the project

Project management processes and product-oriented management processes must be integrated throughout the project's life cycle, given their close relationship. In some cases, it's difficult to distinguish between the two. For example, knowing how the project will be created aids in determining the project's scope. [Executing]

PMI®, *PMBOK® Guide*, 2008, 15–21

32. d. Documentation that completed deliverables have been accepted

Documentation that the completed deliverables have been accepted is prepared as an output of verify scope. The close project or phase procedures provides a listing of necessary activities, including: confirmation that the project has met sponsor, customer, and other stakeholder requirements; satisfaction and validation that the completion and exit criteria have been met; the transfer of deliverables to the next phase or to production/operations has been accomplished; and activities to collect, audit, and archive project information and gather lessons learned have been addressed. [Closing]

PMI®, *PMBOK® Guide*, 2008, 99–100

33. c. A sponsor external to the project

The project charter should be issued by a project initiator or sponsor outside the project but at a level appropriate to the project's needs. Because it provides the project manager with the authority to apply organizational resources to project activities, the project charter should not be issued by the project manager, although, the project manager can assist in its development. Functional managers should have approval authority. [Initiating]

PMI®, *PMBOK® Guide*, 2008, 74

34. c. Prepare a change request

The change request should detail the nature of the change and its effect on the project. Documentation is critical to provide a record of the change and who approved it, in case differences of opinion arise later. A change request is an output from the direct and manage project execution process and an input to the perform integrated change control process. [Monitoring and Controlling]

PMI®, *PMBOK® Guide*, 2008, 93

35. c. Esteem

Other examples of esteem needs include self-respect, recognition, and a sense of equity. [Executing]

Maslow 1954, 80–92; Verma 1996, 60–63

36. b. Kurt Lewin

Kurt Levin, who developed force field analysis, thought that change is not just an event but is a dynamic balance of opposing forces. He reasoned that any situation can reach a state of equilibrium resulting from a balance of forces pushing against each other. Mr. Levin advanced the idea that behavior change follows a three-step process: unfreezing, changing, and refreezing. [Monitoring and Controlling]

Verma, 1997, 28–30

37. c. Conduct an immediate review of the work packages

A thorough review of the work packages will provide a complete accounting of the physical progress achieved on the project. This is the first step in attempting to improve performance. [Closing]

Cleland and Ireland 2007, 365–375

38. c. There are misunderstandings regarding what was agreed to

Using a formal, documented approach to change management reduces the level of misunderstanding or uncertainty regarding the nature of the change and its impact on cost and schedule. For large projects, change control boards are recommended. [Monitoring and Controlling]

Meredith and Mantel 2009, 574

39. b. There are new stakeholders.

As long as the new stakeholders agree with the project's business case, the work should continue. However, if any of the other events occur, termination should be considered. [Closing]

Cleland and Ireland 2007, 365–375

40. b. Configuration management plan

A configuration management plan is part of a project management plan to document how configuration management will be performed on the project.

PMI®, *PMBOK® Guide*, 2008, 82

PROJECT SCOPE MANAGEMENT

Study Hints

The Project Scope Management questions on the PMP® certification exam cover a diverse, yet fundamental, set of project management topics. Collecting requirements, creating the WBS, defining the project life cycle, developing a project scope statement, scope verification, developing a requirements management plan, creating a scope management plan, and managing scope changes are among the topics covered.

PMI® views Project Scope Management as a five-step process that consists of collect requirements, define scope, create WBS, verify scope, and control scope. *PMBOK® Guide* Figure 5-1 provides an overview of this structure. Know this chart thoroughly.

The Project Scope Management questions on the exam are straightforward. Historically, most people have found them to be relatively easy; however, do not be lulled into a false sense of security by past results. These questions cover a wide breadth of material, and you must be familiar with the terminology and perspectives adopted by PMI®.

Following is a list of the major Project Scope Management topics. Use it to help focus your study efforts on the areas most likely to appear on the exam.

Major Topics

Project scope management plan

Collect requirements

- Tools and techniques
- Requirements documentation
- Requirements management plan
- Requirements traceability matrix

Define scope

- Product analysis
- Alternatives analysis
- Facilitated workshops
- Project scope statement

Create WBS

- Benefits
- Uses
- Development/decomposition
- WBS dictionary
- Scope baseline

Verify scope

- Inspection
- Accepted deliverables

Control scope

- Variance analysis
- Work performance measurements
- Updates to the project management plan and to the project documents

Practice Questions

INSTRUCTIONS: Note the most suitable answer for each multiple-choice question in the appropriate space on the answer sheet.

1. Progressive elaboration of product characteristics on your project must be coordinated carefully with the—

   a. Proper project scope definition
   b. Project stakeholders
   c. Scope change control system
   d. Customer's strategic plan

2. You are examining multiple scope change requests on a project you were asked to take over because the previous project manager decided to resign. To assess the degree to which the project scope will change, you need to compare the requests to which project document?

   a. Preliminary scope statement
   b. WBS
   c. Project plan
   d. Scope management plan

3. You and your project team recognize the importance of project scope management to a project's overall success; therefore, you include only the work required for successful completion of the project. The first step in the Project Scope Management process is to—

   a. Clearly distinguish between project scope and product scope
   b. Prepare a scope management plan
   c. Define and document your stakeholders' needs to meet the project's objectives
   d. Capture and manage both project and product requirements

4. An example of an organizational process asset that could affect how project scope is managed is—

   a. Personnel policies
   b. Marketplace conditions
   c. Project files from previous projects
   d. Organizational culture

5. You are managing a complex project for a new method of heating and air conditioning in vehicles. You will use both solar and wind technologies in this project to reduce energy costs. Therefore, you must ensure that the work of your project will result in delivering the project's specified scope, which means that you should measure completion of the product scope against the—

   a. Scope management plan
   b. Scope statement
   c. Product requirements
   d. Requirements management plan

6. A key tool and technique used in scope definition is—

   a. Templates, forms, and standards
   b. Decomposition
   c. Expert judgment
   d. Project management methodology

7. Alternatives identification often is useful in defining project scope. An example of a technique that can be used is—

   a. Sensitivity analysis
   b. Decision trees
   c. Mathematical model
   d. Lateral thinking

8. Product analysis techniques include all the following EXCEPT—

   a. Value engineering
   b. Value analysis
   c. Systems analysis
   d. Bill of materials

9. The baseline for evaluating whether requests for changes or additional work are contained within or outside the project's boundaries is provided by the—

   a. Project management plan
   b. Project scope statement
   c. Project scope management plan
   d. WBS dictionary

10. Rather than use a WBS, your team developed a bill of materials to define the project's work components. A customer review of this document uncovered that a scope change was needed, because a deliverable had not been defined and a change request was written subsequently. This is an example of a change request that was the result of—

    a. An external event
    b. An error or omission in defining the scope of the product
    c. A value-adding change
    d. An error or omission in defining the scope of the project

11. Collecting requirements is critical in project scope management as it becomes the foundation for the project's—

    a. Scope management plan
    b. WBS
    c. Schedule
    d. Scope change control system

12. The project scope description addresses and documents all the following items EXCEPT—

    a. Characteristics and boundaries of the project
    b. The relationship between the deliverables and the business need
    c. The characteristics of the product
    d. Project management methodology (PMM)

13. The first step in collecting requirements on any project, large or small, is to—

    a. Talk with the project stakeholders through interviews
    b. Review the project charter and stakeholder register
    c. Review the project management plan, especially the scope management plan
    d. Prepare a requirements document template that you and your team can use throughout the collect requirements process

14. You want to structure your project so that each project team member has a discrete work package to perform. The work package is a—

    a. Deliverable at the lowest level of the WBS
    b. Task with a unique identifier
    c. Required level of reporting
    d. Task that can be assigned to more than one organizational unit

15. Quality function deployment is one approach for collecting requirements. Assume that you have studied the work of numerous quality experts, such as Deming, Juran, and Crosby, and your organization has a policy that states the importance of quality as the key constraint of all project constraints. You and your team have decided to use quality function deployment on your new project to manufacture turbines that use alternative fuels. The first step you should use is to—

    a. Determine the voice of the customer
    b. Build the house of quality
    c. Address the functional requirements and how best to meet them
    d. Hold a focus group of prequalified stakeholders

16. On the WBS, the first level of decomposition may be displayed by using all the following EXCEPT—

    a. Phases of the project life cycle
    b. Subprojects
    c. Major deliverables
    d. Project organizational units

17. Change is inevitable on projects. Uncontrolled changes are often referred to as—

    a. Rework
    b. Scope creep
    c. Configuration items
    d. Emergency changes

18. Each WBS component should be assigned a unique identifier from a code of accounts to—

    a. Link the WBS to the bill of materials
    b. Enable the WBS to follow a similar numbering system to that of the organization's units as part of the organizational breakdown structure
    c. Sum costs, schedule, and resource information
    d. Link the WBS to the project management plan

19. In scope control it is important to determine the cause of any unacceptable variance relative to the scope baseline. This can be done through—

    a. Root cause analysis
    b. Control charts
    c. Inspections
    d. Project performance measurements

20. To assist your software development team in collecting requirements from potential users and to ensure that agreement about the stakeholders' needs exists early in the project, you decide to use a group creativity technique. Numerous techniques are available, but you and your team choose a voting process to rank the most useful ideas for further prioritization. This approach is known as—

    a. Brainstorming
    b. Nominal group technique
    c. Delphi technique
    d. Affinity diagram

21. You have been appointed project manager for a new project in your organization and must prepare a project plan. You decide to prepare a WBS to show the magnitude and complexity of the work involved. No WBS templates are available to help you. To prepare the WBS, your first step should be to—

    a. Determine the cost and duration estimates for each project deliverable
    b. Identify and analyze the deliverables and related work
    c. Identify the components of each project deliverable
    d. Determine the key tasks to be performed

22. Assume that you are a major subcontractor doing work for a prime contractor on a major project. Your change control system should—

    a. Be identical to that of the prime contractor
    b. Follow the rigor of international configuration management standards
    c. Comply with relevant contractual provisions
    d. Only consider approved change requests

23. You are leading a project team to identify potential new products for your organization. One idea was rejected by management because it would not fit with the organization's core competencies. You need to recommend other products using management's guideline as—

    a. An assumption
    b. A risk
    c. A specification
    d. A technical requirement

24. Verify scope—

    a. Improves cost and schedule accuracy, particularly on projects using innovative techniques or technology
    b. Is the last activity performed on a project before handoff to the customer
    c. Documents the characteristics of the product or service that the project was undertaken to create
    d. Differs from quality control in that verify scope is concerned with the acceptance—not the correctness—of the work results

25. Any step recommended to bring expected future performance in line with the project management plan is called—

    a. Performance evaluation
    b. Corrective action
    c. Preventive action
    d. Defect repair

26. Written change orders should be required on—

    a. All projects, large and small
    b. Only large projects
    c. Projects with a formal configuration management system in place
    d. Projects for which the cost of a change control system can be justified

27. Updates of organizational process assets that are an output of control scope include all the following EXCEPT—

    a. Causes of variations
    b. Lessons learned
    c. Work authorization system
    d. Reasons certain corrective actions were chosen

28. Work performance information includes all the following EXCEPT—

    a. Personnel training results
    b. Costs authorized and incurred
    c. Resource utilization data
    d. Completed deliverables

29. Your project is now under way, and you recognize that, given the nature of project work, scope change is inevitable. You meet with your team and decide to establish a change control system, which is—

    a. A collection of formal, documented procedures to define the steps by which official project documents may be changed
    b. The establishment of a board of individuals for approving or rejecting change requests
    c. A set of procedures by which project scope and product scope may be changed
    d. Mandatory for use on projects so that the scope management plan cannot be changed without prior review and sign-off

30. You are project manager on a systems engineering project designed to last six years and to develop the next-generation corvette for use in military operations. You and your team recognize that requirements may change as new technologies, especially in sonar systems, are developed. You are concerned that these new technologies may lead to changes in the scope of your product, which then will affect the scope of your project. Therefore your requirements traceability matrix should include tracing requirements to all the following project elements EXCEPT—

    a. Business needs
    b. Product design
    c. Product development
    d. Project verification

31. Your customer signed off on the requirements definition document and scope statement of your video game project last month. Today she stated she would like to make it an interactive game that can be played on a television and on a computer. This represents a requested scope change that, at a minimum—

    a. Should be reviewed according to the perform integrated change control process
    b. Results in a change to all project baselines
    c. Requires adjustments to cost, time, quality, and other objectives
    d. Results in a lesson learned

32. The key inputs to the verify scope process include all the below items EXCEPT—

    a. The project management plan (WBS, WBS dictionary, scope baseline)
    b. Change requests
    c. Validated deliverables
    d. Requirements documentation and traceability matrix

33. Modifications may be needed to the WBS and WBS dictionary due to approved change requests, which shows that—

    a. Replanning is an output of control scope
    b. Scope creep is common on projects
    c. Rebaselining will be necessary
    d. Variance is relative to the scope baseline

34. Your team has been working on a contract for three years. Yesterday you were informed that your client depleted its resources and will terminate the contract for convenience. Your first action is to—

    a. Submit the work products to date to your client's representative
    b. Document lessons learned
    c. Establish and document the level and extent of completion
    d. Shut down the project office and reassign all personnel

35. Which following item is NOT an input to control scope?

    a. Requirements traceability matrix
    b. Work performance information
    c. Deliverables
    d. Project scope management plan

36. You are the project manager for a subcontractor on a major contract. The prime contractor has asked that you manage your work in a detailed manner. Your first step is to—

    a. Follow the WBS that the prime contractor developed for the project and use the work packages you identified during the proposal
    b. Develop a subproject WBS for the work package that is your company's responsibility
    c. Establish a similar coding structure to the prime contractor's to facilitate use of a common project management information system
    d. Develop a WBS dictionary to show specific staff assignments

37. The project scope statement is important in scope control because it—

    a. Is a critical component of the scope baseline
    b. Provides information on project performance
    c. Alerts the project team to issues that may cause problems in the future
    d. Is expected to change throughout the project

38. Project exclusions are documented as part of the project's scope statement. They are important to document because they—

    a. Facilitate the project acceptance process
    b. Describe specific constraints associated with the project
    c. Manage stakeholder expectations
    d. Provide more details about the product or service deliverables as well as ancillary results

39. The key outputs of collect requirements include all the following items EXCEPT—

    a. Requirements documentation
    b. Traceability matrix
    c. Scope management plan
    d. Requirements management plan

40. You are establishing a PMO that will have a project management information system that will be an online repository of all program data. You will collect descriptions of all work components for each project under the PMO's jurisdiction. This information will form an integral part of the—

    a. Chart of accounts
    b. WBS dictionary
    c. WBS structure template
    d. Earned value management reports

Answer Sheet

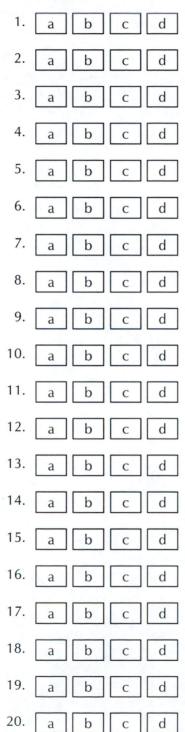
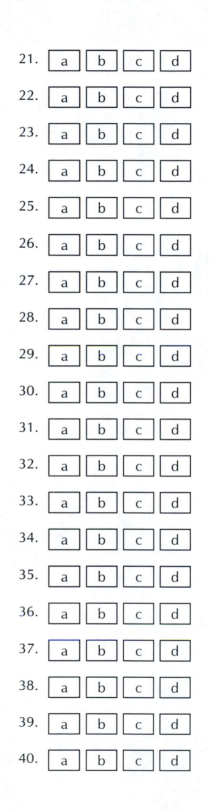

1. a b c d   21. a b c d
2. a b c d   22. a b c d
3. a b c d   23. a b c d
4. a b c d   24. a b c d
5. a b c d   25. a b c d
6. a b c d   26. a b c d
7. a b c d   27. a b c d
8. a b c d   28. a b c d
9. a b c d   29. a b c d
10. a b c d   30. a b c d
11. a b c d   31. a b c d
12. a b c d   32. a b c d
13. a b c d   33. a b c d
14. a b c d   34. a b c d
15. a b c d   35. a b c d
16. a b c d   36. a b c d
17. a b c d   37. a b c d
18. a b c d   38. a b c d
19. a b c d   39. a b c d
20. a b c d   40. a b c d

Answer Key

1. a. Proper project scope definition

Progressive elaboration of a project's specification must be coordinated carefully with proper scope definition, particularly when the project is performed under contract. When properly defined, the project scope—the work to be done—should remain constant even when the product characteristics are elaborated progressively. [Planning]

PMI®, *PMBOK® Guide*, 2008, 7 and 112

2. b. WBS

The WBS, along with the detailed scope statement and the WBS dictionary, defines the project's scope baseline, which provides the basis for any changes that may occur on the project. [Planning]

PMI®, *PMBOK® Guide*, 2008, 121–122

3. b. Prepare a scope management plan

The work involved in the five Project Scope Management processes is preceded by preparing a scope management plan, which is a subsidiary plan for the project management plan. It describes the Project Scope Management processes from definition to control. [Planning]

PMI®, *PMBOK® Guide*, 2008, 104

4. c. Project files from previous projects

Organizational process assets include formal and informal policies, procedures, and guidelines impacting project scope management. Project files from previous projects are one example and may be located in the lessons learned knowledge base. [Planning]

PMI®, *PMBOK® Guide*, 2008, 114

5. c. Product requirements

Completion of the project scope is measured against the project management plan, and completion of the product scope is measured against the requirements. In the project context, product scope consists of features and functions that characterize the product, service, or result. Project scope is the work that must be done to deliver the product, service, or result with specified features and functions. [Planning]

PMI®, *PMBOK® Guide*, 2008, 103 and 105

6. c.   Expert judgment

Expert judgment is used to analyze the information needed to develop a project scope statement. It is applied to any technical details. [Planning]

PMI®, *PMBOK® Guide*, 2008, 114

7. d.   Lateral thinking

Lateral thinking, brainstorming, and pairwise comparison are examples of general management techniques that can be used to generate different approaches to execute and perform the project's work. [Planning]

PMI®, *PMBOK® Guide*, 2008, 114

8. d.   Bill of materials

Product analysis techniques vary by application area, and each application area generally has accepted methods to translate project objectives into tangible deliverables and requirements. Other product analysis techniques include product breakdown, requirements analysis, and systems engineering. [Planning]

PMI®, *PMBOK® Guide*, 2008, 114

9. b.   Project scope statement

Project boundaries identify generally what is included within the project, and state explicitly what is excluded from the project, if a stakeholder might assume that a particular product, service, or result could be a project component. Project boundaries are described as part of the detailed project scope statement. [Planning]

PMI®, *PMBOK® Guide*, 2008, 115–116

10. b.   An error or omission in defining the scope of the project

The bill of materials provides a hierarchical view of the physical assemblies, subassemblies, and components needed to build a manufactured product, whereas the WBS is a deliverable-oriented grouping of project components used to define the total scope of the project. Using a bill of materials where a WBS would be more appropriate may result in an ill-defined scope and subsequent change requests. [Monitoring and Controlling]

PMI®, *PMBOK® Guide*, 2008, 121; Ward 2008, 40

11. b. WBS

Collecting requirements is defining and managing customer expectations. It also involves defining and documenting stakeholder needs to meet project objectives. The requirements become the foundation for the WBS; moreover, cost, schedule, and quality planning are built upon the requirements. [Planning]

PMI®, *PMBOK® Guide*, 2008, 105

12. d. Project management methodology (PMM)

The PMM is an organization-approved approach for project management that is used on every project. It is not part of the project scope descriptions, which addresses and documents the project and deliverable requirements, product requirements, and project boundaries. [Initiating]

PMI®, *PMBOK® Guide*, 2008, 115

13. b. Review the project charter and stakeholder register

Both the project charter and the stakeholder register are inputs to the collect requirements process. You should review them because the charter provides high-level project requirements and a high-level product description, and the stakeholder register provides information on stakeholders who may be helpful in providing additional information about the requirements. [Planning]

PMI®, *PMBOK® Guide*, 2008, 106

14. a. Deliverable at the lowest level of the WBS

A work package is the lowest or smallest unit of work division in a project or WBS. The work package can be scheduled, cost estimated, monitored, and controlled. [Planning]

PMI®, *PMBOK® Guide*, 2008, 116

15. a. Determine the voice of the customer

Quality function deployment is an example of a facilitated workshop used in the manufacturing industry as a tool and technique to collect requirements. It helps to determine the critical characteristics for new product development and starts by collecting customer needs, known as the voice of the customer. [Planning]

PMI®, *PMBOK® Guide*, 2008, 107

16. d. Project organizational units

The WBS includes all work needed to be done to complete the project. The organizational breakdown structure (OBS) includes the organizational units responsible for completing the work. [Planning]

PMI®, *PMBOK® Guide*, 2008, 118

17. b. Scope creep

Project scope creep is typically the result of uncontrolled changes. Scope control works to control the impact of any project scope changes. [Monitoring and Controlling]

PMI®, *PMBOK® Guide*, 2008, 125

18. c. Sum costs, schedule, and resource information

The key document generated from the create WBS process is the actual WBS. Each WBS component is assigned a unique identifier to provide a structure for hierarchical summation of costs, schedule, and resource information. [Planning]

PMI®, *PMBOK® Guide*, 2008, 121

19. d. Project performance measurements

Variance analysis is a tool and technique for scope control. Project performance measurements are used to assess the magnitude of variance, to determine the cause of the variance, and to decide whether corrective action is required. [Monitoring and Controlling]

PMI®, *PMBOK® Guide*, 2008, 127

20. b. Nominal group technique

The nominal group technique enhances brainstorming with a voting process, which is used to rank the most useful ideas for further brainstorming or for prioritization. [Planning]

PMI®, *PMBOK® Guide*, 2008, 108

21. b.   Identify and analyze the deliverables and related work

Identifying and analyzing the deliverables and related work is the first step in the decomposition of a project. The deliverables should be defined in terms of how the project will be organized. For example, the major project deliverables may be used as the first level with the phases of the project repeated at the second level. [Planning]

PMI®, *PMBOK® Guide*, 2008, 118

22. c.   Comply with relevant contractual provisions

In addition to complying with any relevant contractual provisions, scope change control must be integrated with the project's overall change control system and with any systems in place to control project and product scope. [Monitoring and Controlling]

PMI®, *PMBOK® Guide*, 2008, 97 and 115

23. a.   An assumption

Assumptions are factors that, for planning purposes, are considered to be true, real, or certain. They are listed in the project scope statement. [Planning]

Ward 2008, 24; PMI®, *PMBOK® Guide*, 2008, 116 and 419

24. d.   Differs from quality control in that verify scope is concerned with the acceptance—not the correctness—of the work results

Documentation that the customer has accepted completed deliverables is an output of verify scope. [Monitoring and Controlling]

PMI®, *PMBOK® Guide*, 2008, 123

25. b.   Corrective action

Recommended corrective action is an output from control scope. In addition to bringing expected future performance in line with the project management plan, it also serves to bring expected future performance in line with the project scope statement. [Monitoring and Controlling]

PMI®, *PMBOK® Guide*, 2008, 92

26. a. All projects, large and small

A system is needed for careful monitoring of changes made to the requirements. Use of written change orders encourages the individuals asking for changes to take responsibility for their requests and reduces frivolous requests that may adversely affect the project. [Monitoring and Controlling]

PMI®, *PMBOK® Guide*, 2008, 71, 83–88

27. c. Work authorization system

The work authorization system is an example of an enterprise environmental factor. The others are examples of organizational process assets that may require update as a result of scope control. [Monitoring and Controlling]

PMI®, *PMBOK® Guide*, 2008, 128

28. a. Personnel training results

Work performance information is any data or information describing work accomplishment, including cost, quality, and schedule performance. Personnel training schedule is an administrative matter not directly related to work accomplishment. [Monitoring and Controlling]

PMI®, *PMBOK® Guide*, 2008, 127

29. c. A set of procedures by which project scope and product scope may be changed

In addition to complying with any relevant contractual provisions, scope change control must be integrated with the project's overall change control system and with any systems in place to control project and product scope. [Monitoring and Controlling]

PMI®, *PMBOK® Guide*, 2008, 80

30. d. Project verification

The requirements traceability matrix is an output of the collect requirements process. It includes tracing requirements to business needs, opportunities, and objectives; project objectives; project scope/WBS deliverables; product design; product development; test strategy and scenarios; as well as high-level requirements to more detailed requirements. [Planning]

PMI®, *PMBOK® Guide*, 2008, 111

31. a. Should be reviewed according to the perform integrated change control process

A requested change is an output from the control scope process. Such a change should be handled according to the integrated change control process and may result in an update to the scope baseline. [Monitoring and Controlling]

PMI®, *PMBOK® Guide*, 2008, 93

32. b. Change request

The change requests are not an input of the verify scope process, but an output. The other items are all inputs to help the project manager verify the scope of the project. [Monitoring and Controlling]

PMI®, *PMBOK® Guide*, 2008, 124–125

33. d. Variance is relative to the scope baseline

Approved changes will most likely impact and cause updates to the WBS, WBS dictionary, and project scope statement. In other words, they will cause variance to the scope baseline. [Monitoring and Controlling]

PMI®, *PMBOK® Guide*, 2008, 125

34. c. Establish and document the level and extent of completion

Stakeholders' official acceptance of project scope is part of the verify scope process. If a project is terminated before it is complete, the degree to which the project has been completed should be established and documented. [Monitoring and Controlling]

PMI®, *PMBOK® Guide*, 2008, 342

35. c. Deliverables

Deliverables that fully or partially completed are inputs to scope verification. [Monitoring and Controlling]

PMI®, *PMBOK® Guide*, 2008, 128–129

36. b. Develop a subproject WBS for the work package that is your company's responsibility

Work packages are items at the lowest level of the WBS. A subproject WBS breaks down work packages into greater detail. A subproject WBS generally is used when the project manager assigns a scope of work to another organization, and the project manager at that organization must plan and manage the scope of work in greater detail. [Planning]

PMI®, *PMBOK® Guide*, 2008, 118

37. a. Is a critical component of the scope baseline

The project scope statement, along with the WBS and WBS dictionary, is a key input to scope control. [Monitoring and Controlling]

PMI®, *PMBOK® Guide*, 2008, 124

38. c. Manage stakeholder expectations

The project scope statement describes the deliverables and the work required to create them. It also provides a common understanding of the scope among stakeholders. By including explicit scope exclusions to show what is out of scope for the project, the project team can better manage stakeholder expectations. [Planning]

PMI®, *PMBOK® Guide*, 2008, 115

39. c. Scope management plan

The scope management plan includes the processes, documentation, tracking systems, and approval levels necessary for authorizing changes. [Monitoring and Controlling]

PMI®, *PMBOK® Guide*, 2008, 109–111

40. b. WBS dictionary

The WBS dictionary typically includes a code of accounts identifier, a statement of work, responsible organization, and a list of schedule milestones, among other items. [Planning]

PMI®, *PMBOK® Guide*, 2008, 121

PROJECT TIME MANAGEMENT

Study Hints

The Project Time Management questions on the PMP® certification exam focus heavily on the program evaluation and review technique (PERT), the critical path method (CPM), the precedence diagramming method (PDM), and the critical chain method; the differences between these four techniques; and the appropriate circumstances for their use. The exam tests your knowledge of how PERT/CPM networks are constructed, how schedules are computed, what the critical path is, and how networks are used to analyze and solve project scheduling, and resource allocation and leveling issues. There is a good chance that you will be presented with a network diagram that will be the subject of five or more questions. Therefore, detailed knowledge of network scheduling is essential. There also seems to be a focus on fast-tracking as a method to accelerate the project schedule. You must know the advantages offered by networks over bar charts and network diagrams. You also should understand the concept of float (or slack) and how it presents challenges and opportunities to project schedulers.

Because a thorough understanding of networks and scheduling is required to successfully answer questions on Project Time Management, you should take a course relating to that topic, preferably the ESI *Scheduling and Cost Control* course. If you cannot take a course, you may want to consult the user's manual for one of the more popular desktop software project management packages. Typically, you will find plenty of illustrations and short, easy-to-understand scheduling exercises at the level of detail required to correctly answer the exam questions.

The *PMBOK® Guide* separates the function of Project Time Management into six processes: define activities, sequence activities, estimate activity resources, estimate activity durations, develop schedule, and control schedule. Review *PMBOK® Guide* Figure 6-1 before taking the ESI practice test. Know this chart thoroughly.

Following is a list of the major Project Time Management topics. Use it to help focus your study efforts on the areas most likely to appear on the exam.

Major Topics

Schedule management plan

Define activities

- Activity list
- Activity attributes
- Milestone list

Sequence activities

- PDM
- Dependencies
- Leads and lags

Estimate activity resources

- Activity resource requirements
- Resource breakdown structure
- Resource calendars

Estimate activity durations

- Expert judgment
- Analogous estimating
- Parametric estimates
- Three-point estimates
- Reserve analysis

Develop schedule

- Schedule network analysis
- Critical path method
- Critical chain method
- Resource leveling
- What-if scenario analysis
- Leads and lags
- Crashing and fast-tracking
- Project schedule
- Schedule baseline

Control schedule

- Performance reviews
- Variance analysis
- Work performance measurements
- Change requests
- Updates
  - Project management plan
  - Project documents

Practice Questions

INSTRUCTIONS: Note the most suitable answer for each multiple-choice question in the appropriate space on the answer sheet.

Use the following network diagram to answer questions 1 through 4. Activity names and duration are provided.

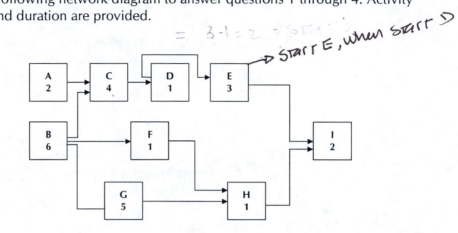

= 3-1 = 2 = Start ? → Start E, when start D

1. What is the duration of the critical path in this network?

    a. 10
    b. 12
    c. 14
    d. 15

2. What is the float for Activity G?

    a. −2
    b. 0
    c. 1
    d. 4

3. If a project planner imposes a finish time of 14 on the project with no change in the start date or activity durations, what is the total float of Activity E?

    a. −1
    b. 0
    c. 2
    d. Cannot be determined

4. If the imposed finish time in question 3 above is removed and reset to 16 and the duration of Activity H is changed to 3, what is the late finish for Activity G?

   a. −11
   b. 11
   c. −13
   d. 13

5. Your company, which operates one of the region's largest chemical processing plants, has been convicted of illegally dumping toxic substances into the local river. The court has mandated that the required cleanup activities be completed by February 15. This date is an example of—

   a. A key event
   b. A milestone
   c. A discretionary dependency
   d. An external dependency

6. You are managing a construction project for a new city water system. The contract requires you to use special titanium piping equipment that is guaranteed not to corrode. The titanium pipe must be resting in the ground a total of 10 days before connectors can be installed. In this example, the 10-day period is defined as—

   a. Lag
   b. Lead
   c. Float
   d. Slack

7. Of the following, which one is NOT a tool or technique used for schedule control?

   a. Variance analysis
   b. Three-point estimate
   c. What-if scenario analysis
   d. Schedule change control system

8. You are planning to conduct the team-building portion of your new project management training curriculum out-of-doors in the local park. You are limited to scheduling the course at certain times of the year, and the best time for the course to begin is mid-July. One of the more common date constraints to use as you develop the project schedule is—

   a. "Start no earlier than"
   b. "Finish no later than"
   c. "Fixed late start"
   d. "Fixed early finish"

9. Project schedule development is an iterative process. If the start and finish dates are not realistic, the project probably will not finish as planned. You are working with your team to define how to manage schedule changes. You documented your decisions in which of the following?

   a. Schedule change control procedures
   b. Schedule management plan
   c. Schedule risk plan
   d. Service-level agreement

10. If, when developing your project schedule, you want to define a distribution of probable results for each schedule activity and use that distribution to calculate another distribution of probable results for the total project, the most common technique to use is—

    a. PERT
    b. Monte Carlo analysis
    c. Linear programming
    d. Concurrent engineering

11. Your lead engineer estimates that a work package will most likely require 50 weeks to complete. It could be completed in 40 weeks if all goes well, but it could take 180 weeks in the worst case. What is the PERT estimate for the expected duration of the work package?

    a. 45 weeks
    b. 70 weeks
    c. 90 weeks
    d. 140 weeks

12. Your customer wants the project to be completed six months earlier than planned. You believe you can meet this target by overlapping project activities. The approach you plan to use is known as—

    a. Critical chain
    b. Fast-tracking
    c. Leveling
    d. Crashing

13. Activity A has a duration of three days and begins on the morning of Monday the 4th. The successor activity, B, has a finish-to-start relationship with A. The finish-to-start relationship has three days of lag, and activity B has a duration of four days. Sunday is a nonworkday. Such data can help to determine—

    a. The total duration of both activities is 8 days
    b. Calendar time between the start of A to the finish of B is 11 days
    c. The finish date of B is Wednesday the 13th
    d. Calendar time between the start of A to the finish of B is 14 days

14. You can use various estimating approaches to determine activity durations. When you have a limited amount of information available about your project, especially when in the early phases, the best approach to use is—

    a. Bottom-up estimating
    b. Analogous estimating
    c. Reserve analysis
    d. Parametric analysis

15. "I cannot test the software until I code the software." This expression describes which of the following dependencies?

    a. Discretionary
    b. Rational
    c. Preferential
    d. Mandatory or hard

16. Working with your team to provide the basis for measuring and reporting schedule progress, you agree to use the—

    a. Schedule management plan
    b. Network diagram
    c. Project schedule
    d. Technical baseline

17. Your approved project schedule was based on resource leveling due to a scarcity of resources. Management has now mandated that the project be completed as soon as possible. Which of the following methods will you use to recalculate the schedule?

    a. Resource manipulation
    b. Reverse resource allocation
    c. Critical chain scheduling
    d. Resource reallocation

18. Review the following network diagram and table. Of the various activities, which ones would you crash and in what order?

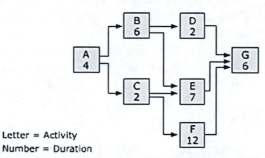

Letter = Activity
Number = Duration

Activity	Time Required, Weeks		Cost $		Crashing Cost Per Weeks, $
	Normal	Crash	Normal	Crash	
A	4	2	10,000	14,000	2,000
B	6	5	30,000	42,500	12,500
C	2	1	8,000	9,500	1,500
D	2	1	12,000	18,000	6,000
E	7	5	40,000	52,000	6,000
F	12	3	20,000	29,000	3,000
G	6	2	5,000	30,000	6,000

a. A, C, E, and F
b. A, B, D, and F
c. A, B, E, and F
d. C, A, F, and G

19. You are remodeling your kitchen and decide to prepare a network diagram for this project. Your appliances must be purchased and available for installation by the time the cabinets are completed. In this example, these relationships are—

a. Start-to-finish
b. Finish-to-start
c. Start-to-start
d. Finish-to-finish

20. Decomposition is a technique used for both WBS development and activity definition. Which following statement best describes the role decomposition plays in activity definition as compared to creating the WBS?

a. Final output is described in terms of work packages in the WBS.
b. Final output is described as deliverables or tangible items.
c. Final output is described as schedule activities.
d. Decomposition is used the same way in scope definition and activity definition.

21. When sequencing project activities in the schedule, all the following are true EXCEPT—

    a. There may be scheduled dates for specific milestones
    b. Every activity is connected to at least one predecessor and one successor
    c. Lead or lag time may be required
    d. Necessary sequencing of events may be described by the activity attributes

22. A schedule performance index of less than 1.0 indicates that the—

    a. Project is running behind the monetary value of the work it planned to accomplish
    b. Earned value physically accomplished thus far is 100%
    c. Project has experienced a permanent loss of time
    d. Project may not be on schedule, but the project manager need not be concerned

23. Various tools and techniques are available to sequence activities, and several factors can help to determine which tool or technique to select. When a project manager decides to include *subnetworks* or a *fragment network* as part of his or her scheduling technique, what does this decision say about the project?

    a. The work is unique requiring special network diagrams at various stages.
    b. Software that manages resources is available over an existing electronic network.
    c. Several identical or nearly identical series of activities are repeated throughout the project.
    d. Multiple critical paths exist in the project.

24. To meet regulatory requirements, you need to crash your project schedule. Your first step is to compute—

    a. The cost and time slope for each critical activity that can be expedited
    b. The cost of additional resources to be added to the project's critical path
    c. The time saved in the overall schedule when tasks are expedited on the critical path
    d. Three probabilistic time estimates of PERT for each critical path activity

25. Which one of the following is the primary input to the define activities process?

    a. Project management plan
    b. Project scope statement
    c. Project scope baseline
    d. Project charter

26. Unlike bar charts, milestone charts show—

    a. Scheduled start or completion of major deliverables and key external interfaces
    b. Activity start and end dates of critical tasks
    c. Expected durations of the critical path
    d. Dependencies between complementary projects

27. Project managers should pay attention to critical and subcritical activities when evaluating project time performance. One way to do this is to analyze 10 subcritical paths in order of ascending float. This approach is part of—

    a. Variance analysis
    b. Simulation
    c. Earned value management
    d. Trend analysis

28. An activity has an early start date of the 10th and a late start date of the 19th. The activity has a duration of four days. There are no nonworkdays. From the information given, what can be concluded about the activity?

    a. Total float for the activity is nine days.
    b. The early finish date of the activity is the end of the day on the 14th.
    c. The late finish date is the 25th.
    d. The activity can be completed in two days if the resources devoted to it are doubled.

29. In project development, schedule information such as who will perform the work, where the work will be performed, activity type, and WBS classification are examples of—

    a. Activity attributes
    b. Constraints
    c. Data in the WBS repository
    d. Refinements

30. Which of the following is a primary input to define activities?

    a. Project management plan
    b. Project scope management plan
    c. Scope baseline
    d. Project management software

31. The purpose of using What-if analysis in schedule control is to—

    a. Review scenarios to bring the schedule in line with the plan
    b. Document requested changes
    c. Provide additional details as to when the schedule baseline should be updated
    d. Update the activity attributes

32. Several types of float are found in project networks. Float that is used by a particular activity and does NOT affect the float in later activities is called—

    a. Extra float
    b. Free float
    c. Total float
    d. Expected float

33. All the following statements regarding critical chain method are true EXCEPT—

    a. It modifies the schedule to account for limited resources
    b. The first step is to use conservative estimates for activity durations
    c. Duration buffers are added on the critical path
    d. It focuses on managing buffer activity durations

34. You are managing a new technology project designed to improve the removal of hazardous waste from your city. You are in the planning phase of this project and have prepared your network diagram. Your next step is to—

    a. Describe any unusual sequencing in the network
    b. State the number resources required to complete each activity
    c. Establish a project calendar and link it to individual resource calendar
    d. Determine which schedule compression techniques is the most appropriate, because your customer requests that the project be completed as soon as possible

35. The risk register may need to be updated as an output of which following process:

    a. Define activities
    b. Sequence activities
    c. Estimate activity resources
    d. Control schedule

36. You are managing a project that will use a virtual team with team members on three different continents. Your company is looking to use the virtual team to provide a lower cost product by using resources in countries that have a favorable exchange rate to that of your country. To assist in this process as you estimate resource requirements, it is helpful to consider—

    a. Bottom-up estimating
    b. Published estimating data
    c. Analogous estimating
    d. Reserve analysis

37. Activity A has a pessimistic *(P)* estimate of 36 days, a most likely *(ML)* estimate of 21 days, and an optimistic *(O)* estimate of 6 days. What is the probability that activity A will be completed in 16 to 26 days?

    a. 55.70 percent
    b. 68.26 percent
    c. 95.46 percent
    d. 99.73 percent

38. You are managing a project to redesign a retail store layout to improve customer throughput and efficiency. Much project work must be done on site and will require the active participation of store employees who are lifelong members of a powerful union with a reputation for labor unrest. One important component of your schedule must be—

    a. A resource capabilities matrix
    b. Buffers and reserves
    c. A resource calendar
    d. A resource histogram

39. To account for uncertainty in a schedule, reserve analysis may be used. All the following are examples of contingency reserves EXCEPT—

    a. Fixed number of work periods
    b. Percent of the estimated activity duration
    c. Buffers
    d. Productivity metrics

40. The reason that the schedule performance index (SPI) is shown as a ratio is to—

    a. Enable a detailed analysis of the schedule regardless of the value of the schedule variance
    b. Distinguish between critical path and noncritical path work packages
    c. Provide the ability to show performance for a specified time period for trend analysis
    d. Measure the actual time to complete the project

Answer Sheet

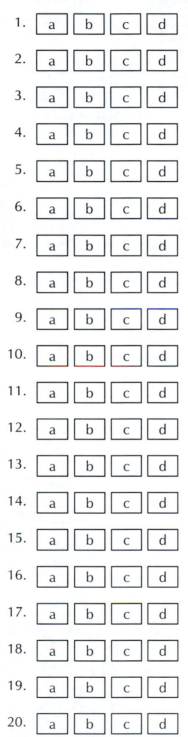

1. a b c d
2. a b c d
3. a b c d
4. a b c d
5. a b c d
6. a b c d
7. a b c d
8. a b c d
9. a b c d
10. a b c d
11. a b c d
12. a b c d
13. a b c d
14. a b c d
15. a b c d
16. a b c d
17. a b c d
18. a b c d
19. a b c d
20. a b c d

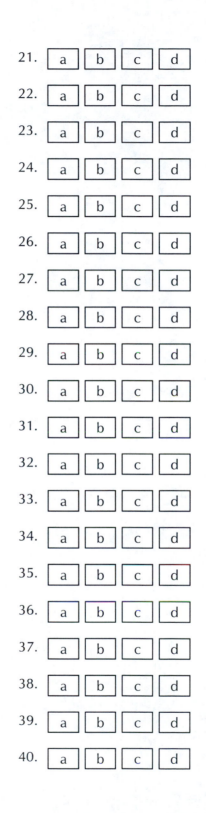

21. a b c d
22. a b c d
23. a b c d
24. a b c d
25. a b c d
26. a b c d
27. a b c d
28. a b c d
29. a b c d
30. a b c d
31. a b c d
32. a b c d
33. a b c d
34. a b c d
35. a b c d
36. a b c d
37. a b c d
38. a b c d
39. a b c d
40. a b c d

Answer Key

1. d. 15

The total duration for the path B-C-D-E-I is 15. The duration of any other path in the network is less than 15. [Planning]

Meredith and Mantel 2009, Chapter 8

2. c. 1

Float = (late finish – early finish) or

(late start – early start)

Activity G   LF = 12   (12 – 11) = (1)

EF = 11

LS = 7   (7 – 6) = (1)

ES = 6

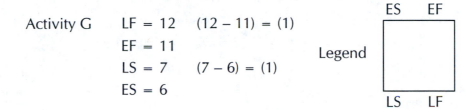

Legend

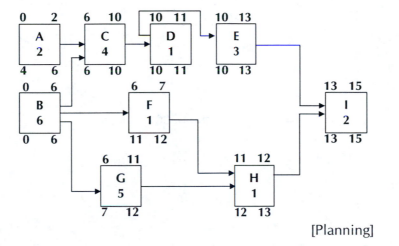

[Planning]

Meredith and Mantel 2009, Chapter 8

3. a. −1

The imposed finish date becomes the late finish for Activity I. The late dates for each activity need to be recalculated. The dates for Activity E become—

ES = 10
EF = 13
LS = 9
LF = 12

Total float = LS − ES or 9 − 10 = (−1) or
                       LF − EF or 12 − 13 = (−1)

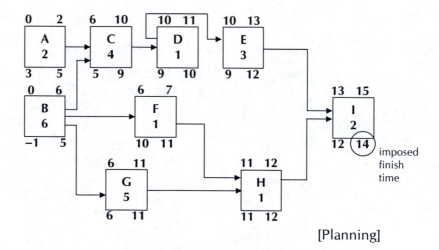

[Planning]

Meredith and Mantel 2009, Chapter 8

4. b. 11

The late dates for all activities need to be recalculated given the changed duration. Activity G's revised late dates are—

LF = 11
LS = 6

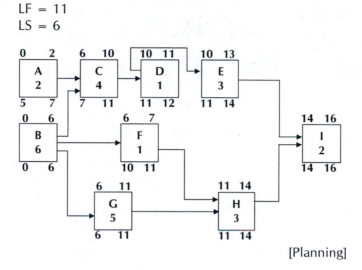

[Planning]

Meredith and Mantel 2009, Chapter 8

5. b. A milestone

A milestone is a significant point or event in the project. Milestones may be required by the project sponsor, customer, or other external factors for the completion of certain deliverables. [Planning]

PMI®, *PMBOK® Guide*, 2008, 136

6. a. Lag

For example, in a finish-to-start dependency with a 20-day lag, the successor activity cannot start until 20 days after the predecessor has finished. [Planning]

PMI®, *PMBOK® Guide*, 2008, 140

7. c. What-if scenario analysis

What-if scenario analysis is a tool used in schedule development. [Planning]

PMI®, *PMBOK® Guide*, 2008, 156

8. a. **"Start no earlier than"**

Imposed dates on schedule activity starts of finishes can be used to restrict the start of finish to occur either no earlier than a specified date or no later than a specified date. Although all four date constraints typically are available in project management software, "start no earlier than" and "finish no later than" constraints are more commonly used. [Planning]

PMI®, *PMBOK® Guide*, 2008, 428

9. b. **Schedule management plan**

The schedule management plan is part of the overall project management plan and defines, among other things, how schedule changes will be managed. Whether it is formal or informal, highly detailed or broadly framed, it generally is based on specific project needs. [Planning]

PMI®, *PMBOK® Guide*, 2008, 130

10. b. **Monte Carlo analysis**

What-if scenarios (simulation) is a tool and technique for developing schedules by which multiple project durations with different sets of activity assumptions are calculated. Monte Carlo analysis is the most commonly used simulation technique. [Planning]

PMI®, *PMBOK® Guide*, 2008, 156

11. b. **70 weeks**

$$E(t) = \frac{\text{Optimistic} + (4 \times \text{Most likely}) + \text{Pessimistic}}{6}$$

$$= \frac{40 + 200 + 180}{6} = \frac{420}{6} = 70 \text{ weeks}$$

[Planning]

PMI®, *PMBOK® Guide*, 2008, 150

12. b. **Fast-tracking**

Fast-tracking is a way to accelerate the project schedule. [Planning]

PMI®, *PMBOK® Guide*, 2008, 157 and 427

13. b. Calendar time between the start of A to the finish of B is 11 days

The duration of A, which is three, is added to the duration of B, which is four, for a total of seven. The three days between the activities is lag and not duration. The lag is a constraint and must be taken into account as part of the network calculations, but it does not consume resources. The total time by the calendar is 11 days as counted from the morning of Monday the 4th. The lag occurs over Thursday, Friday, and Saturday. Sunday is a nonworkday, so activity B does not start until Monday the 11th. Therefore, the calendar time is 11 days, and activity B ends on Thursday the 14th. [Planning]

PMI®, *PMBOK® Guide*, 2008, 140 and 156

14. b. Analogous estimating

Although limitations exist with all estimating approach, analogous estimating is often used when there is a limited amount of information for the project. It uses historical information and expert judgment. [Planning]

PMI®, *PMBOK® Guide*, 2008, 149

15. d. Mandatory or hard

Mandatory dependencies may be required contractually or be inherent in the nature of the project work. They describe a relationship in which the successor activity cannot be started because of physical constraints until the predecessor activity has been finished. For example, software cannot be tested until it has been developed (or coded). [Planning]

PMI®, *PMBOK® Guide*, 2008, 139

16. c. Project schedule

The approved project schedule is a key input to schedule control. It is the schedule baseline, and it provides the basis for measuring and reporting schedule performance. [Monitoring and Controlling]

PMI®, *PMBOK® Guide*, 2008, 161

17. d. Resource reallocation

While resource leveling will often result in a project duration that is longer than the preliminary schedule, it can also be used to get a schedule back on track by reassigning activities from noncritical to critical path activities. [Planning]

PMI®, *PMBOK® Guide*, 2008, 156

18. d. C, A, F, and G

First, it is necessary to determine the critical path, which is A, C, F, and G. To determine the lowest weekly crashing cost, start with C at $1,500 per week. The next activity is A, followed by F and G. [Planning]

PMI®, *PMBOK® Guide*, 2008, 154; Kerzner 2006, 494–495

19. d. Finish-to-finish

The completion of the work of the successor activity depends upon the completion of the work of the predecessor activity. [Planning]

PMI®, *PMBOK® Guide*, 2008, 138

20. c. Final output is described as schedule activities.

In the create WBS process, final output is described as deliverables or tangible items. [Planning]

PMI®, *PMBOK® Guide*, 2008, 134

21. b. Every activity is connected to at least one predecessor and one successor

The sequence activity process involves identifying and documenting relationships among the project activities. However, the first and last activity and milestone are not connected to at least one predecessor or successor. [Planning]

PMI®, *PMBOK® Guide*, 2008, 136

22. a. Project is running behind the monetary value of the work it planned to accomplish

The SPI represents how much of the originally scheduled work has been accomplished at a given period in time, thus providing the project team with insight as to whether the project is on schedule. [Monitoring and Controlling]

PMI®, *PMBOK® Guide*, 2008, 183

23. c. Several identical or nearly identical series of activities are repeated throughout the project.

When identical network descriptions are repeated throughout a project, templates of those activities can be developed. If those series of tasks are repeated several times, the template can be updated several times. Software can be used with the templates to facilitate documenting and adapting them for future use. [Planning]

PMI®, *PMBOK® Guide*, 2008, 141

24. a. The cost and time slope for each critical activity that can be expedited

Slope = (Crash cost – Normal cost) / (Crash time – Normal time). This calculation shows the cost per day of crashing the project. The slope is negative to indicate that as the time required for a project or task decreases, the cost increases. If the costs and times are the same regardless of whether they are crashed or normal, the activity cannot be expedited. [Planning]

Meredith and Mantel 2009, 386

25. c. The scope baseline

The scope baseline—made up of the scope statement, WBS, and WBS dictionary–is the primary input to the define activities process and are used to develop the activity list that subsequently will help to create the schedule. [Planning]

PMI®, *PMBOK® Guide*, 2008, 134

26. a. Scheduled start or completion of major deliverables and key external interfaces

Milestones are singular points in time, such as the start or completion of a significant activity or group of activities. [Planning]

PMI®, *PMBOK® Guide*, 2008, 157

27. a. Variance analysis

Performance of variance analysis during the schedule monitoring process is a key element of time control. Float variance is an essential planning component for evaluating project time performance. [Monitoring and Controlling]

PMI®, *PMBOK® Guide*, 2008, 163

28. a. Total float for the activity is nine days.

Total float or slack is computed by subtracting the early start date from the late start date, or 19 – 10 = 9. To compute the early finish date given a duration of 4, we would start counting the activity on the morning of the 10th; therefore, the activity would be completed at the end of day 13, not 14 (10, 11, 12, 13). If we started the activity on its late start date on the morning of the 19th, we would finish at the end of day 22, not 25. Insufficient information is provided to determine whether this activity can be completed in 2 days if the resources are doubled. [Planning]

Meredith and Mantel 2009, 346–350; PMI®, *PMBOK® Guide*, 2008, 155

29. a. Activity attributes

Identifying activity attributes is helpful for further selection and sorting of planned activities. They are used for schedule development and for report formatting purposes. [Planning]

PMI®, *PMBOK® Guide*, 2008, 136

30. c. Scope baseline

The scope statement, WBS, and WBS dictionary are considered explicitly to schedule activity definition and are used to develop the activity list. [Planning]

PMI®, *PMBOK® Guide*, 2008, 134

31. a. Review scenarios to bring the schedule in line with the plan

A corrective action is anything that is done to bring expected future schedule performance in line with the schedule baseline. Regarding the project schedule, it usually means taking action to speed up the project. One way to determine why the schedule performance is not in line with the plan is What-if analysis, which may address schedule activities and other scenarios other than the activity that is actually causing the variance. [Monitoring and Controlling]

PMI®, *PMBOK® Guide*, 2008, 156, 163

32. b. Free float

Free float is defined as the amount of time an activity can be delayed without delaying the early start of any immediately succeeding activities. [Planning]

PMI®, *PMBOK® Guide*, 2008, 155

33. b. The first step is to use conservative estimates for activity durations

When using critical chain techniques, the initial project schedule is developed using duration estimates with required dependencies and defined constraints as inputs. [Planning]

PMI®, *PMBOK® Guide*, 2008, 155

34. a. Describe any unusual sequencing in the network

A summary narrative should accompany the schedule network diagram and describe the approach used to sequence the activities in the network. This narrative also should describe any unusual sequences in the network. [Planning]

PMI®, *PMBOK® Guide*, 2008, 141

35. b. Sequence activities

The risk register may require updates in both the sequence activities and develop schedule processes. In the sequence activity process, the activity lists and activity attributes may need updates as well. [Planning]

PMI®, *PMBOK® Guide*, 2008, 141

36. b. Published estimating data

In estimating activity resources, published estimating data is a tool and technique that is used as many companies routinely publish updated production rates and unit costs of resources. This includes labor trades, material, and equipment for different countries and geographic locations in these countries. [Planning]

PMI®, *PMBOK® Guide*, 2008, 144

37. b. 68.26 percent

First, compute the standard deviation:

$$\sigma = \frac{P-O}{6} \text{ or } \frac{36-6}{6} = 5 \text{ days}$$

Next, compute PERT expected time:

$$\frac{P+4(ML)+O}{6} \text{ or } \frac{36+4(21)+6}{6} = 21 \text{ days}$$

Finally, determine range of outcomes using 1σ:

$$21 - 5 = 16 \text{ days, and } 21 + 5 = 26 \text{ days}$$

Simply defined, 1σ is the amount on either side of the mean of a normal distribution that will contain approximately 68.26% of the population. [Planning]

Meredith and Mantel 2009, 355–361

38. c. A resource calendar

Project and resource calendars identify periods when work is allowed. Project calendars affect all resources. Resource calendars affect a specific resource or a resource category, such as a labor contract that requires certain workers to work on certain days of the week. [Planning]

PMI®, *PMBOK® Guide*, 2008, 148 and 438

39. d. Productivity metrics

Duration estimates may include contingency reserves, and contingency should be identified clearly in schedule documentation. They are built into the overall project schedule to account for uncertainty. They also may be developed using quantitative analysis methods. When more information is known about the project, the contingency reserve may be used, reduced, or eliminated. [Planning]

PMI®, *PMBOK® Guide*, 2008, 151

40. c. **Provide the ability to show performance for a specified time period for trend analysis**

Because schedule performance index (SPI) and cost performance index (CPI) are expressed as ratios, they can be used to show performance for a specific time period or trends over a long-time horizon. Additionally, there is no need to disclose confidential financial data to convey the project's status to one's customers; they should not have a need to know such information [Monitoring and Controlling]

Kerzner 2006, 618–619

PROJECT COST MANAGEMENT

Study Hints

You do not need to be a certified public accountant to successfully answer the Project Cost Management questions on the PMP® certification exam. PMI® addresses cost management from a project manager's perspective, which is much more general than that of an accountant. However, these questions are not easy. Far from it! Exam takers find the Project Cost Management questions more difficult than most of the others because they address such a broad range of cost issues (for example, cost estimating, earned value, and creating and interpreting S-curves) and require a significant amount of study time.

You may find questions relating to contract cost management. Because cost considerations are heavily affected by contract type and Project Procurement Management is one of the nine *PMBOK® Guide* areas on which you will be tested, time spent studying that area will help to prepare you for the cost questions on the exam and vice versa.

The exam may include several questions that require you to know and solve specific, albeit simple, formulas. You *must* have a thorough knowledge of earned value—what it is and how it is computed. You also should be knowledgeable about variance analysis.

PMI® views Project Cost Management as a three-step process comprising estimate costs, determine budgets, and control costs. See *PMBOK® Guide* Figure 7-1 for an overview of this structure. Know this chart thoroughly.

Important: PMI® allows the use of standard six-function ($+$, $-$, $\times$, $\div$, $\sqrt{}$, %) business calculators. These calculators must be silent and have a self-contained power source. They are NOT to include a printing mechanism or a full alphabetic character set. Programmable calculators, which are instruments that can store mathematical formulas, are prohibited. The testing center will provide calculators for your use during the exam.

Following is a list of the major Project Cost Management topics. Use it to help focus your study efforts on the areas most likely to appear on the exam.

Major Topics

Project cost management

Life-cycle cost (LCC)

Cost management plan

Estimate costs

- Scope baseline
- Human resource plan
- Risk register
- Cost estimating methods
    - Analogous estimating
    - Parametric modeling
    - Bottom-up estimating
    - Three-point estimates
    - Vendor bid analysis
    - Reserve analysis
    - Cost of quality
- Accuracy of estimates
    - Order of magnitude
    - Budget
    - Definitive
- Direct versus indirect costs
- Contingency/management reserve
- Activity cost estimates
- Basis of estimates

Cost risk and contract type

Determine budgets

- Cost aggregation
- Reserve analysis
- Funding limit reconciliation

Cost performance baseline

Control costs

- Performance reviews
- Variance analysis
- Forecasting

Major Topics (continued)

Earned value management (EVM)

- The most rudimentary building blocks
- Cost variance (CV)
- Schedule variance (SV)
- Cost performance index (CPI)
- Forecasting
  - Schedule performance index (SPI)
  - Budget at completion (BAC)
  - Variance at completion (VAC)
  - Estimate to complete (ETC)
  - Estimate at completion (EAC)
  - To-complete performance index (TCPI)

Earned value measurement techniques

- Weighted milestones
- Fixed formula
- Percent complete
- Work performance measurements
- Budget forecasts
- Change requests
- Document updates

Practice Questions

INSTRUCTIONS: Note the most suitable answer for each multiple-choice question in the appropriate space on the answer sheet.

You are using earned value progress reporting for your current project in an effort to teach your software developers the benefits of earned value. You plan to display project results on the cafeteria bulletin board so that the team knows how the project is progressing. Use the current status, listed below, to answer questions 1 through 4:

$$PV \ = \ \$2,200$$
$$EV \ = \ \$2,000$$
$$AC \ = \ \$2,500$$
$$BAC \ = \ \$10,000$$

1. According to earned value analysis, the SV and status of the project described above is—

   a. −$300; the project is ahead of schedule
   b. +$8,000; the project is on schedule
   c. +$200; the project is ahead of schedule
   d. −$200; the project is behind schedule

2. What is the CPI for this project, and what does it tell us about cost performance thus far?

   a. 0.20; actual costs are exactly as planned
   b. 0.80; actual costs have exceeded planned costs
   c. 0.80; actual costs are less than planned costs
   d. 1.25; actual costs have exceeded planned costs

3. The CV for this project is—

   a. 300
   b. −$300
   c. 500
   d. −$500

4. What is the EAC for this project, and what does it represent?

   a. $12,500; the revised estimate for total project cost (based on performance thus far)
   b. $10,000; the revised estimate for total project cost (based on performance thus far)
   c. $12,500; the original project budget
   d. $10,000; the original project budget

5. Your first task on your project is to prepare a cost estimate. You decided to use analogous estimating. Which of the following is NOT characteristic of analogous estimating?

   a. Supports top-down estimating
   b. Is a form of expert judgment
   c. Has an accuracy rate of ±10% of actual costs
   d. Involves using the cost of a previous, similar project as the basis for estimating current project cost

6. All the following are outputs of the estimate cost process EXCEPT—

   a. Activity cost estimates
   b. Basis of estimates
   c. Documented constraints
   d. Cost performance baseline

7. You must consider direct costs, indirect costs, overhead costs, and general and administrative costs during cost estimating. Which of the following is NOT an example of a direct cost?

   a. Salary of the project manager
   b. Subcontractor expenses
   c. Materials used by the project
   d. Electricity

8. If the cost variance is the same as the schedule variance and both numbers are greater than zero, then—

   a. The cost variance is due to the schedule variance
   b. The variance is favorable to the project
   c. The schedule variance can be easily corrected
   d. Labor rates have escalated since the project began

9. You are responsible for preparing a cost estimate for a large World Bank project. You decide to prepare a bottom-up estimate because your estimate needs to be as accurate as possible. Your first step is to—

   a. Locate a computerized tool to assist in the process
   b. Use the cost estimate from a previous project to help you prepare this estimate
   c. Identify and estimate the cost for each work package or activity
   d. Consult with subject matter experts and use their suggestions as the basis for your estimate

10. Management has grown weary of the many surprises, mostly negative, that occur on your projects. In an effort to provide stakeholders with an effective performance metric, you will use the to-complete performance index (TCPI). Its purpose is to—

   a. Determine the schedule and cost performance needed to complete the remaining work within management's financial goal for the project
   b. Determine the cost performance needed to complete the remaining work within management's financial goal for the project
   c. Predict final project costs
   d. Predict final project schedule and costs

11. If operations on a work package were estimated to cost $1,500 and finish today but, instead, have cost $1,350 and are only two-thirds complete, the cost variance is—

   a. $150
   b. –$150
   c. –$350
   d. –$500

12. When you review cost performance data on your project, different responses will be required depending on the degree of variance or control thresholds from the baseline. For example, a variance of 10 percent might not require immediate action, whereas a variance of 100 percent will require investigation. A description of how you plan to manage cost variances should be included in the—

   a. Cost management plan
   b. Change management plan
   c. Performance measurement plan
   d. Variance management plan

13. As of the fourth month on the Acme project, cumulative planned expenditures were $100,000. Actual expenditures totaled $120,000. How is the Acme project doing?

   a. It is ahead of schedule.
   b. It is in trouble because of a cost overrun.
   c. It will finish within the original budget.
   d. The information is insufficient to make an assessment.

14. On your project, you need to assign costs to the time period in which they are incurred. To do this, you should—

   a. Identify the project components so that costs can be allocated
   b. Use the project schedule as an input to determine budget
   c. Prepare a detailed and accurate cost estimate
   d. Prepare a cost performance plan

15. You have a number of costs to track and manage because your project is technically very complex. They include direct costs and indirect (overhead) costs. You have found that managing overhead costs is particularly difficult because they—

    a. Are handled on a project-by-project basis
    b. Represent only direct labor costs
    c. Represent only equipment and materials needed for the project
    d. Are usually beyond the project manager's control

16. If you want to calculate the ETC based on your expectations that similar variances to those noted to date will not occur, you should use which of the following formulas?

    a. ETC = BAC - EV
    b. ETC = (BAC - EV) / CPI
    c. ETC = AC + EAC
    d. ETC = AC + BAC - EV

17. You receive a frantic phone call from your vice president who says she is going to meet with a prospective client in 15 minutes to discuss a large and complex project. She asks you how much the project will cost. You quickly think of some similar past projects, factor in a few unknowns, and give her a number. What type of estimate did you just provide?

    a. Definitive
    b. Budget
    c. Order-of-magnitude
    d. Detailed

18. Your approved cost baseline has changed because of a major scope change on your project. Your next step should be to—

    a. Estimate the magnitude of the scope change
    b. Issue a budget update
    c. Document lessons learned
    d. Execute the approved scope change

19. Which of the following is a tool for analyzing a design, determining its functions, and assessing how to provide those functions' cost effectively?

    a. Pareto diagram
    b. Value analysis
    c. Configuration management
    d. Value engineering

20. The cumulative CPI has been shown to be relatively stable after what percentage of project completion?

    a. 5% to 10%
    b. 15% to 20%
    c. 25% to 35%
    d. 50% to 75%

21. The undistributed budget is part of the—

    a. Management reserve
    b. Performance measurement baseline
    c. Level-of-effort cost accounts
    d. General and administrative accounts

22. It is expensive to lease office space in cities around the world. Office space can cost approximately USD $80 per square foot in Tampa, Florida. And it can cost approximately ¥50,000 per square meter in Tokyo. These "averages" can help a person to determine how much it will cost to lease office space in these cities based on the amount of space leased. These estimates are examples of—

    a. Variance analysis
    b. Parametric estimating
    c. Bottom-up estimating
    d. Reserve analysis

23. Your project manager has requested that you provide him with a forecast of project costs for the next 12 months. He needs this information to determine if the budget should be increased or decreased on this major construction project. In addition to the usual information sources, which of the following should you also consider?

    a. Cost estimates from similar projects
    b. WBS
    c. Project schedule
    d. Approved change requests

24. There are a number of different earned value management rules of performance measurement that can be established as part of the cost management plan. Which one of the following is NOT an example of such a rule?

    a. Code of accounts allocation provision
    b. Formulas to determine the ETC
    c. Earned value credit criteria
    d. Definition of the WBS level

25. Which of the following calculations CANNOT be used to determine EAC?

    a. EV to date plus the remaining project budget
    b. AC to date plus a new estimate for all remaining work
    c. AC to date plus the remaining budget
    d. AC to date plus the remaining budget modified by a performance factor

26. Typically, the statement "no one likes to estimate, because they know their estimate will be proven incorrect" is true. However, you have been given the challenge of estimating the costs for your nuclear reactor project. A basic assumption that you need to make early in this process is—

    a. How direct and indirect costs will be handled
    b. Whether or not experts will be available to assist you in this process
    c. If there will be a multiyear project budget
    d. Whether the project has required delivery dates

27. By reviewing cumulative cost curves, the project manager can monitor—

    a. EV
    b. PV
    c. CVs
    d. CPI

28. Control accounts—

    a. Are charge accounts for personnel time management
    b. Summarize project costs at level 2 of the WBS
    c. Identify and track management reserves
    d. Represent the basic level at which project performance is measured and reported

29. Performance review meetings are held to assess schedule activity and work package or control account status and progress. Typically, they are used in conjunction with all but which of the following performance reporting techniques?

    a. Variance analysis
    b. Trend analysis
    c. Time reporting systems
    d. Earned value analysis

30. Overall cost estimates must be allocated to individual activities or work packages to establish the project cost performance baseline. In an ideal situation, a project manager would prefer to prepare estimates—

    a. Before the budget is requested
    b. After the budget is approved by management
    c. Using a parametric estimating technique and model specific for that project type
    d. Using a bottom-up estimating technique

31. According to learning curve theory, when many items are produced repetitively—

    a. Unit costs decrease geometrically as production rates increase linearly
    b. Unit costs decrease as production rates increase
    c. Unit costs decrease in a regular pattern as more units are produced
    d. Costs of training increase as the level of automation increases

32. The method of calculating the EAC by adding the remaining project budget (modified by a performance factor) to the actuals to date is used most often when the—

    a. Current variances are viewed as atypical ones
    b. Original estimating assumptions are no longer reliable because conditions have changed
    c. Current variances are viewed as typical of future variances
    d. Original estimating assumptions are considered to be fundamentally flawed

33. Increased attention to return on investment (ROI) now requires you to complete a financial analysis of the payback period on your project. Such an analysis identifies the—

    a. Ratio of discounted revenues over discounted costs
    b. Future value of money invested today
    c. Amount of time before net cash flow becomes positive
    d. Point in time where costs exceed profit

34. A revised cost baseline may be required in cost control when—

    a. CVs are severe, and a realistic measure of performance is needed
    b. Updated cost estimates are prepared and distributed to stakeholders
    c. Corrective action must be taken to bring expected future performance in line with the project plan
    d. EAC shows that additional funds are needed to complete the project even if a scope change is not needed

35. As project manager, you identified a number of acceptable tolerances as part of your earned value management system. During execution, some "unacceptable" variances occurred. After each "unacceptable" variance occurred, you did which one of the following first?

    a. Updated the budget
    b. Prepared a revised cost estimate
    c. Adjusted the project plan
    d. Documented lessons learned

36. Assume that the project cost estimates have been prepared for each activity and the basis of these estimates has been determined. Now, as the project manager for your nutrition awareness program in your hospital, you are preparing your budget. Because you have estimates for more than 1,200 separate activities, you have decided to first—

    a. Aggregate these estimates by work packages
    b. Aggregate these estimates by control accounts to facilitate the use of earned value management
    c. Use the results of previous projects to predict total costs
    d. Set your cost performance baseline

37. The cumulative cost curve for planned and actual expenditures—

    a. Helps to monitor project performance at a glance
    b. Is used for calculating the CPI
    c. Is also known as a histogram
    d. Forecasts total project expenditures

38. The reason that the cost performance index (CPI) is shown as a ration is to—

    a. Enable a detailed analysis of the schedule regardless of the value of the schedule variance
    b. Distinguish between critical path and noncritical path work packages
    c. Provide the ability to show performance for a specified time period for trend analysis
    d. Measure the actual time to complete the project

39. Assume that your actual costs are $800; your planned value is $1,200; and your earned value is $1,000. Based on these data, what can be determined regarding your schedule variance?

    a. At +$200, the situation is favorable as physical progress is being accomplished ahead of your plan.
    b. At –$200, the physical progress is being accomplished at a slower rate than is planned, indicating an unfavorable situation.
    c. At +$400, the situation is favorable as physical progress is being accomplished at a lower cost than was forecasted.
    d. At –$200, you have a behind-schedule condition, and your critical path has slipped.

40. The CPI on your project is 0.84. This means that you should—

    a. Place emphasis on improving the timeliness of the physical progress
    b. Reassess the life-cycle costs of your product, including the length of the life-cycle phase
    c. Recognize that your original estimates were fundamentally flawed and your project is in an atypical situation
    d. Place emphasis on improving the productivity by which work was being performed

Answer Sheet

1. a b c d
2. a b c d
3. a b c d
4. a b c d
5. a b c d
6. a b c d
7. a b c d
8. a b c d
9. a b c d
10. a b c d
11. a b c d
12. a b c d
13. a b c d
14. a b c d
15. a b c d
16. a b c d
17. a b c d
18. a b c d
19. a b c d
20. a b c d

21. a b c d
22. a b c d
23. a b c d
24. a b c d
25. a b c d
26. a b c d
27. a b c d
28. a b c d
29. a b c d
30. a b c d
31. a b c d
32. a b c d
33. a b c d
34. a b c d
35. a b c d
36. a b c d
37. a b c d
38. a b c d
39. a b c d
40. a b c d

Answer Key

1. d. −$200; the project is behind schedule

SV is calculated as EV − PV (in this case, $2,000 − $2,200). A negative variance means that the work completed is less than what was planned for at that point in the project. [Monitoring and Controlling]

PMI®, *PMBOK® Guide*, 2008, 182

2. b. 0.80; actual costs have exceeded planned costs

CPI is calculated as EV / AC (in this case, $2,000 / $2,500). EV measures the budgeted dollar value of the work that has actually been accomplished, whereas AC measures the actual cost of getting that work done. If the two numbers are the same, work on the project is being accomplished for exactly the budgeted amount of money (and the ratio will be equal to 1.0). If actual costs exceed budgeted costs (as in this example), AC will be larger than EV and the ratio will be less than 1.0. CPI is also an index of efficiency. In this example, an index of 0.80 (or 80 percent) means that for every dollar spent on the project only 80 cents worth of work is actually accomplished. [Monitoring and Controlling]

PMI®, *PMBOK® Guide*, 2008, 183

3. d. −$500

CV is calculated as EV − AC (in this case, $2,000 − $2,500). A negative CV means that accomplishing work on the project is costing more than was budgeted. [Monitoring and Controlling]

PMI®, *PMBOK® Guide*, 2008, 182

4. a. $12,500; the revised estimate for total project cost (based on performance thus far)

EAC is calculated as BAC / CPI (in this case, $10,000 / 0.80). It is now known that the project will cost more than the original estimate of $10,000. The project has been getting only 80 cents worth of work done for every dollar spent (CPI), and this information has been used to forecast total project costs. This approach assumes that performance for the remainder of the project will also be based on a CPI of 0.80. [Monitoring and Controlling]

PMI®, *PMBOK® Guide*, 2008, 184–185

5. c. Has an accuracy rate of $\pm$10% of actual costs

A frequently used method of estimate costs, the analogous technique relies on experience and knowledge gained to predict future events. This technique provides planners with some idea of the magnitude of project costs but generally not within $\pm$10%. [Planning]

PMI®, *PMBOK® Guide*, 2008, 171

6. d. Cost performance baseline

Cost baseline is an output from the determine budget process. [Monitoring and Controlling]

PMI®, *PMBOK® Guide*, 2008, 188

7. d. Electricity

Direct costs are incurred for the exclusive benefit of a project (for example, salary of the project manager, materials used by the project, and subcontractor expenses). Indirect costs, also called overhead costs, are allocated to a project by its performing organization as a cost of doing business. These costs cannot be traced to a specific project and are accumulated and allocated equitably over multiple projects (for example, security guards, fringe benefits, and electricity). [Planning]

PMI®, *PMBOK® Guide*, 2008, 169

8. b. The variance is favorable to the project

A positive schedule variance indicates that the project is ahead of schedule. A positive cost variance indicates that the project has incurred less cost than estimated for the work accomplished; therefore, the project is under budget. [Monitoring and Controlling]

PMI®, *PMBOK® Guide*, 2008, 182

9. c. Identify and estimate the cost for each work package or activity

Bottom-up estimating is derived by first estimating the cost of the project's elemental tasks at the lower levels of the WBS or for an activity and then aggregating those estimates at successively higher levels of the WBS for subsequent reporting and tracking purposes. [Planning]

PMI®, *PMBOK® Guide*, 2008, 172

10. b. Determine the cost performance needed to complete the remaining work within management's financial goal for the project

The TCPI takes the value of work remaining and divides it by the value of funds remaining to obtain the cost performance factor needed to complete all remaining work according to a financial goal set by management. [Monitoring and Controlling]

PMI®, *PMBOK® Guide*, 2008, 185

11. c. −$350

CV is calculated by EV − AC, or $1,500(2/3) − $1,350 = −$350. [Monitoring and Controlling]

PMI®, *PMBOK® Guide*, 2008, 182

12. a. Cost management plan

The management and control of costs focuses on variance thresholds. Certain variances are acceptable, and others, usually those falling outside a particular range, are unacceptable. The actions taken by the project manager for variances are described in the cost management plan. [Planning]

PMI®, *PMBOK® Guide*, 2008, 166

13. d. The information is insufficient to make an assessment.

The information provided tells us that, as of the fourth month, more money has been spent than was planned. However, we need to know how much work has been completed to determine how the project is performing. In earned value terms, we are missing the EV. [Monitoring and Controlling]

PMI®, *PMBOK® Guide*, 2008, 182

14. b. Use the project schedule as an input to determine budget

Accurate project performance measurement depends on accurate cost and schedule information. The project schedule includes planned start and finish dates for all activities tied to work packages and control accounts. This information is used to aggregate costs to the calendar period for which the costs are planned to be incurred. [Planning]

PMI®, *PMBOK® Guide*, 2008, 176

15. d. Are usually beyond the project manager's control

Overhead includes costs such as rent, insurance, or heating, that pertain to the project as a whole and cannot be attributed to a particular work item. The amount of overhead to be added to the project is frequently decided by the performing organization and is beyond the control of the project manager. [Monitoring and Controlling]

Meredith and Mantel 2009, 299, 306–307

16. a. ETC = BAC - EV

This formula assumes that the estimate to complete is based on atypical variances. [Monitoring and Controlling]

PMI®, *PMBOK® Guide*, 2008, 184–185

17. c. Order-of-magnitude

An order-of-magnitude estimate, which is referred to also as a ballpark estimate, has an accuracy range of −50% to 100% and is made without detailed data. [Planning]

PMI®, *PMBOK® Guide*, 2008, 168; Ward 2008, 295

18. b. Issue a budget update

Budget updates reflect changes to an approved cost baseline. These changes generally are made in response to an approved scope change. [Monitoring and Controlling]

PMI®, *PMBOK® Guide*, 2008, 188–189

19. d. Value engineering

Value engineering considers possible cost trade-offs as a design evolves. The technique entails identifying the functions that are needed and analyzing the cost effectiveness of the alternatives available for providing them. [Monitoring and Controlling]

PMI®, *PMBOK® Guide*, 2008, 444

20. b.   15% to 20%

The CPI has been proven to be an accurate and reliable forecasting tool. Researchers have found that the cumulative CPI does not change by more than 10% once a project is approximately 20% complete. The CPI provides a quick statistical forecast of final project costs. [Monitoring and Controlling]

Fleming and Koppelman 2000, 134

21. b.   Performance measurement baseline

The undistributed budget is applied to project work that has not yet been linked to WBS elements at or below the lowest level of reporting. It is, therefore, part of the performance measurement baseline and is expected to be used in the performance of project work. [Monitoring and Controlling]

PMI®, *PMBOK® Guide*, 2008, 177

22. b.   Parametric estimating

Parametric estimating involves using statistical relationships between historical data and other variables to calculate or estimate for activity parameters, such as cost, budget, or duration. The example is representative of a simple parametric model. [Planning]

PMI®, *PMBOK® Guide*, 2008, 150, 172, 177–178

23. d.   Approved change requests

An approved change request from the perform integrated change control process can include modifications to the cost terms of the contract project scope, cost baseline, or cost management plan. [Monitoring and Controlling]

PMI®, *PMBOK® Guide*, 2008, 187

24. a.   Code of accounts allocation provision

Three recognized earned value management rules of performance measurement are to (1) determine the ETC calculation to be used on the project, (2) establish how EV credit will be determined (for example, 0–100, 0–50–100, and so on), and (3) define the WBS level at which the earned value analysis will be performed. [Planning]

PMI®, *PMBOK® Guide*, 2008, 166

25. a. EV to date plus the remaining project budget

EAC is a forecast of the most likely total value based on project performance and risk quantification. To calculate EAC, the AC of a project must be known and used in the calculation. Any calculation that relies solely on the EV will not yield an accurate measure of cost performance. [Monitoring and Controlling]

PMI®, *PMBOK® Guide*, 2008, 184–185

26. a. How direct and indirect costs will be handled

The scope statement is a key input in the estimate costs process and should be reviewed. It provides the project description, acceptance criteria, key deliverables, boundaries, assumptions, and constraints about the project. It also notes one basic assumption that must be made as costs are estimated is whether the estimates will be limited only to direct project costs or whether they also will include indirect project costs. [Planning]

PMI®, *PMBOK® Guide*, 2008, 169

27. c. CVs

Cumulative cost curves, or S-curves, enable the project manager to monitor cost variances at a glance. The difference in height between the planned-expenditure curve and the actual-expenditure curve represents the monetary value of variances at any given time. [Monitoring and Controlling]

PMI®, *PMBOK® Guide*, 2008, 183

28. d. Represent the basic level at which project performance is measured and reported

Control accounts represent a management control point where scope, budget (resource plans), actual costs, and schedule are integrated and compared to earned value for performance measurement. [Planning]

PMI®, *PMBOK® Guide*, 2008, 166 and 422

29. c. Time reporting systems

Performance review meetings are conducted to determine schedule, budget, and quality performance among other important issues. Time reporting systems are a performance reporting tool and technique in project communications management used to record and provide time expended for the project. [Monitoring and Controlling]

PMI®, *PMBOK® Guide*, 2008, 186

30. a.   Before the budget is requested

Often project cost estimates are prepared after budgetary approval is provided. However, work package cost estimates should be prepared before the budget request if at all possible, to enhance accuracy. [Planning]

PMI®, *PMBOK® Guide*, 2008, 174–175

31. c.   Unit costs decrease in a regular pattern as more units are produced

Learning curve theory indicates that human performance usually improves when a task is repeated. Specifically, each time output doubles, worker hours per unit decrease by a fixed percentage. This percentage is called the learning rate. [Planning]

Meredith and Mantel 2009, 308–310

32. c.   Current variances are viewed as typical of future variances

Past performance is indicative of future performance; therefore, using a performance indicator to modify the remaining project budget yields the most accurate estimate. [Monitoring and Controlling]

PMI®, *PMBOK® Guide*, 2008, 184

33. c.   Amount of time before net cash flow becomes positive

Payback period analysis determines the time required for a project to recover the investment in it and become profitable. A weakness of this approach is a lack of emphasis on the magnitude of the profitability. [Planning]

Meredith and Mantel 2009, 47; PMI® *PMBOK® Guide*, 2008, 165–168; Ward 2008, 305

34. a.   CVs are severe, and a realistic measure of performance is needed

After the CVs exceed certain ranges, the original project budget may be questioned and changed as a result of new information. [Monitoring and Controlling]

PMI®, *PMBOK® Guide*, 2008, 188

35. d. Documented lessons learned

Lessons learned but not documented are "lessons lost." The lessons learned knowledge database will help current project members, as well as people on future projects, make better decisions. Accordingly, the reasons for the variance, the rationale supporting the corrective action, and other related information must be documented. [Monitoring and Controlling]

PMI®, *PMBOK® Guide*, 2008, 91

36. a. Aggregate these estimates by work packages

The WBS provides the relationship among all the project deliverables and their components and should be reviewed before the budget is developed. As the budget is determined, the cost estimates for the activities should be aggregated by the work packages in the WBS. Then, later, they are aggregated for the control accounts and finally for the entire project. [Planning]

PMI®, *PMBOK® Guide*, 2008, 177

37. a. Helps to monitor project performance at a glance

Cost curves for planned and actual expenditures are created by adding each month's costs to the previous reporting period's expenditures. By doing so, one can quickly see how the project is performing. [Monitoring and Controlling]

PMI®, *PMBOK® Guide*, 2008, 183

38. c. Provide the ability to show performance for a specified time period for trend analysis

Because schedule performance index (SPI) and cost performance index (CPI) are expressed as ratios, they can be used to show performance for a specific time period or trends over a long-time horizon. Additionally, there is no need to disclose confidential financial data to convey the project's status to one's customers; they should not have a need to know such information. [Monitoring and Controlling]

Kerzner 2006, 618–619

39. **b.** **At −$200, the physical progress is being accomplished at a slower rate than is planned, indicating an unfavorable situation.**

Schedule variance is calculated: EV − PV or $1,000 − $1,200 = −$200. Because the SV is negative, physical progress is being accomplished at a slower rate than planned. [Monitoring and Controlling]

Kerzner 2006, 616; PMI®, *PMBOK® Guide*, 2008, 183

40. **d.** **Place emphasis on improving the productivity by which work was being performed**

CPI = EV / AC and measures the efficiency of the physical progress accomplished compared to the baseline. A CPI of 0.84 means that for every dollar spent, you're only receiving 84 cents of progress. Therefore, you should focus on improving the productivity by which work is being performed. [Monitoring and Controlling]

Kerzner 2006, 618; PMI®, *PMBOK® Guide*, 2008, 183

PROJECT QUALITY MANAGEMENT

Study Hints

The Project Quality Management questions on the PMP® certification exam are straightforward—especially if you know definitions of terms and understand statistical process control. You are not required to solve quantitative problems, but there are questions on statistical methods of measuring and controlling quality.

The exam is likely to reflect a heavy emphasis on customer satisfaction and continuous improvement through the use of quality tools such as Pareto analysis and cause-and-effect diagrams. You must also know the differences among plan quality, perform quality assurance, and perform quality control.

The *PMBOK® Guide* includes all quality-related activities under the term Project Quality Management, which comprises the three quality processes mentioned above. Review *PMBOK® Guide* Figure 8-1 for an overview of the Project Quality Management structure before taking the practice test. Know this chart thoroughly.

Following is a list of the major Project Quality Management topics. Use it to help focus your study efforts on the areas most likely to appear on the exam.

Major Topics

Key **PMBOK**® **Guide** *concepts*

Quality defined

Quality management

Quality policy

Plan quality tools

- Cost-benefit analysis
- Benchmarking
- Design of experiments
- Cost of quality
- Control charts
- Statistical sampling
- Flowcharts
- Proprietary quality management methodologies
- Brainstorming
- Affinity diagrams
- Force field analysis
- Nominal group technique
- Prioritization matrixes

Key quality planning documents

- Quality management plan
- Quality metrics
- Quality checklists
- Process improvement plan

Quality assurance

- Quality control measurements
- Quality audits
- Process analysis
- Quality improvement
- Continuous process improvement
- Use of quality improvement standards and definitions

Major Topics (continued)

Quality control

- Variable
- Attribute
- Prevention
- Probability
- Standard deviation
- Process control
- Sampling
- Tolerance

Quality control tools

- Cause-and-effect diagrams
- Control charts
- Flowcharting
- Histograms
- Pareto charts
- Run charts
- Scatter diagrams
- Statistical sampling
- Inspection

Approved change requests review

Validated changes and deliverables

Impact of motivation on quality

Priority of quality versus cost and schedule

Design and quality

Practice Questions

INSTRUCTIONS: Note the most suitable answer for each multiple-choice question in the appropriate space on the answer sheet.

1. Quality is very important to your company. Each project has a quality statement that is consistent with the organization's vision and mission. Both internal and external quality assurance are provided on all projects to—

   a. Ensure confidence that the project will satisfy relevant quality standards
   b. Monitor specific project results to note whether they comply with relevant quality standards
   c. Identify ways to eliminate causes of unsatisfactory results
   d. Use inspection to keep errors out of the process

2. Benchmarking is a technique used in—

   a. Inspections
   b. Root cause analysis
   c. Plan quality
   d. Perform quality control

3. In quality management, the practice "rework" is—

   a. Acceptable under certain circumstances
   b. An adjustment made that is based on quality control measurements
   c. Action taken to bring a defective or nonconforming component into compliance
   d. Not a concern if errors are detected early

4. The quality function deployment process is used to—

   a. Provide better product definition and product development
   b. Help products to succeed in the marketplace
   c. Improve the functional characteristics of a product
   d. Support production planning and the just-in-time approach

5. As it applies to quality, the law of diminishing returns says that—

   a. 100% quality is unattainable
   b. 100% inspection is not cost effective
   c. Beyond a certain point, additional investment in quality has a negative ROI
   d. Providing quality products will stop, or at least diminish, the number of returned items

6. You are leading a research project that will require between 10 and 20 aerospace engineers. Some senior-level aerospace engineers are available. They are more productive than junior-level engineers, who cost less and who are available as well. You want to determine the optimal combination of senior- and junior-level personnel. In this situation, the appropriate technique to use is to—

   a. Conduct a design of experiments
   b. Use the Ishikawa diagram to pinpoint the problem
   c. Prepare a control chart
   d. Analyze the process using a Pareto diagram

7. The purpose of the Taguchi method is to—

   a. Manage the flow of material for better visibility and control
   b. Use statistical techniques to compute a "loss function" to determine the cost of producing products that fail to achieve a target value
   c. Design, group, and manage production operations as self-contained flexible cells capable of start-to-finish processing of a family of items
   d. Regulate coordination and communication among process stages

8. Quality assurance promotes quality improvement. A "breakthrough" is the accomplishment of any improvement that takes the organization to unprecedented levels of performance by attacking—

   a. Special causes of variation
   b. Common causes of variation
   c. Inspection over prevention
   d. Specific tolerances

9. Which of the following statements best describes attribute sampling versus variables sampling?

   a. Attribute sampling is concerned with prevention, whereas variables sampling is concerned with inspection.
   b. Attribute sampling is concerned with conformance, whereas variables sampling is concerned with the degree of conformity.
   c. Attribute sampling is concerned with special causes, whereas variables sampling is concerned with any causes.
   d. Both are the same concept.

10. Your project scheduler has just started working with your project and has produced defective reports for the past two accounting cycles. If this continues, these defective reports could provide the potential for customer dissatisfaction and lost productivity due to rework. You discovered that the project scheduler needs additional training on using the scheduling tool that is used on your project. The cost of training falls under which one of the following categories?

    a. Overhead costs
    b. Failure costs
    c. Prevention costs
    d. Indirect costs

11. When a process is within acceptable limits, it—

    a. Should not be adjusted
    b. May not be changed to provide improvements
    c. Shows differences caused by expected events or normal causes
    d. Should not be inspected or reworked for any reason

12. The project team should have a working knowledge of statistical process control to help evaluate quality control outputs. Of all the topics involved, which of the following is the most important for the team to understand?

    a. Sampling and probability
    b. Attribute sampling and variables sampling
    c. Tolerances and control limits
    d. Special causes and random causes

13. Rank ordering of defects should be used to guide corrective action. This is the underlying principle behind—

    a. Trend analysis
    b. Inspections
    c. Control charts
    d. Pareto diagrams

14. Project quality management was once thought to include only inspection or quality control. In recent years, the concept of project quality management has broadened. Which statement is NOT representative of the new definition of quality management?

    a. Quality is designed into the product or service, not inspected into it.
    b. Quality is the concern of the quality assurance staff.
    c. Customers require a documented and, in some cases, registered quality assurance system.
    d. National and international standards and guidelines for quality assurance systems are available.

15. In order to monitor the number of errors or defects that have been identified and the number that remain undetected, you should—

    a. Design an experiment
    b. Use a checklist
    c. Conduct a trend analysis
    d. Perform an audit

16. Your quality assurance department recently performed a quality audit of your project and identified a number of findings and recommendations. One recommendation seems critical and should be implemented because it affects successful delivery of the product to your customer. Your next step should be to—

    a. Call a meeting of your project team to see who is responsible for the problem
    b. Reassign the team member who had responsibility for oversight of the problem
    c. Perform product rework immediately
    d. Issue a change request to implement the needed corrective action

17. Six sigma refers to the aim of setting tolerance limits at six standard deviations from the mean, whereas the normally expected deviation of a process is—

    a. One standard deviation
    b. Two standard deviations
    c. Three standard deviations
    d. Undeterminable because of the unique nature of every process

18. You recognize the importance of quality control on your project. However, you also know that quality control has costs associated with it and that the project has a limited budget. One way to reduce the cost of quality control is to—

    a. Work to ensure that the overall quality program is ISO compliant
    b. Use statistical sampling
    c. Conduct inspections throughout the process
    d. Use trend analysis

19. Deming's Fourteen Points provides a way for an organization to create and sustain a culture of continuous improvement. As such it should be directed by—

    a. The project manager
    b. Top management
    c. Employees participating in quality circles
    d. Stakeholders

20. Quality inspections also may be called—

    a. Control tests
    b. Walk-throughs
    c. Statistical sampling
    d. Checklists

21. Your management has prescribed that a quality audit be conducted at the end of every phase in a project. This audit is part of the organization's—

    a. Quality assurance process
    b. Quality control process
    c. Quality improvement program
    d. Process adjustment program

22. You are managing a major international project, and your contract requires you to prepare both a project plan and a quality management plan. Your core team is preparing a project quality management plan. Your first step in developing this plan is to—

    a. Determine specific metrics to use in the quality management process
    b. Identify the quality standards for the project
    c. Develop a quality policy for the project
    d. Identify specific quality management roles and responsibilities for the project

23. Recently your company introduced a new set of "metal woods" to its established line of golfing equipment. However, in the past weeks many of the clubs have been returned due to quality problems. You decide to conduct a failure mode and criticality analysis to—

    a. Analyze the product development cycle after product release to determine strengths and weaknesses
    b. Evaluate failure modes and causes associated with the design and manufacture of an existing product
    c. Evaluate failure modes and causes associated with the design and manufacture of a new product
    d. Help management set priorities in its existing manufacturing processes to avoid failures

24. The "rule of seven" as applied to statistical process control charts means that—

    a. Seven rejects typically occur per thousand inspections
    b. Seven consecutive measurements are ascending, descending, or the same
    c. At least seven inspectors should be in place for every thousand employees
    d. A process is not out of control even though seven measurements fall outside the lower and upper control limits

25. Long-term contracting is an important aspect of project quality management because it—

    a. Provides incentives to vendors to make quality commitments
    b. Improves quality through the use of benefit-cost ratio
    c. Usually results in lower costs and increased profitability
    d. Provides for periodic, yet mandatory quality audits

26. Even though your project is vastly different from a manufacturing operation, you believe the principles of *kaizen* will work well. The *kaizen* approach to continuous improvement emphasizes—

    a. The greater importance of customer satisfaction over cost
    b. Radical changes in operating practices
    c. Incremental improvement
    d. The use of quality circles to improve morale

27. Results of quality control testing and measurement are used—

    a. As an input to quality planning
    b. To prepare an operational definition
    c. To prepare a control chart
    d. As an input to quality assurance

28. The statistical control chart is a tool used primarily to help—

    a. Monitor process variation over time
    b. Measure the degree of conformance
    c. Determine whether results conform
    d. Determine whether results conform to requirements

29. The area where the project manager can have the greatest impact on the quality of his or her project is in—

    a. Quality planning
    b. Quality assurance
    c. Quality control
    d. Quality improvement

30. You are a project manager for residential construction. As a project manager, you must be especially concerned with building codes—particularly in the quality planning process. You must ensure that building codes are reflected in your project plans because—

    a. Standards and regulations are an input to plan quality
    b. Quality audits serve to ensure there is compliance with regulations
    c. They are a cost associated with quality initiatives
    d. Compliance with standards is the primary objective of perform quality control

31. You work as a project manager in the largest hospital in the region. Studies have shown that patients have to wait for long periods before being treated. To assist in identifying the factors contributing to this problem, you and your team have decided to use which of the following techniques?

    a. Cause-and-effect diagrams
    b. Pareto analysis
    c. Scatter diagrams
    d. Control charts

32. The ISO 9000 standards provide—

    a. A description of how products should be produced
    b. Specifics for the implementation of quality systems
    c. A framework for quality systems
    d. The maximum process requirements necessary to ensure that customers receive a good product

33. All of the following will assure that a good quality audit has been completed EXCEPT—

    a. Products are safe and fit for use
    b. Improvement opportunities are identified
    c. Proper preventive action is taken when required
    d. Project team members are adequately trained for their jobs

34. There are three uses and types of Pareto analysis. If you wish to provide a measure of significance to factors that at first may not appear to be significant at all, you should use a—

    a. Basic Pareto analysis
    b. Comparative Pareto analysis
    c. Weighted Pareto analysis
    d. Trend Pareto analysis

35. Constancy of purpose is a core concept for continuous improvement. An organization displaying constancy of purpose must have all the following elements EXCEPT—

    a. Documented and well-disseminated statements of purpose and vision
    b. A set of strategic and tactical plans
    c. An awareness by all members of the organization of the purpose, vision, goals, and objectives and their roles in achieving them
    d. Separate quality assurance and quality control departments reporting to senior management

36. Quality objectives of the project are recorded in—

    a. Process improvement plan
    b. Quality management plan
    c. Quality baseline
    d. Quality metrics

37. The below Pareto chart indicates defects in areas associated with billing a client for project services. Based on this Pareto analysis, which area, or areas, indicate the greatest opportunity for improvement?

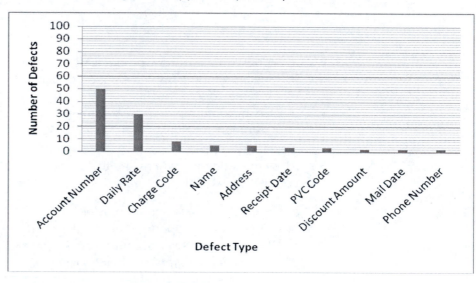

    a. The account number, because if it is incorrect, the invoice may be sent to the wrong client.
    b. The daily rate, because if it is incorrect, the total amount of the invoice will be wrong, which impacts the cash flow.
    c. The charge code, name, address, receipt date , pvc code, discount amount, mail date, and phone number, because they are fairly easy to confirm and correct, thereby significantly reducing the types of defects.
    d. The account number and daily rate, because they account for 80 percent of all defects.

38. You have decided to use a fishbone diagram to identify the relationship between an effect and its causes. To begin, you should first—

    a. Select an interdisciplinary team who has used the technique before to help brainstorm the problem
    b. Determine the major categories of defects
    c. Set up a process analysis using HIPO charts
    d. Identify the problem

39. Assume that your project in the food service industry involves the need for the presence of the required food label as specified by the Food and Drug Administration. In this situation, you plan to use control charts as a quality control tool, so you should prepare a(n)—

    a. Variables chart
    b. Attribute chart
    c. Trend chart
    d. Run chart

40. The quality management plan describes all the following EXCEPT the—

    a. Method for implementing the quality policy
    b. QA, QC, and continuous process improvement for the project
    c. Efforts at the front end of a project to ensure that earlier decisions are correct
    d. Procedures used to conduct trade-off analyses among cost, schedule, and quality

Answer Sheet

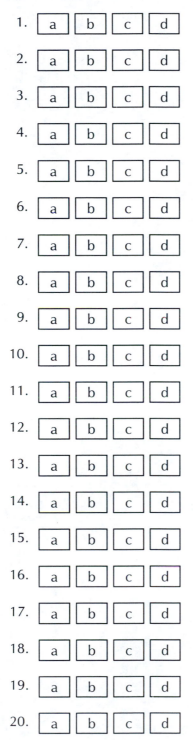

1. a b c d
2. a b c d
3. a b c d
4. a b c d
5. a b c d
6. a b c d
7. a b c d
8. a b c d
9. a b c d
10. a b c d
11. a b c d
12. a b c d
13. a b c d
14. a b c d
15. a b c d
16. a b c d
17. a b c d
18. a b c d
19. a b c d
20. a b c d

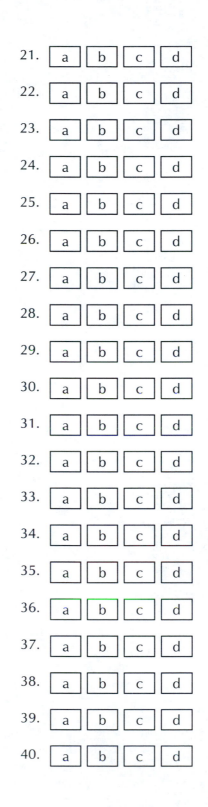

21. a b c d
22. a b c d
23. a b c d
24. a b c d
25. a b c d
26. a b c d
27. a b c d
28. a b c d
29. a b c d
30. a b c d
31. a b c d
32. a b c d
33. a b c d
34. a b c d
35. a b c d
36. a b c d
37. a b c d
38. a b c d
39. a b c d
40. a b c d

Answer Key

1. a. Ensure confidence that the project will satisfy relevant quality standards

Quality assurance increases project effectiveness and efficiency and provides added benefits to project stakeholders. It includes all the planned and systematic quality activities to ensure that the project uses all the processes to meet requirements. Quality assurance should be performed throughout the project. [Executing]

PMI®, *PMBOK® Guide*, 2008, 201–202, 204

2. c. Plan quality

Benchmarking involves comparing actual or planned practices to those practices of comparable projects to identify best practices, to note ideas for improvement, and to provide a way to measure performance. [Planning]

PMI®, *PMBOK® Guide*, 2008, 197

3. c. Action taken to bring a defective or nonconforming component into compliance

Rework is a frequent cause of project overruns. The project team must make every reasonable effort to control and minimize rework so that defective or nonconforming components are brought into compliance with requirements or specifications. [Monitoring and Controlling]

PMI®, *PMBOK® Guide*, 2008, 438

4. a. Provide better product definition and product development

Quality function deployment helps a design team to define, design, manufacture, and deliver a product or service to meet or exceed customer needs. Its main features are to capture the customer's requirements, ensure cross-functional teamwork, and link the main phases of product development—product planning, part deployment, process planning, and production planning. It is a propriety quality management methodology in the plan quality process. [Planning]

Evans and Lindsay 2005, 568–569; PMI®, *PMBOK® Guide*, 2008, 199

5. **c. Beyond a certain point, additional investment in quality has a negative ROI**

   If a company has paid $100,000 to gain 98% quality and it would cost an additional $25,000 to gain the other 2%, this is known as the law of diminishing returns. [Monitoring and Controlling]

   Ward 2008, 240

6. **a. Conduct a design of experiments**

   This technique is used to identify which variables have the most influence. It is a statistical method to identify the factors that may influence specific variables of a product or process under development or in production. For example, roller blade designers might want to determine which combination of number of wheels and titanium ball bearings would produce the most desirable "ride" characteristics at a reasonable cost. This technique, however, can be applied to project management issues such as cost and schedule trade-offs. An appropriately designed "experiment" often will help project managers to find an optimal solution from a relatively limited number of options, and often it help to determine the number and type of tests to use and their impact on quality. [Planning]

   PMI®, *PMBOK® Guide*, 2008, 197

7. **b. Use statistical techniques to compute a "loss function" to determine the cost of producing products that fail to achieve a target value**

   The Taguchi method is used to estimate the loss associated with controlling or failing to control process variability. It is based on the principle that by carefully selecting design parameters to produce robust designs, an organization can produce products that are more forgiving and tolerant. The tool helps determine the value or break-even point of improving a process to reduce variability. [Monitoring and Controlling]

   Ward 2008, 432

8. **b. Common causes of variation**

   Quality improvement includes action taken to increase project effectiveness and efficiency in order to provide added benefits to stakeholders. A breakthrough attacks chronic losses, or in Deming's terminology, common causes of variation. [Executing]

   Evans and Lindsay 2005, 486

9. b. Attribute sampling is concerned with conformance, whereas variables sampling is concerned with the degree of conformity.

Attribute sampling determines whether a result does or does not conform. Variables sampling rates a result on a continuous scale to measure the degree of conformity. [Monitoring and Controlling]

PMI®, *PMBOK® Guide*, 2008, 206

10. c. Prevention costs

Prevention costs include any expenditure directed toward ensuring that quality is achieved the first time. [Planning]

Rose 2005 8–9

11. a. Should not be adjusted

Processes should be changed only through established change procedures. If the process is outside acceptable limits, it should be adjusted. [Monitoring and Controlling]

PMI®, *PMBOK® Guide*, 2008, 209

12. a. Sampling and probability

Sampling and probability form the basis of statistical process control, which helps the team monitor project results for compliance with relevant quality standards so that methods can be identified to eliminate causes of unsatisfactory results. [Monitoring and Controlling]

PMI®, *PMBOK® Guide*, 2008, 198

13. d. Pareto diagrams

Pareto diagrams are histograms, ordered by frequency of occurrence, that show how many results were generated by type or category of identified cause. The project team should take action to fix the problems that are causing the greatest number of defects first. Pareto diagrams are based on Pareto's Law, which holds that a relatively small number of causes will typically produce a large majority of defects, also called the "solzo rule." [Monitoring and Controlling]

PMI®, *PMBOK® Guide*, 2008, 210–211

14. b.   Quality is the concern of the quality assurance staff.

Quality concerns all levels of management and staff. Its success requires participation from all members of the project team with management providing the needed resources to succeed. [Planning]

PMI®, *PMBOK® Guide*, 2004, 191

15. c.   Conduct a trend analysis

Trend analysis involves using mathematical techniques to forecast future outcomes based on historical results. It is performed using run charts. It is used to monitor technical performance, as well as cost and schedule performance. [Monitoring and Controlling]

PMI®, *PMBOK® Guide*, 2008, 211–212

16. d.   Issue a change request to implement the needed corrective action

The information obtained from a quality audit can be used to improve quality systems and performance. In most cases, implementing quality improvements requires preparation of change requests. [Executing]

PMI®, *PMBOK® Guide*, 2008, 204–205

17. c.   Three standard deviations

When the results of a sample of items measured falls within three standard deviations and that sample is representative of the entire population, you can assume that more than 99% of all items fall within that range. This generally accepted range of results has been used by quality control professionals through the years. Six sigma is a program started by Motorola that, from a statistical standpoint, indicates a quality standard of only 3.4 defects per million. [Executing]

PMI®, *PMBOK® Guide*, 2008, 209

18. b.   Use statistical sampling

Statistical sampling uses part of a population to draw conclusions about the total population. It is a well-proven technique that can significantly reduce the cost of quality control. [Monitoring and Controlling]

PMI®, *PMBOK® Guide*, 2008, 198

19. b. Top management

Deming is known as a quality pioneer. His approach to quality is not only statistically based but focuses on what management's responsibilities should be with respect to quality. His Fourteen Points for management are goals of quality for transforming business. [Executing]

Rose 2005, 28–29

20. b. Walk-throughs

Inspections comprise an examination of a work product to determine if it conforms to standards. Additional names for inspections are audits, reviews, or peer reviews (in some application areas, these terms may have narrow and specific meanings). [Monitoring and Controlling]

PMI®, *PMBOK® Guide*, 2008, 213

21. a. Quality assurance process

Quality assurance is a managerial function that establishes processes or procedures in an organization or project to assist in determining whether quality standards are being met. It is the application of planned, systematic quality activities to ensure that the project will use all processes needed to meet requirements and is performed throughout the life of the project. [Executing]

PMI®, *PMBOK® Guide*, 2008, 201–202

22. c. Develop a quality policy for the project

The quality policy includes the overall intentions and direction of the organization with regard to quality, as formally expressed by top management. If the performing organization lacks a formal quality policy or if the project involves multiple performing organizations, as in a joint venture, the project management team must develop a quality policy for the project as an input to plan quality. [Planning]

PMI®, *PMBOK® Guide*, 2004, 194

23. **c.** **Evaluate failure modes and causes associated with the design and manufacture of a new product**

This technique is a method of analyzing design reliability. A list of potential failure modes is developed for each element, and then each mode is given a numeric rating for frequency of occurrence, criticality, and probability of detection. These data are used to assign a risk priority number for prioritizing problems and guiding the design effort. [Monitoring and Controlling]

Evans and Lindsay 2005, 582–594

24. **b.** **Seven consecutive measurements are ascending, descending, or the same**

Consecutive points on a process control chart that are ascending, descending, or the same indicate an abnormal trend in the process and must be investigated. [Monitoring and Controlling]

PMI®, *PMBOK® Guide*, 2008, 209

25. **a.** **Provides incentives to vendors to make quality commitments**

Vendors that have long-term relationships with buyers are generally more inclined to invest in process and quality improvement, because they have a higher probability of recovering their costs. The stability provided through longer-term contracts permits better planning and encourages better communication and partnering between the buyer and the seller. Long-term contracting with fewer vendors also reduces buyer-related costs by simplifying accounting, collections, and other administrative tasks. [Planning]

Rose 2005, 87–88

26. **c.** **Incremental improvement**

Imai, a Japanese engineer, coined the word *kaizen* to describe an approach to quality that means making small improvements every time a process is repeated. [Executing]

Evans and Lindsay 2005, 347—348

27. d.   As an input to quality assurance

Quality control activities result in measurements that are used as inputs to the QA process. Such quality control measurements are used to reevaluate and analyze the quality standards and processes of the organization. [Executing]

PMI®, *PMBOK® Guide*, 2008, 201–202

28. a.   Monitor process variation over time

Used to monitor process variation and to detect and correct changes in process performance, the statistical control chart helps people understand and control their processes and work. [Monitoring and Controlling]

PMI®, *PMBOK® Guide*, 2008, 196

29. b.   Quality assurance

Quality assurance is the management section of quality management. It is the collective term for the formal activities and managerial processes that attempt to ensure that products and services meet the required quality level. The project manager should establish administrative processes and procedures necessary to ensure and often prove that the scope statement conforms to the customer's actual requirements, to determine which processes will be used to ensure that stakeholders have confidence that the quality activities will be properly performed, and to ensure that all legal and regulatory requirements will be met. [Executing]

Kerzner 2006, 846

30. a.   Standards and regulations are an input to plan quality

During the plan quality process, the project management team must consider any application area-specific standards, regulations, rules, and guidelines that may affect the project as part of the enterprise environmental factors. Building codes are an example of regulations. [Planning]

PMI®, *PMBOK® Guide*, 2008, 14 and 194

31. a.   Cause-and-effect diagrams

Cause-and-effect diagrams, also called Ishikawa diagrams or fishbone diagrams, are used to illustrate how various causes and subcauses interact to create a special effect. It is named for its developer, Kaoru Ishikawa. [Monitoring and Controlling]

Ward 2008, 226; PMI®, *PMBOK® Guide*, 2008, 208–209

32. c. A framework for quality systems

ISO 9000 provides a basic set of requirements for a quality system, without specifying the particulars for implementation. [Planning]

Evans and Lindsay 2005, 128–132; PMI®, *PMBOK® Guide*, 2008, 190

33. d. Project team members are adequately trained for their jobs

The purpose of the quality audit is to evaluate whether the project is conforming to the project's quality requirements and is following established quality procedures and policies. It looks at the outputs of the work processes and not on the individuals performing the job. [Executing]

Kerzner 2006, 847

34. c. Weighted Pareto analysis

The weighted Pareto analysis gives a measure of significance to factors that may not appear significant at first, using such additional factors as cost, time, and criticality. A basic Pareto analysis identifies the vital few contributors that account for most quality problems, and the comparative Pareto analysis focuses on any number of program options or actions. [Monitoring and Controlling]

Kerzner 2006, 855–856

35. d. Separate quality assurance and quality control departments reporting to senior management

Top management should provide constancy of purpose so that it can be infused throughout the organization. Constancy of purpose also requires a shared belief among organization members that management's behavior clearly signals its commitment to and support of achievement of the vision. Quality assurance and control are functions that must be performed by everyone, not just those assigned to specific departments. [Executing]

Rose 2005, 29

36. b. Quality management plan

The quality management plan describes how the team will implement the quality policy, which describes the objectives of the project regarding quality management. [Planning]

PMI®, *PMBOK® Guide*, 2008, 200

37. d. The account number and daily rate, because they account for 80 percent of all defects.

Pareto analysis focuses on what Joseph Juran called the vital few. Named after Vilfredo Pareto, an Italian economist whose studies showed that 80 percent of the wealth was held by 20 percent of the population, quality analysis typically shows that 80 percent of the all problems (defects) are found in 20 percent of the items or areas studied.

Rose 2005, 86–87

38. d. Identify the problem

There are typically six steps in this process but the first and most important is to identify the problem. This step often involves the use of other statistical process control tools, such as Pareto analysis, the histogram, and control charts as well as brainstorming. The result of this step is a clear, concise problem statement. [Monitoring and Controlling]

PMI®, *PMBOK® Guide*, 2008, 208–209; Kerzner 2006, 853

39. b. Attribute chart

There are two types of control charts: variable charts, which are used with continuous data, and attribute charts, for use with discrete data. Attribute data have only two values (conforming/nonconforming, pass/fail, go/no-go, or present/absent). In this situation, you are looking for the presence of the required food label. [Monitoring and Controlling]

Kerzner 2006, 862–863

40. d. Procedures used to conduct trade-off analyses among cost, schedule, and quality

A part of the overall project management plan, the quality management plan should address all aspects of how quality management will be implemented on the project and how the project team will implement the quality policy. Trade-off analyses are business judgments and, as such, are not procedural steps to be included in the quality management plan. [Planning]

PMI®, *PMBOK® Guide*, 2008, 200

PROJECT HUMAN RESOURCE MANAGEMENT

Study Hints

The Project Human Resource Management questions on the PMP® certification exam focus heavily on organizational structures, roles and responsibilities of the project manager, team building, and conflict resolution. Many of the questions are taken from the *PMBOK® Guide* and the following PMI® handbooks, which have been consolidated into one publication available from PMI® entitled *Principles of Project Management* (1997).

- *Conflict Management for Project Managers* by John R. Adams and Nicki S. Kirchof

- *Organizing for Project Management* by Dwayne P. Cable and John R. Adams

- *Roles and Responsibilities of the Project Manager* by John R. Adams and Brian W. Campbell

- *Team Building for Project Managers* by Linn C. Stuckenbruck and David Marshall

- *The Project Manager's Work Environment: Coping with Time and Stress* by Paul C. Dinsmore, Martin Dean Martin, and Gary T. Huettel

Six other publications also are useful for questions in this area as noted by PMI® in Appendix G of the *PMBOK® Guide*:

- *Essential People Skills for Project Managers* by Ginger Levin and Steven Flannes

- *Organizing Projects for Success*, vol. 1 of *The Human Aspects of Project Management* by Vijay K. Verma

- *Human Factors in Project Management* (Revised Edition) by Paul C. Dinsmore

- *Human Resource Skills for the Project Manager*, vol. 2 of *The Human Aspects of Project Management* by Vijay K. Verma

- *Managing the Project Team*, vol. 3 of *The Human Aspects of Project Management* by Vijay K. Verma

- *Seven Habits of Highly Effective People* by Stephen R. Covey

In contrast to other areas of the *PMBOK® Guide* in which commonly known terms are used, some terminology developed for Project Human Resource Management appears to be peculiar to PMI®. (In fact, much of the terminology has been used in project management literature for many years, but that literature has not always been widely disseminated.) For example, in the area of project organizational structures, some experts with years of experience in the field have not encountered such terms or concepts as *project expeditor* or *weak matrix*. Accordingly, committing to memory PMI®'s definition and classification of the following subject areas is imperative:

- Project organizational structures
- Stages of team development
- Decision-making guidelines
- Influencing guidelines
- Negotiation skills
- Conflict management concepts

In spite of the unfamiliarity of some of the terminology, most exam takers do not find the human resource questions on the exam difficult.

PMI® views Project Human Resource Management as having four elements: develop human resource plan, acquire project team, develop project team, and manage project team. See *PMBOK® Guide* Figure 9-1 for an overview of this structure. Know it cold!

Following is a list of the major Project Human Resource Management topics. Use it to help focus your study efforts on the areas most likely to appear on the exam.

Major Topics

Overall PMBOK® Guide approach to project human resource management

Forms of organization

- Functional
- Project expeditor
- Project coordinator
- Weak matrix
- Strong matrix
- Balanced matrix
- Projectized
- Composite

Develop human resource plan tools and techniques

- Organization chart and position descriptions
  - Hierarchical-type charts
  - Organizational breakdown structure
  - Resource breakdown structure
- Matrix-based charts
  - Responsibility assignment matrix
- Text-oriented formats
  - Role/responsibility authority forms
  - Resource calendars
  - Resource histogram
- Networking plan
- Organizational theory

Develop human resource plan outputs

- Human resource plan
  - Role and responsibility assignments
  - Staffing management plan
  - Organization chart

Acquire project team

Project manager roles and responsibilities

- Functions
- Roles
- Negotiation

Types of power

Acquisition

Major Topics (continued)

Virtual teams

Project staff assignments

Develop project team objectives

Interpersonal skills

- Empathy
- Influence
- Creativity
- Group facilitation

Training

Team-building activities

- Approaches
- Stages of team development
    - Goals and results of project team building
    - Symptoms of poor teamwork
    - Ground rules for project team building
    - The team-building process

Ground rules

Motivation theories

- Maslow's Hierarchy of Needs
- McGregor's Theory X and Theory Y
- Herzberg's Theory of Motivation
- Expectancy Theory
- McClellan Needs Theory

Reward and recognition systems

Team Performance Assessment

Manage Project Team

- Project conflict
    - Why conflict is unavoidable on projects
    - Seven sources of conflict in project environments
- Conflict and the project life cycle
- Conflict management
    - Problem solving (or confrontation)
    - Compromising
    - Smoothing
    - Withdrawal
    - Forcing

Major Topics (continued)

Observation and Conversation

Project Performance Approval Issue Log

Interpersonal skills

- Leadership
- Influencing
- Effective decision making

Practice Questions

INSTRUCTIONS: Note the most suitable answer for each multiple-choice question in the appropriate space on the answer sheet.

1. You have been assigned as project manager on what could be a "bet the company" project. You realize that to be successful you need to exercise maximum control over project resources. Which form of project organization should you establish for this project?

   a. Strong matrix
   b. Projectized
   c. Project coordinator
   d. Weak matrix

2. Which of the following is a ground rule for project team building?

   a. Perform frequent performance appraisals
   b. Ensure that each team member reports to his or her functional manager in addition to the project manager
   c. Start early
   d. Try to solve team political problems

3. Project A is being administered using a matrix form of organization. The project manager reports to a senior vice president who provides visible support to the project. In this scenario, which of the following statements best describes the relative power of the project manager?

   a. The project manager will probably not be challenged by project stakeholders.
   b. In this strong matrix, the balance of power is shifted to the functional line managers.
   c. In this tight matrix, the balance of power is shifted to the project manager.
   d. In this strong matrix, the balance of power is shifted to the project manager.

4. You are leading a team to recommend an equitable reward and recognition system for project managers. Before finalizing the plan, you want to ensure that executives understand the basic objective of reward systems. This objective is to—

   a. Be comparable with the award system established for functional managers to indicate parity and to show the importance of project management to the company
   b. Make the link between project performance and reward clear, explicit, and achievable
   c. Motivate project managers to work toward common objectives and goals as defined by the company
   d. Attract people to join the organization's project management career path

5. Which of the following factors contributes the most to team communication?

   a. External feedback
   b. Performance appraisals
   c. Smoothing over of team conflicts by the project manager
   d. Colocation

6. You are managing a virtual team. The project has been under way for several months, and you believe your team members do not view themselves as a team or unified group. To help rectify this situation, you should—

   a. Ensure that every member of the project team uses e-mail as a form of communication
   b. Mandate that the team follow the vision and mission statement of his or her organization
   c. Create symbols and structures that solidify the unity of the dispersed work group
   d. Provide team members with the latest in communications technology and mandate its use

7. Major difficulties arise when multiple projects need to be managed in the functional organizational structure because of—

   a. The level of authority of the project manager
   b. Conflicts over the relative priorities of different projects in competition for limited resources
   c. Project team members who are focused on their functional specialty rather than on the project
   d. The need for the project manager to use interpersonal skills to resolve conflicts informally

8. The team you have organized for your new project consists of three people who will work full-time and five people who will support the project on a part-time basis. All team members know one another and have worked together in the past. To ensure a successful project start-up, your first step should be to—

    a. Meet with each team member individually to discuss assignments
    b. Prepare a responsibility assignment matrix and distribute it to each team member
    c. Distribute the project plan and WBS to the team
    d. Hold a project kickoff meeting

9. In negotiating, knowing your points and issues and addressing them with confidence and assertiveness is known as—

    a. Attitudinal structuring
    b. Firm competition
    c. Soft competition
    d. Rough bargaining

10. As you prepare your human resource plan, you need to determine the skill and capacity required to complete the activities in the project. This should be documented in the—

    a. Roles and responsibilities section
    b. Staffing management plan
    c. Staff acquisition section
    d. Compliance section

11. The primary result of effective team development is—

    a. Improved project performance
    b. An effective, smoothly running team
    c. An understanding by project team members that the project manager is ultimately responsible for project performance
    d. Enhancement of the ability of stakeholders to contribute as individuals and team members

12. The team members on your project have been complaining that they do not have any sense of identity as a team because they are located in different areas of the building. To remedy this situation, you developed a project logo and had it printed on T-shirts to promote the project, but this action has not worked. Your next step is to—

    a. Initiate a newsletter
    b. Create an air of mystery about the project
    c. Establish a "team meeting room"
    d. Issue guidelines on how team members should interact with other stakeholders

13. The project team directory is an output from which of the following processes?

    a. Develop project team
    b. Acquire project team
    c. Develop human resource plan
    d. Manage project team

14. Team-building activities include management and individual actions taken specifically and primarily to improve team performance. Many of these actions may enhance team performance as a secondary effect. An example of some action that may enhance team performance as a secondary effect is—

    a. Establishing team performance goals and holding off-site retreats to review ways of best achieving these goals
    b. Colocating all team members in a single physical location
    c. Establishing a team-based reward and recognition system
    d. Involving nonmanagement-level team members in the planning process

15. Given that you are neighbors, you and the CEO of your company have established a friendly personal relationship. Recently your company appointed you project manager for a new project that is crucial to achieving next year's financial targets. Which type of power available to project managers might you be able to rely upon?

    a. Referent
    b. Reward
    c. Formal
    d. Expert

16. You have been a project manager for seven years. You now are managing the construction of a new facility that must comply with the government's newly issued environmental standards. You want to ensure that your team members are able to select methods to complete various activities on the project without needing to involve you in each situation. As you prepare your human resource plan, you should document this information in which of the following—

    a. Roles and responsibilities section
    b. Resource assignment matrix
    c. Resource breakdown structure
    d. Staffing management plan

17. It is important on all projects to determine when and how human resources will be met. Assume that you are managing a project to assess methods for streamlining the regulatory approval process for new medical devices in your government agency. Because the agency has undergone downsizing during the past three years, subject matter experts are in short supply. You must determine whether the needed subject matter experts can be acquired from inside the agency or whether you must use contractors. This information should be documented in the—

    a. Make-or-buy decisions in the procurement management plan
    b. Contracts management plan
    c. Staffing management plan
    d. Resource management plan

18. In both the weak and strong matrix organizational structures, the primary condition leading to conflict is—

    a. Communication barriers
    b. Conflicting interests
    c. Need for consensus
    d. Ambiguous jurisdictions

19. As project manager, you are primarily responsible for implementing the project management plan by authorizing the execution of project activities. Because you do not work in a projectized organization, you do not have direct access to human resource administrative activities. Therefore you need to—

    a. Outsource these functions
    b. Prepare a project team charter that is signed off by a member of the human resources department to delineate responsibilities
    c. Ensure that your team is sufficiently aware of administrative requirements to ensure compliance
    d. Ask the head of human resources to approve your project human resource plan personally

20. Constant bickering, absenteeism, and substandard performance have characterized the behavior of certain members of your team. You have planned an off-site retreat for the team to engage in a variety of activities. Your primary objective for investing time and money in this event is to improve—

    a. Team performance
    b. Morale
    c. Quality
    d. Individual performance

21. Two team members on your project often disagree. You need a conflict resolution method that provides a long-term resolution. You decide to use which one of the following approaches?

    a. Confronting
    b. Problem solving
    c. Collaborating
    d. Smoothing

22. Which of the following is an enterprise environmental factor that may influence the development of the human resource plan?

    a. The organizational structure of the performing organization
    b. Poor communication among team members
    c. Ambiguous staffing requirements
    d. Team morale

23. As a project manager, you believe in using a "personal touch" to further team development. One approach that has proven effective toward this goal is—

    a. Creating a team name
    b. Providing flexible work time
    c. Issuing a project charter
    d. Celebrating special occasions

24. Your project has been under way for some time, but indicators show that it is in trouble. You have observed all the following symptoms of poor teamwork in your project team EXCEPT—

    a. Frustration
    b. Excessive meetings
    c. Lack of trust or confidence in the project t manager
    d. Unproductive meetings

25. You are the project manager for a two-year project that is now beginning its second year. The mix of team members has changed, and there is confusion as to roles and responsibilities. In addition, several of the completed work packages have not received the required sign-offs and three work packages are five weeks behind schedule. To gain control of this project, you need to—

    a. Rebaseline your original human resource plan with current resource requirements
    b. Change to a projectized organizational structure for maximum control over resource assignments
    c. Work with your team to prepare a responsibility assignment matrix
    d. Create a new division of labor by assigning technical leads to the most critical activities

26. You are part of a team that is working to develop a new medical implant device. Your project manager is an expert in medical implantation devices, yet he continually seeks opinions from the team about a wide variety of project and product issues. Team members often run project meetings while he sits silently at the head of the table. Which one of the following best characterizes his leadership style?

    a. Laissez-faire
    b. Team directed
    c. Collaborative
    d. Shared leadership

27. The major difference between the project coordinator and project expeditor forms of organization is that—

    a. Strong commitment to the project usually does not exist in the project expeditor form of organization
    b. The project coordinator cannot personally make or enforce decisions
    c. The project expeditor acts only as an intermediary between management and the project team
    d. The project coordinator reports to a higher-level manager in the organization

28. Which one of the following represents a constraint on the acquire project team process?

    a. Preassignment of staff to the project
    b. Recruitment practices of the organizations involved
    c. Use of outsourcing
    d. Team member training requirements

29. During a recent status review meeting for your project, one team member was critical of some others and seemed to try to diminish their status on the team. This person was assuming which one of the following destructive team roles?

    a. Recognition seeker
    b. Blocker
    c. Aggressor
    d. Dominator

30. Objectives for conducting performance appraisals during the course of a project can include all the following EXCEPT—

    a. Initial establishment of roles and responsibilities
    b. Discovery of unknown or unresolved issues
    c. Development of individual training plans
    d. Establishment of goals for future time periods

31. Your organization is adopting a project-based approach to business, which has been difficult. Although project teams have been created, they are little more than a collection of functional and technical experts who focus on their specialties. You are managing the company's most important project. As you begin this project, you must place a high priority on—

    a. Creating an effective team
    b. Identifying the resources needed to finish the project on time
    c. The best way to communicate status to the CEO
    d. Establishing firm project requirements

32. In organizing a project, a project manager must deal with conflict. Which statement is TRUE regarding conflict in projects?

    a. A matrix form of organization can produce a lack of clear role definitions and lead to ambiguous jurisdictions between and among functional leaders and project managers
    b. Sources of conflict include project priorities, PERT/CPM schedules, contract administrative procedures, and type of contract
    c. Conflict is to be avoided whenever possible
    d. Strong matrix project managers have few human resource conflicts, because they can dictate their needs to functional managers

33. The chances for successful completion of a multidisciplinary project are increased if project team members are—

    a. Problem oriented
    b. Politically sensitive to top management's needs
    c. Focused on individual project activities
    d. Focused on customer demands

34. The terms strong matrix, balanced matrix, and weak matrix when applied to the matrix structure in project organization refer to the—

    a. Ability of the organization to achieve its goals
    b. Physical proximity of project team members to one another and to the project manager
    c. Degree of the project manager's authority
    d. Degree to which team members bond together

35. The key way for a project manager to promote optimum team performance in project teams whose members are not colocated is to—

    a. Build trust
    b. Establish a reward and recognition system
    c. Obtain the support of the functional managers in the other locations
    d. Exercise his or her right to control all aspects of the project

36. Hierarchical-type charts are a tool and technique for use in human resource planning. Which one of the following is helpful in tracking project costs and can be aligned with the organization's accounting system?

    a. RACI
    b. RAM
    c. RBS
    d. OBS

37. When choosing the most appropriate form of project organization, the first step is to—

    a. Create the WBS and let it determine the project organizational structure
    b. Produce an initial project management plan and determine the functional areas responsible for each task
    c. Refer to the project charter developed by top management
    d. Develop a project schedule, including a top-down flowchart, and identify the functional areas to perform each task

38. Conflicts in which following three areas represent the majority of all project conflicts?

    a. Personalities, cost objectives, and schedules
    b. Cost objectives, administrative procedures, and scarce resources
    c. Scarce resources, scheduling priorities, and personal work styles
    d. Personal work styles, project priorities, and cost objectives

39. Which of the following qualifications is the most important for a project manager?

    a. Supervisory experience
    b. Negotiation skill
    c. Education in a technical field
    d. Ability to work well with others

40. Determining the method and the timing of releasing team members should be included in the—

    a. Staff acquisition plan
    b. Human resource plan
    c. Staffing management plan
    d. Project training plan

Answer Sheet

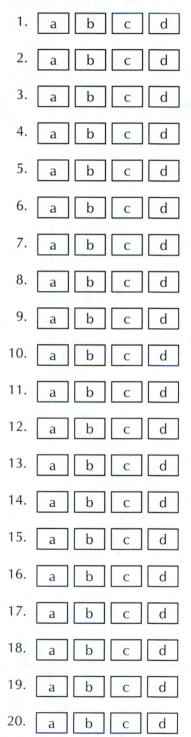

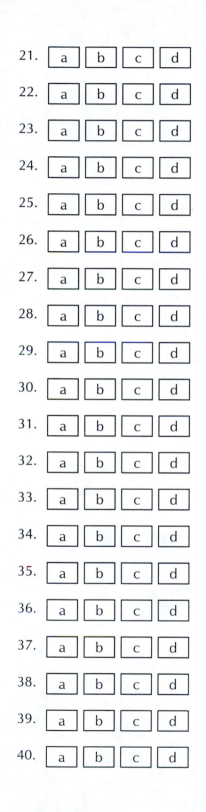

1. a b c d
2. a b c d
3. a b c d
4. a b c d
5. a b c d
6. a b c d
7. a b c d
8. a b c d
9. a b c d
10. a b c d
11. a b c d
12. a b c d
13. a b c d
14. a b c d
15. a b c d
16. a b c d
17. a b c d
18. a b c d
19. a b c d
20. a b c d

21. a b c d
22. a b c d
23. a b c d
24. a b c d
25. a b c d
26. a b c d
27. a b c d
28. a b c d
29. a b c d
30. a b c d
31. a b c d
32. a b c d
33. a b c d
34. a b c d
35. a b c d
36. a b c d
37. a b c d
38. a b c d
39. a b c d
40. a b c d

Answer Key

1. b. Projectized

In a projectized organizational structure, all project team members report directly and solely to the project manager. He or she has complete control over these resources and therefore, exercises more authority over them than when in any other project organizational structure. [Planning]

PMI®, *PMBOK® Guide*, 2008, 28–31

2. c. Start early

Starting the team-building process early in the project is crucial for setting the right tone and preventing bad habits and patterns from developing. [Executing]

Adams et al. 1997, 137; PMI®, *PMBOK® Guide*, 2008, 410

3. d. In this strong matrix, the balance of power is shifted to the project manager.

The project manager's ability to influence project decisions increases the higher up he or she—and the person to whom he or she reports—is placed in the organization. In the strong matrix, the project manager's authority ranges from moderate to high. [Planning]

PMI®, *PMBOK® Guide*, 2008, 28; Verma 1995, 156–157

4. b. Make the link between project performance and reward clear, explicit, and achievable

Reward and recognition systems are formal management actions that provide an incentive to behave in a particular way, usually with respect to achieving certain goals. Such systems are described in the staffing management plan. [Executing]

PMI®, *PMBOK® Guide*, 2008, 225 and 234

5. d. Colocation

Colocation is the placement of team members in the same physical location to enhance their ability to perform as a team, primarily through increased communication. [Executing]

PMI®, *PMBOK® Guide*, 2008, 234

6. c. Create symbols and structures that solidify the unity of the dispersed work group

Because the dispersed project team does not share the same physical space each day, team members need symbols and structures to identify them as a unified group. As the group works together, symbols should be developed to show accomplishments as a group. These symbols should be visible throughout the organization. [Executing]

Kostner 1994, 53–54 and 170; PMI®, *PMBOK® Guide*, 2008, 228

7. b. Conflicts over the relative priorities of different projects in competition for limited resources

When a finite group of resources must be distributed across multiple projects, conflicts in work assignments will occur. [Executing]

PMI®, *PMBOK® Guide*, 2008, 239

8. d. Hold a project kickoff meeting

An indispensable tool in project management, the kickoff or launch meeting is held at the outset of the project and is designed to get the project rolling. The meeting provides the opportunity not only to present the project charter and discuss the project's goals and objectives but also to establish rapport among team members. [Executing]

Meredith and Mantel, 2009, 243

9. d. Rough bargaining

Rough bargaining is the third stage in negotiations that occurs during the negotiation meeting phase. It follows protocol and probing and is important for successful negotiations. [Executing]

Verma 1996, 153

10. a. Roles and responsibilities section

Roles and responsibilities are listed in the human resource plan. This section describes roles and authority, responsibility, and competency or the skill and capacity required to complete project activities. When team members do not have the required competencies, project performance may be jeopardized and the project manager must have proactive responses to handle these situations. [Planning]

PMI®, *PMBOK® Guide*, 2008, 223

11. a. Improved project performance

Improved project performance not only increases the likelihood of meeting project objectives, it also creates a positive team experience contributing to the enhancement of team capabilities. [Executing]

PMI®, *PMBOK® Guide*, 2008, 235

12. c. Establish a "team meeting room"

Colocating team members, even on a temporary basis, enhances communications, thereby contributing to improved project performance. In addition, the "team meeting room" provides a sense of identity to the project team and raises the visibility of the project within the organization. Creating a newsletter is simply applying another organizational process asset, which has proven ineffective. [Executing]

PMI®, *PMBOK® Guide*, 2008, 234

13. b. Acquire project team

The project team directory is part of project staff assignments, an output from the acquire project team process. Other outputs are resource calendars and updates to the human resource plan. [Executing]

PMI®, *PMBOK® Guide*, 2008, 229

14. d. Involving nonmanagement-level team members in the planning process

Team-building activities vary from breakfast review meetings to golf outings to off-site sessions designed to improve interpersonal relationships. The purpose of all team-building activities, however, is to improve team performance. Many actions, such as involving nonmanagement-level team members in the planning process or establishing ground rules for surfacing and dealing with conflict, may enhance team performance as a secondary effect. [Executing]

PMI®, *PMBOK® Guide*, 2008, 232

15. a. Referent

Referent power is based on a less powerful person's identification with a more powerful person. This type of power is useful in terms of persuasion and helps the project manager exert influence over individuals from whom he or she needs support. [Planning]

Adams et al. 1997, 174–180

16. a.   Roles and responsibilities section

Authority refers to the right to apply project resources, make decisions, and sign approvals. Examples include selecting methods to complete activities, quality acceptance, and responding to variances in the project. The individual authority of each team member should match their individual responsibilities. This is documented in the roles and responsibilities section in the human resource plan. [Planning]

PMI®, *PMBOK® Guide*, 2008, 223

17. c.   Staffing management plan

The staffing management plan is part of the human resource plan. One section of it involves staff acquisition. Among other things, this section includes whether the human resources will come from within the organization or from external, contracted sources. These data then help to plan the acquisition of project team members. [Planning]

PMI®, *PMBOK® Guide*, 2008, 223

18. d.   Ambiguous jurisdictions

Ambiguous jurisdictions exist when two or more parties have related responsibilities, but their work boundaries and role definitions are unclear. This situation is found frequently in weak and strong matrix organizations because of the "two-boss" concept. [Executing]

Filley 1975, 9; PMI®, *PMBOK® Guide*, 2008, 239–240

19. c.   Ensure that your team is sufficiently aware of administrative requirements to ensure compliance

A projectized work environment is unusual because project managers rarely have every function under their control. But compliance with administrative requirements, government regulations, union contract provisions, and other constraints is a consideration in human resource management. [Planning]

PMI®, *PMBOK® Guide*, 2008, 28

20. a.   Team performance

Team development leads to improved team performance, which ultimately results in improved project performance. Improvements in team performance can come from many sources and can affect many areas of project performance. For example, improved individual skill levels such as enhanced technical competence may enable team members to perform their assigned activities more effectively. Team development efforts have greater benefit when conducted early but should take place throughout the project life cycle. [Executing]

PMI®, *PMBOK® Guide*, 2008, 229–230

21. c.   Collaborating

Collaborating is an effective technique for managing conflict when a project is too important to be compromised. It involves incorporating multiple ideas and viewpoints from people with different perspectives and offers a good opportunity to learn from others. It provides a long-term resolution. [Executing]

PMI®, *PMBOK® Guide*, 2008, 240; Verma 1996, 119–120

22. a.   The organizational structure of the performing organization

Enterprise environmental factors can influence the develop human resource plan process. The organizational structure of the performing organization determines whether the project manager's role is a strong one (as in a strong matrix) or a weak one (as in a weak matrix). Other examples of enterprise environmental factors are existing human resources, personnel administration functions, and marketplace conditions. [Planning]

PMI®, *PMBOK® Guide*, 2008, 219

23. d.   Celebrating special occasions

Project managers can show interest in their team members by celebrating occasions such as birthdays, anniversaries with the organization, and special achievements. Other approaches include being supportive, being clear, learning some information about each team member, and being accessible. Through observation and conversation, the project management team monitors indicators such as progress toward project deliverables, accomplishments that are a source of pride for team members, and interpersonal issues. [Executing]

PMI®, *PMBOK® Guide*, 2008, 234

24. b. Excessive meetings

The problem is not too many meetings, but unproductive ones. The purpose of project meetings is to focus the skills and resources of the project team on project performance. Meetings that are considered "gripe sessions" or a time for the project manager to "lay down the law" are demoralizing to the team. [Executing]

Adams et al. 1997, 131

25. c. Work with your team to prepare a responsibility assignment matrix

The responsibility assignment matrix defines project roles and responsibilities in terms of work packages and activities. It can be used to show who is a participant, who is accountable, who handles review, who provides input, and who must sign off on specific work packages or project phases. [Planning]

PMI®, *PMBOK® Guide*, 2008, 221

26. d. Shared leadership

Shared leadership is more than participatory management or collaboration; it involves letting the project team take over as much of the leadership role as it will accept. [Executing]

Verma 1997, 159

27. d. The project coordinator reports to a higher-level manager in the organization

The relative position of the project coordinator in the organization is thought to lead to an increased level of authority and responsibility. [Executing]

Adams et al. 1997, 15–17; Verma 1995, 153–156

28. b. Recruitment practices of the organizations involved

Staff assignments in organizations are governed by the policies, procedures, or guidelines of individual components. These policies will constrain the project manager's actions in acquiring a project team. The more familiar the project manager is with such policies, the easier it will be for him/her to assemble a team. [Executing]

PMI®, *PMBOK® Guide*, 2008, 227

29. c. Aggressor

The aggressor is destructive in that he or she criticizes others and attempts to deflate their status. Other destructive team roles are the blocker, withdrawer, recognition seeker, topic jumper, dominator, and, in some cases, devil's advocate. Destructive behavior, if allowed to continue, can endanger a team-building effort. [Executing]

Adams et al. 1997, 145–147

30. a. Initial establishment of roles and responsibilities

Project performance appraisals are a tool and technique for the manage project team process and are used, among other objectives, to reclarify roles and responsibilities. It is critical that team members receive positive feedback in what might otherwise be a hectic environment. [Executing]

PMI®, *PMBOK® Guide*, 2008, 238

31. a. Creating an effective team

An effective team is critical to project success, but such a team is not born spontaneously. In early project phases, it is vitally important for the project manager to place a high priority on initiating and implementing the team-building process. [Executing]

PMI®, *PMBOK® Guide*, 2008, 232; Verma 1997, 137

32. a. A matrix form of organization can produce a lack of clear role definitions and lead to ambiguous jurisdictions between and among functional leaders and project managers

Matrix management is useful but complex, involving difficult communication because of the use of borrowed and often part-time resources who are spread throughout the organization. [Executing]

Adams et al. 1997, 189–194; *PMBOK® Guide*, 2008, 239–240

33. a. Problem oriented

Problem-oriented people tend to learn and use whatever problem-solving techniques appear helpful. Although the project manager must be politically sensitive, team members need not have developed this skill to the extent required of the project manager; and rather than focusing on individual activities, team members should take a systems approach focusing on the entire project. [Executing]

Meredith and Mantel 2009, 118–119; PMI®, *PMBOK® Guide*, 2008, 412

34. c. Degree of the project manager's authority

In a strong matrix organization, the balance of power shifts toward the project manager. In a weak matrix organization, the balance of power shifts toward the functional or line manager. [Planning]

PMI®, *PMBOK® Guide*, 2008, 28

35. a. Build trust

Team members who are physically separate from one another tend not to know each other well. They have few opportunities to develop trust in the traditional way, and they tend to communicate poorly with one another. Trust then must become the foundation upon which all team-building activities are built. [Executing]

PMI®, *PMBOK® Guide*, 2008, 230

36. c. RBS

The resource breakdown structure (RBS) is a variation of the organizational breakdown structure (OBS) and is used to show which work elements are assigned to individuals and other resource categories. As an example, it can show all crane operators and cranes even though they may be scattered throughout the OBS and WBS, which can help to track project costs. [Planning]

PMI®, *PMBOK® Guide*, 2008, 220

37. b. Produce an initial project management plan and determine the functional areas responsible for each task

All effort on a project starts from the project management plan, which details the work that must be accomplished. [Planning]

Meredith and Mantel 2009 203

38. c. Scarce resources, scheduling priorities, and personal work styles

Although all areas listed contain potential conflicts, the majority (over 50%) of all conflict in a project environment is caused by scarce resources, scheduling priorities, and personal work styles. [Executing]

PMI®, *PMBOK® Guide*, 239

39. d. Ability to work well with others

Project management requires getting things done through people who generally do not report directly to the project manager. The ability to influence project team members, as well as other key stakeholders, is crucial for success. [Executing]

PMI®, *PMBOK® Guide*, 2008, 13, 409–413

40. c. Staffing management plan

The staffing management plan is a document that describes when and how human resources will become part of the project team and when they will return to their organizational units. It addresses how staff members will be acquired, how long they will remain on the project, how and when they will be released, training needs, and other important aspects of forming and disbanding the team. [Planning]

PMI®, *PMBOK® Guide*, 2008, 223–224

PROJECT COMMUNICATIONS MANAGEMENT

Study Hints

The Project Communications Management questions on the PMP® certification exam are relatively basic and are taken primarily from the *PMBOK® Guide* and other PMI®-published reference materials. Common sense and your own experience will play a large role in your ability to answer the questions on this topic. There will be questions that test your specific knowledge of *PMBOK® Guide* terms and concepts. However, there will also be many general questions that require you to choose the "best" answer. To answer these questions correctly, you must apply common sense.

The questions focus on formal and informal communication, verbal versus written communication, conflict resolution, and management styles. PMI® considers management style to be an essential component of how a project manager communicates.

The PMI® handbooks (which are now included in *Principles of Project Management*, PMI®, 1997), *Roles and Responsibilities of the Project Manager* by John R. Adams and Brian W. Campbell, *Conflict Management for Project Managers* by John R. Adams and Nicki S. Kirchof, and *Team Building for Project Managers* by Linn C. Stuckenbruck and David Marshall, should be studied thoroughly for this section of the PMP® certification exam. The PMI® publication *Human Resource Skills for the Project Manager,* which is volume 2 of *The Human Aspects of Project Management* by Vijay K. Verma, is another useful reference. PMI® considers the kickoff meeting one of the most effective mechanisms in Project Communications Management. The nature and purpose of this meeting are discussed in *Team Building for Project Managers*.

PMI® views Project Communications Management as a process consisting of five elements: identify stakeholders, plan communications, distribute information, manage stakeholder expectations, and report performance. See *PMBOK® Guide* Figure 10-1 for an overview of this structure. Know this chart thoroughly.

Following is a list of the major Project Communications Management topics. Use it to help focus your study efforts on the areas most likely to appear on the exam.

Major Topics

Importance of project communications management

Indentify stakeholders

- Typical project stakeholders
  - Customers/users
  - Sponsor
  - Portfolio manager/portfolio review board
  - Program managers
  - Project management office
  - Project managers
  - Project team
  - Functional managers
  - Operations management
  - Sellers' business partners
- Stakeholder analysis
  - Classification models
- Stakeholder register
- Stakeholder management strategy

Communication dimensions

Communication channels

Communication skills

Plan communications

- The communications model
  - Encode
  - Message and feedback-message
  - Medium
  - Noise
  - Decode
- Communications requirements analysis
- Communications technology
- Communication methods
- Communications management plan

Distribute information

- Sender-feedback model
- Choice of media
- Writing style
- Meeting management techniques
- Presentation techniques
- Facilitation techniques

Major Topics (continued)

Distribute information (continued)

- Stakeholder notifications
- Reports, presentations, records
- Stakeholder feedback
- Lessons learned documents

Barriers to communication

Manage stakeholder expectations

- Issue log
- Change log
- Interpersonal skills
  - Building trust
  - Resolving conflict
  - Listening actively
  - Overcoming resistance to change
- Management skills
  - Presentation
  - Negotiating
  - Writing
  - Public speaking

Report Performance

- Status reports
  - Simple
  - Elaborate
- Work performance information
- Work performance measurements
- Budget forecasts
- Variance analysis
- Forecasting methods
  - Time-series
  - Casual/econometric
  - Judgmental
  - Simulation, probabilistic, and ensemble
- Communication methods
- Reporting systems
- Performance reports
- Change requests
  - Corrective actions
  - Preventive actions

Documentation

Practice Questions

INSTRUCTIONS: Note the most suitable answer for each multiple-choice question in the appropriate space on the answer sheet.

1. As project manager, you plan to conduct a "kickoff" meeting at which you will discuss all the following EXCEPT—

   a. Establishing working relationships and standard formats for global communication
   b. Reviewing project plans
   c. Establishing individual and group responsibilities and accountabilities
   d. Discussing specific legal issues regarding the contract

2. One purpose of the communications management plan is to provide information about the—

   a. Methods that will be used to convey information
   b. Methods that will be used for releasing team members from the project when they are no longer needed
   c. Project organization and stakeholder responsibility relationships
   d. Experience and skill levels of each team member

3. Project managers for international projects should recognize key issues in cross-cultural settings and place special emphasis on—

   a. Establishing a performance reporting system
   b. Developing a system to manage communications
   c. Establishing and following a production schedule for information distribution to avoid responding to requests for information between scheduled communications
   d. Using translation services for formal, written project reports

4. You are managing a project with team members located at customer sites on three different continents. You have a number of stakeholders on your project, and most of them are located outside of the corporate office. Who should be responsible for stakeholder management?

   a. A specific team member in each of the three locations
   b. You, because you are the project manager
   c. The project sponsor
   d. A core team including you, as the project manager, and three representatives from the three different locations

5. Analyzing stakeholders is a part of the identify stakeholders process. Common approaches for analyzing stakeholders in a qualitative manner includes all the following two-axis grids, EXCEPT—

   a. Comparing power and influence
   b. Comparing power and interest
   c. Comparing influence and location
   d. Comparing influence and impact

6. As a project manager, you try to use empathic listening skills to help understand another person's frame of reference. In following this approach, you should—

   a. Mimic the content of the message
   b. Probe, then evaluate the content
   c. Evaluate the content, then advise
   d. Rephrase the content and reflect the feeling

7. Statements of organizational policies and philosophies, position descriptions, and constraints are examples of—

   a. Downward communication
   b. Lateral communication
   c. External communication
   d. Horizontal communication

8. You have decided to organize a study group of other project managers in your organization to help prepare for the PMP® exam. What type of communication are you employing in your efforts to organize this group?

   a. Horizontal
   b. Vertical
   c. Formal
   d. External

9. Your company CEO just sent you an e-mail asking you to make a presentation on your project, which has been in progress for 18 months, to over 50 identified internal and external stakeholders. He scheduled the presentation for next Monday. The first step in preparing the presentation is to—

   a. Define the audience
   b. Determine the objective
   c. Decide on the general form of the presentation
   d. Plan a presentation strategy

10. You are responsible for a project in your organization that has multiple internal customers. Because many people in your organization are interested in this project, you decide to prepare a stakeholder management strategy. Before preparing this strategy, you should—

    a. Conduct a stakeholder analysis to assess information needs
    b. Determine a production schedule to show when each stakeholder needs each type of information produced
    c. Determine the potential impact that each stakeholder may generate
    d. Prioritize each stakeholder's level of interest and influence

11. Project managers spend a great deal of time communicating with the team, the stakeholders, the client, and the sponsor. One can easily see the challenges involved, especially if one team member must communicate a technical concept to another team member in a different country. The first step in this process is to—

    a. Encode the message
    b. Decode the message
    c. Determine the feedback loops
    d. Determine the medium

12. On your project, scope changes, constraints, assumptions, integration and interface requirements, and overlapping roles and responsibilities pose communications challenges. The presence of communication barriers is most likely to lead to—

    a. Reduced productivity
    b. Increased hostility
    c. Low morale
    d. Increased conflict

13. The most common communication problem that occurs during negotiation is that—

    a. Each side may misinterpret what the other side has said
    b. Each side may give up on the other side
    c. One side may try to confuse the other side
    d. One side may be too busy thinking about what to say next to hear what is being said

14. You finally have been appointed project manager for a major company project. One of your first activities as project manager will be to create the communications management plan. As you match the stakeholder with the appropriate communication methods for that stakeholder, you could use any one of the following methods EXCEPT—

    a. Interactive communications
    b. Passive communications
    c. Pull communications
    d. Push communications

15. As an output of plan communications, it may be necessary to update the project documents, which include the—

    a. Stakeholder register
    b. Corporate policies, procedures, and processes
    c. Knowledge management system
    d. Overall product improvements

16. Sample attributes of a communications management plan include which one of the following?

    a. Roles
    b. Responsibilities
    c. Ethics
    d. Authority

17. The process of conferring with others to come to terms or reach an agreement is called—

    a. Win-win
    b. Negotiation
    c. Getting to "yes"
    d. Confrontation

18. At the end of each project, the project team should prepare a lessons learned summary that focuses on all the following EXCEPT—

    a. Sharing best practices with other project teams in the organization
    b. Warning others of potential problems
    c. Suggesting methods to mitigate risks effectively to ensure success
    d. Sharing only positive aspects of the project for future replication elsewhere in the organization

19. The most important requirement for ensuring that issues get resolved is that they are—

    a. Included in the WBS
    b. Included in the project's risk register
    c. Assigned an owner and a target date for closure
    d. Brought to the project manager's attention immediately

20. As head of the PMO, you will participate in performance reviews for all major projects. To ensure these reviews are productive, you believe project managers must ensure that—

    a. Work performance information on the status of deliverables is collected
    b. Earned value analysis is used for all projects
    c. All project documents are available to meeting attendees before the meeting
    d. The focus is on cost and schedule variances rather than scope, resources, quality, and risks

21. Performance reports provide information on—

    a. Scope, schedule, cost, and quality
    b. Customer satisfaction
    c. Unacceptable variances
    d. Scope creep

22. Communication is important when setting and managing expectations with the stakeholders. Which one of the following statements is NOT true regarding the importance of communications within a project?

    a. Communications is one of the single biggest contributors to project success or failure.
    b. Communications (including listening) is important in projects, but cannot be attributed directly to the success or failure of a project.
    c. Effective communications includes awareness of communication styles, cultural issues, relationships, personalities, and the context of the situation
    d. Listening is part of communicating and is a way to gain insight into problem areas, managing conflicts, and making decisions.

23. In person-to-person communication, messages are sent on verbal levels and nonverbal levels simultaneously. As a general rule, what percentage of the message actually is sent through nonverbal cues?

    a. 5 percent to 15 percent
    b. 20 percent to 30 percent
    c. 40 percent to 50 percent
    d. Greater than 50 percent

24. As an output from plan communications, it may be necessary to update the—

    a. Project schedule
    b. Corporate policies, procedures, and processes
    c. Knowledge management system
    d. WBS

25. In project communications, the first step in a written communication is to—

    a. Analyze the facts and assumptions that have a bearing on the purpose of the message
    b. Collect needed materials
    c. Develop a logical sequence of the topics to be addressed
    d. Establish the basic purpose of the message

26. A communications management plan includes which one of the following sample contents?

    a. Resources allocated for cost control
    b. Escalation processes, including time frames and the management chains
    c. Dimensions
    d. Project assumptions and constraints

27. Your organization has decided to use project management for all of its endeavors. It has established a Center of Excellence for Project Management to support the movement into management by projects and has appointed you as its director. Since you work in a matrix environment, which of the following types of communications is the most essential for success?

    a. Upward
    b. Lateral
    c. Downward
    d. Diagonal

28. You have heard recently that the client calls your progress reports the "Code of Hammurabi" because they seem to be written in hieroglyphics and are completely indecipherable to all but an antiquities scholar. This situation could have been avoided by—

    a. Informing the client at the start of the project about the types of reports they will receive
    b. Using risk management techniques to identify client issues
    c. Hiring an expert report writer to prepare standard reports
    d. Engaging in communications planning

29. In the manage stakeholder expectations process, lessons learned focus on—

    a. Updated policies and procedures
    b. Improved business skills
    c. Knowledge management
    d. Causes of issues and reasons corrective actions were chosen

30. You want to ensure that the information you collect showing project progress and status is meaningful to stakeholders. To determine specific metrics, you will conduct a stakeholder analysis and then determine the level of detail stakeholders require. You will document this information in the—

    a. WBS
    b. Project management methodology
    c. Project charter
    d. Communications management plan

31. An issue log or action-item log is an output of which following process?

    a. Manage risks
    b. Manage stakeholder expectations
    c. Report performance
    d. Close project

32. The project management plan is an input to the distribute information process. Which part of the plan is most relevant to this process?

    a. Configuration management process
    b. Communications techniques
    c. Work breakdown structure
    d. Performance measurement baseline

33. Information received from stakeholders concerning project operations can be distributed and used to modify or improve future performance of the project. This modification or improvement is done as an update to organizational process assets during which following process?

    a. Plan communications
    b. Distribute information
    c. Report performance
    d. Manage stakeholder expectations

34. General management skills relevant to the distribute information process include—

    a. Operational planning
    b. Organizational behavior
    c. Managing stakeholder requirements
    d. Influencing the organization

35. Changes in the distribute information process should trigger changes to the—

    a. Project management plan and performance reporting system
    b. Integrated change control system and the communications management plan
    c. Monitor and control project process and the project management plan
    d. Organizational process assets updates

36. The most effective means for communicating and resolving issues with stakeholders are—

    a. Video conferences
    b. Portals
    c. Face-to-face meetings
    d. E-mail

37. Lessons learned must be documented as part of the historical database not only for the project but also for the performing organization. Lessons learned documentation is an output of the—

    a. Execute project plan process
    b. Monitor and control project process
    c. Perform quality assurance process
    d. Distribute information process

38. Because communications planning often is linked tightly with enterprise environmental factors, which one of the following statements is true?

    a. The project's organizational structure has a major effect on the project's communications requirements.
    b. Standardized guidelines, work instructions, and performance measurement criteria are key items to consider.
    c. Procedures for approving and issuing work authorizations should be taken into consideration.
    d. Criteria and guidelines to tailor standard processes to the specific needs of the project should be stated explicitly.

39. You are working on a project with 15 stakeholders. The number of communication channels on this project is—

    a. 15
    b. 105
    c. 210
    d. 225

40. Which of the following formulas calculates the number of communication channels in a project?

    a. $\dfrac{n(n-1)}{2}$

    b. $\dfrac{n^2-1}{2}$

    c. $\dfrac{n^2-1}{n}$

    d. $\dfrac{2^n-2}{1^n}$

Answer Sheet

1. a b c d
2. a b c d
3. a b c d
4. a b c d
5. a b c d
6. a b c d
7. a b c d
8. a b c d
9. a b c d
10. a b c d
11. a b c d
12. a b c d
13. a b c d
14. a b c d
15. a b c d
16. a b c d
17. a b c d
18. a b c d
19. a b c d
20. a b c d

21. a b c d
22. a b c d
23. a b c d
24. a b c d
25. a b c d
26. a b c d
27. a b c d
28. a b c d
29. a b c d
30. a b c d
31. a b c d
32. a b c d
33. a b c d
34. a b c d
35. a b c d
36. a b c d
37. a b c d
38. a b c d
39. a b c d
40. a b c d

Answer Key

1. d.   Discussing specific legal issues regarding the contract

Conducted after contract award or approval of the project, the kickoff meeting provides an opportunity for project participants to get to know each other and review information about the project. It is not a forum to discuss detailed project issues. [Executing]

Meredith and Mantel, 2009, 243; PMI®, *PMBOK® Guide*, 2008, 257

2. a.   Methods that will be used to convey information

The plan should also contain a distribution structure that shows the methods that will be used to distribute various types of information and the individuals or organizations to which the information will be distributed, production schedules showing when each type of communication will be produced, and methods to access information between scheduled communications. Also included is a discussion of how the plan will be updated and revised as needs change. The communications management plan is a component of the project management plan. The level of detail of its content should be commensurate with the size and complexity of the project. [Planning]

PMI®, *PMBOK® Guide*, 2008, 257

3. b.   Developing a system to manage communications

Project stakeholders must receive information in a timely fashion. Global communications that use standard formats through a communications management system may reduce the impact of cultural differences. [Executing]

PMI®, *PMBOK® Guide*, 2008, 259–260

4. b.   You, because you are the project manager

Stakeholder management refers to any action taken by the project manager or project team to satisfy the needs of and resolve issues with project stakeholders. The project manager is responsible for stakeholder management. [Monitoring and Controlling]

PMI®, *PMBOK® Guide*, 2008, 261–262

5. c. Comparing influence and location

Identifying and analyzing the stakeholders helps to classify them better for developing a strategy to help manage them and their expectations throughout the project. The most common comparison elements are: power, influence, interest, and impact. The location of the person may have an impact on one of the other measures, but it is not easily quantifiable on a low, medium, high, type scale. [Initiating]

PMI®, *PMBOK® Guide*, 249

6. d. Rephrase the content and reflect the feeling

Empathic listening requires seeing the world the way the other person sees it, with the goal of understanding that person's views and feelings. Unlike sympathetic listening, empathic listening contains no element of value judgment. [Executing]

Covey 2004, 239–243

7. a. Downward communication

Downward communication provides direction and control for project team members and other employees. It contains job-related information, such as actions required, standards, the time activities should be performed, activities to be completed, and progress measurement. [Executing]

PMI®, *PMBOK® Guide*, 2008, 244

8. a. Horizontal

Communication skills are used to exchange information between the sender and the receiver. Horizontal communication occurs between or among peers, that is, across, rather than up and down, the organization. [Executing]

PMI®, *PMBOK® Guide*, 2008, 244

9. b. Determine the objective

Only after the objective is determined can the other issues listed be addressed effectively. The information must be relevant to audience needs. [Monitoring and Controlling]

PMI®, *PMBOK® Guide*, 2008, 261; Verma 1997, 18–19

10. a. Conduct a stakeholder analysis to assess information needs

Stakeholder analysis is used to analyze the information needs of the stakeholders and to determine the sources for meeting those needs. It helps to determine whose interests should be taken into account throughout the project. [Initiating]

PMI®, *PMBOK® Guide*, 2008, 248

11. a. Encode the message

As the first step in the basic communication model, it is essential to translate thoughts or ideas into a language that is understood by others. Then, the message is sent using various technologies, and the receiver decodes it or translates it back into meaningful thoughts or ideas. [Planning]

PMI®, *PMBOK® Guide*, 2008, 255

12. d. Increased conflict

Barriers to communication lead to a poor flow of information. Accordingly, messages are misinterpreted by recipients, thereby creating different perceptions, understanding, and frames of reference. Left unchecked, poor communication increases conflict among project stakeholders, which causes the other problems listed to arise. [Executing]

PMI®, *PMBOK® Guide*, 2008, 239; Verma 1997, 24–25

13. a. Each side may misinterpret what the other side has said

Effective communication is the key to successful negotiation. Misunderstanding is the most common communication problem. A project manager should listen actively, acknowledge what is being said, and speak for a purpose. [Executing]

Fisher et al. 1991, 32–34; Verma 1996, 165

14. b. Passive communications

You can use several different methods to share information. Interactive communications are multidirectional in nature, like conferences and meetings. Pull communications are those methods where the recipient finds the information at their leisure and gets the information that they want at their discretion. Push communications is targeted information sent to a select group, but does not certify that the recipient actually has received the information, like e-mail. Passive communications is more of a style of delivering the content or receiving the content. [Initiating]

PMI®, *PMBOK® Guide*, 256

15. a. Stakeholder register

Although the other items may be updated as well, the stakeholder register is updated most often as a result of plan communications, and you learn more about your various stakeholders. The knowledge management system along with the corporate policies, procedures and processes, are part of the organizational process assets. Overall product improvements are change control and part of perform integrated change control. [Planning]

PMI®, *PMBOK® Guide*, 258

16. b. Responsibilities

The communications management plan should identify the team member charged with distributing information. Other attributes include the information to be communicated and how it will be communicated; the purpose, frequency, and time frame for the communications; and method of transmitting the information. [Planning]

PMI®, *PMBOK® Guide*, 257

17. b. Negotiation

Negotiation involves compromise so that each party feels it has received something of value, even though it has had to make certain sacrifices. [Executing]

PMI®, *PMBOK® Guide*, 2008, 227, 409–413

18. d. Sharing only positive aspects of the project for future replication elsewhere in the organization

The lessons learned summary should document the major positive and negative aspects of the project so that future projects can benefit from the team's successes and failures, by replicating the good things about the project and avoiding the mistakes. [Executing]

Garrett 2007, 188; PMI®, *PMBOK® Guide*, 2008, 261

19. c. Assigned an owner and a target date for closure

If issues are left unresolved, conflicts arise and the project may be delayed. Holding someone accountable to ensure the issue is addressed expedites resolution. [Executing]

PMI®, *PMBOK® Guide*, 2008, 261–265

20. a. Work performance information on the status of deliverables is collected

As an input to performance reporting, work performance information describes the status of the identified project deliverables. It provides detail regarding what has been accomplished to date or for a specific time period. [Monitoring and Controlling]

PMI®, *PMBOK® Guide*, 2008, 266–268

21. a. Scope, schedule, cost, and quality

Project performance focuses on the four main areas of a project: scope, schedule, cost, and quality. It does not focus on one area to the exclusion of the others. [Monitoring and Controlling]

PMI®, *PMBOK® Guide*, 2008, 266–267

22. b. Communications (including listening) is important in projects, but cannot be attributed directly to the success or failure of a project.

Communications is considered one of the single most powerful indicators of project success or failure. Effective communications includes an awareness of all types of filters that may be impeding or straining communications. Listening is vital to good communications. [Executing]

PMI®, *PMBOK® Guide*, 2008, 411

23. d. Greater than 50 percent

Nonverbal cues can be divided into four categories: physical, aesthetic, signs, and symbols. Many studies have demonstrated that most messages are conveyed through such nonverbal cues as facial expression, touch, and body motion, rather than through the words spoken. [Executing]

Verma 1996, 19

24. a. Project schedule

Communications planning often entails the need to update project documents, including the project schedule, stakeholder register, and the stakeholder management strategy. [Planning]

PMI®, *PMBOK® Guide*, 2008, 258

25. d. Establish the basic purpose of the message

The first step is to establish a general or specific purpose before starting to write. There are many reasons to communicate. Some examples include to direct, inform, inquire, or persuade. Project managers should work closely with their team to develop a consensus on the purpose of the message [Executing]

Verma 1996, 20

26. b. Escalation processes, including time frames and the management chains

Numerous items, including escalation processes, are part of the communications management plan. Business issues may arise that cannot be resolved at a lower staff level. During such a time, an escalation process is required to show time frames and the names of people in the management chain who will work to resolve these issues. [Planning]

PMI®, *PMBOK® Guide*, 2008, 257

27. b. Lateral

Lateral or horizontal communication is between the project manager and his or her peers and will be where most of the communications will occur. Accordingly, it is essential for success in a highly competitive environment and requires diplomacy, experience, and mutual respect. [Executing]

Verma 1997, 136

28. d. Engaging in communications planning

The communications management plan is prepared during communications planning. The plan should include a description of the information to be distributed such as format, content, level of detail, as well as conventions and definitions to be used. [Planning]

PMI®, *PMBOK® Guide*, 2008, 256–257

29. d. Causes of issues and reasons corrective actions were chosen

As part of the updates to the organizational process assets, lessons learned should be documented about stakeholder management with a focus on the documentation of issues that were resolved and how they were resolved and closed. [Monitoring and Controlling]

PMI®, *PMBOK® Guide*, 2008, 265 and 271

30. d. Communications management plan

The project team must conduct an analysis of stakeholder communications requirements to ensure that stakeholders are receiving the information required to participate in the project. For example, stakeholders typically require performance reports for information purposes. Such information requirements should be included in the communications management plan. [Planning]

PMI®, *PMBOK® Guide*, 2004, 253 and 257

31. b. Manage stakeholder expectations

Issue logs or action-item logs are used to document and monitor the resolution of issues. [Monitoring and Controlling]

PMI®, *PMBOK® Guide*, 2008, 265

32. d. Performance measurement baseline

This is an approved, time-phased plan against which project scope, schedule, and cost performance are measured on a regular basis. It may also include technical and quality parameters. [Monitoring and Controlling]

PMI®, *PMBOK® Guide*, 2008, 267–268

33. b. Distribute information

Information distribution involves making information available to project stakeholders in a timely manner. It is done through the communications management plan and also through responding to unexpected requests for information. Feedback from stakeholders is used to improve project performance. [Executing]

PMI®, *PMBOK® Guide*, 2008, 243–245

34. c. Managing stakeholder requirements

Communications skills are part of general management skills and include the exchange of information. Regarding information distribution, this means that the right persons get the right information at the right time as defined in the communications management plan. [Executing]

PMI®, *PMBOK® Guide*, 2008, 261–263

35. d. Organizational process assets updates

Any changes regarding how information is distributed would cause a review (or changes) in the organizational process assets, including (but not limited to) stakeholder notifications; project reports, presentations, and records; feedback from stakeholders; and lessons learned documentation. [Executing]

PMI®, *PMBOK® Guide*, 260–261

36. c. Face-to-face meetings

Face-to-face meetings are considered the most effective way to resolve issues with stakeholders because a greater exchange of ideas can take place in a shorter period of time, plus being with the stakeholders in the same room creates a certain dynamic. When face-to-face meetings are not warranted or practical, such as an international project, then telephone calls, e-mails, and other communication methods can be used. [Monitoring and Controlling]

PMI®, *PMBOK® Guide*, 2008, 264

37. d. Distribute information process

This process is concerned with providing stakeholders with project information in a timely manner. Lessons learned documentation is an example of project information. [Executing]

PMI®, *PMBOK® Guide*, 2008, 261

38. a. **The project's organizational structure has a major effect on the project's communications requirements.**

Enterprise environmental factors undoubtedly will influence the project's success and must be considered because communication must be adapted to the project environment. The maturity of the organization with respect to its project management system, culture, style, organizational structure, and project management office can also influence the project. [Planning]

PMI®, *PMBOK® Guide*, 2008, 252–253

39. b. **105**

The formula for determining the number of communication channels is $n(n-1)/2$, where n = the number of stakeholders: $15(15-1)/2 = (15)(14)/2 = 105$. It is important to note that project managers must plan the project's communications requirements carefully, limiting who will communicate with whom given the potential for confusion when multiple communications channels can exist. [Planning]

PMI®, *PMBOK® Guide*, 2008, 253

40. a. $$\frac{n(n-1)}{2}$$

Where n = the number of stakeholders. [Planning]

PMI®, *PMBOK® Guide*, 2008, 253

PROJECT RISK MANAGEMENT

Study Hints

Most exam takers find the Project Risk Management questions on the PMP® certification exam demanding because they address many concepts that project managers may not have been exposed to in their work or education. However, the questions correspond closely to *PMBOK® Guide* material, so you should not have much difficulty if you study the concepts and terminology found there. Although the questions included do not contain mathematically complex work problems, they do require you to know certain theories, such as expected monetary value (EMV) and decision-tree analysis. Additionally, you are likely to encounter questions related to levels of risk faced by both buyer and seller based on various types of contracts.

PMI® views risk management as a six-step process including plan risk management, identify risks, perform qualitative risk analysis, perform quantitative risk analysis, plan risk response, and monitor and control risk. *PMBOK® Guide* Figure 11-1 provides an overview of this approach. Know this chart thoroughly.

Following is a list of the major Project Risk Management topics. Use it to help focus your study efforts on the areas most likely to appear on the exam.

Major Topics

Project risk management

- Risk defined
- Types of risk
  - Known risks
  - Unknown risks
- Risk factors
  - Risk event
  - Probability of occurrence
  - Amount at stake (impact)
  - Risk conditions
  - Risk tolerances

Risk processes

Plan risk management

- Planning meetings and analyses
- Risk management plan
  - Methodology
  - Roles and responsibilities
  - Budget
  - Timing
  - Categories
  - Definitions of probability and impact
  - Probability and impact matrix
  - Revised stakeholder tolerances
  - Reporting formats
  - Tracking

Risk tolerance

Identify risks

- Definition
- Timing
- Plans and baselines
- Project documents

Identify risks tools and techniques

- Documentation reviews
- Brainstorming
- Delphi method
- Interviews
- Root cause analysis
- Strengths-weaknesses-opportunities-threats (SWOT) analysis

Major Topics (continued)

Identify risks tools and techniques (continued)

- Checklists
- Assumption analysis
- Diagramming techniques
- Expert judgment

Risk register

- List of identified risks
- List of potential responses

Perform qualitative risk analysis

- Prioritize risks for further action
- Risk probability and impact assessment
- Probability/impact matrix
- Risk data quality assessment
- Risk categories
- Risk urgency assessment
- Expert judgment
- Risk register updates
  - Relative ranking or priority list of risks
  - Risks by category
  - Causes of risks requiring particular attention
  - Risks requiring near-term responses and additional analysis and responses
  - Watch list of low priority risks
  - Trends

Perform quantitative risk analysis

- Numerical analysis of the effect of identified risks on project objectives
- Interviewing
- Probability distribution
- Sensitivity analysis
- Expected monetary value analysis
- Decision-tree analysis
- Decision-tree analysis guidelines
- Monte Carlo analysis
  - Path convergence
  - Statistical distribution

Major Topics (continued)

Perform quantitative risk analysis (continued)

- Risk register updates
  - Probabilistic analysis of the project
  - Probability of achieving cost and time objectives
  - Prioritized list of risks
  - Trends

Plan risk responses

- Negative risks or threats
  - Avoid
  - Transfer
  - Mitigate
  - Accept
- Positive risks or opportunities
  - Exploit
  - Share
  - Enhance
  - Accept
- Contingent responses
- Risk register updates
  - Risk-related contract decisions
  - Updates to plans and documents

Monitor and control risks

- Definition and purpose
- Tools and techniques
  - Risk reassessment
  - Risk audits
  - Variance and trend analysis
  - Technical performance measurement
  - Reserve analysis
  - Status meetings
- Updates to the risk register
- Change requests
- Updates to organizational process assets, change requests, plans, and documents

Practice Questions

INSTRUCTIONS: Note the most suitable answer for each multiple-choice question in the appropriate space on the answer sheet.

1. As the project manager, you have the option of proposing one of three systems to a client: a full-feature system that not only satisfies the minimum requirements but also offers numerous special functions (the "Mercedes"); a system that meets the client's minimum requirements (the "Yugo"); and a system that satisfies the minimum requirements plus has a few extra features (the "Toyota"). The on-time records and associated profits and losses are depicted on the below decision tree. What is the expected monetary value of the "Toyota" system?

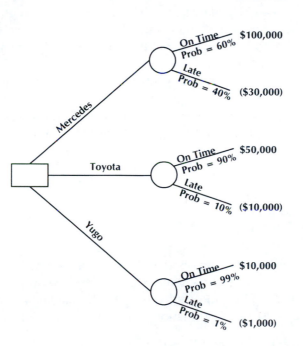

a. $9,900
b. $44,000
c. $45,000
d. $48,000

2. A risk response strategy that can be used for both threats and opportunities is—

   a. Share
   b. Avoid
   c. Accept
   d. Transfer

3. The risk urgency assessment is a tool and technique used for—

   a. Plan risk responses
   b. Identify risks
   c. Perform qualitative risk analysis
   d. Perform quantitative risk analysis

4. Projects are particularly susceptible to risk because—

   a. Murphy's law states that "if something can go wrong, it will"
   b. There is uncertainty in all projects
   c. Project management tools are generally unavailable at the project team level
   d. There are never enough resources to do the job

5. As project manager, you have assembled the team to prepare a comprehensive list of project risks. Which one of the following documents would be the most helpful in this process?

   a. OBS
   b. WBS
   c. RBS
   d. CBS

6. You are working on identifying possible risks to your project to develop a nutritional supplement. You want to develop a comprehensive list of risks that can be addressed later through qualitative and quantitative risk analysis. An information gathering technique used to identify risks is—

   a. Documentation reviews
   b. Probability and impact analysis
   c. Checklist analysis
   d. Brainstorming

7. The Delphi technique is a particularly useful method for identifying risks to—

    a. Present a sequence of decision choices graphically to decision makers
    b. Define the probability of occurrence of specific variables
    c. Reduce bias in the analysis and keep any one person from having undue influence on the outcome
    d. Help take into account the attitude of the decision maker toward risk

8. A workaround is—

    a. An unplanned response to a negative risk event
    b. A plan of action to follow when something unexpected occurs
    c. A specific response to certain types of risk as described in the risk management plan
    d. A proactive, planned method of responding to risks

9. Most statistical simulations of budgets, schedules, and resource allocations use which one of the following approaches?

    a. PERT
    b. Decision-tree analysis
    c. Present value analysis
    d. Monte Carlo analysis

10. In the below path convergence example, if the odds of completing activities 1, 2, and 3 on time are 50 percent, 50 percent, and 50 percent, what are the chances of starting activity 4 on day 6?

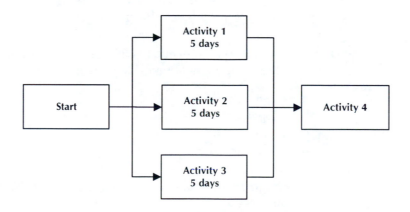

    a. 10 percent
    b. 13 percent
    c. 40 percent
    d. 50 percent

11. A project health check identified a risk that your project would not be completed on time. As a result, you are quantifying the project's risk exposure and determining what cost and schedule contingency reserves might be needed. You performed a schedule risk analysis using Monte Carlo analysis. The basis for your schedule risk analysis is the—

    a. WBS
    b. Gantt chart
    c. Schedule network diagram and duration estimates
    d. Probability/impact risk rating matrix

12. You are developing radio frequency (RF) technology that will improve overnight package delivery. You ask each stakeholder to estimate the most optimistic package delivery time using the RF technology, the most pessimistic time, and the most likely time. This shows that for your next step you plan to—

    a. Use a beta or triangular probability distribution
    b. Conduct a sensitivity analysis
    c. Structure a decision analysis as a decision tree
    d. Determine the strategy for risk response

13. Each one of the following statements about risk avoidance is true EXCEPT that it—

    a. Focuses on changing the project management plan to eliminate entirely the threat
    b. Isolates the project's objectives from the risk's impact
    c. Accepts the consequences of the risk event should it occur
    d. Changes the project objective that is in jeopardy

14. If the probability of event 1 is 80 percent and of event 2 is 70 percent and they are independent events, how likely is it that both events will occur?

    a. 6 percent
    b. 15 percent
    c. 24 percent
    d. 56 percent

15. The project scope statement should be used in the identify risk process because it—

    a. Identifies project assumptions
    b. Identifies all the work that must be done and, therefore, includes all the risks on the project
    c. Helps to organize all the work that must be done on the project
    d. Contains information on risks from prior projects

16. Your project team has identified all the risks on the project and has categorized them as high, medium, and low. The "low" risks are placed on which one of the following for monitoring?

    a. Threat list
    b. Low risk list
    c. Watch list
    d. Low impact list

17. A general contingency is used for—

    a. Risks that are identified at the outset of the project
    b. Risks that are not identified at the outset of the project but are known before they occur
    c. Risks that cannot be known before they occur because they are external risks
    d. Any risks that cannot be known before they occur

18. The simplest form of quantitative risk analysis and modeling techniques is—

    a. Probability analysis
    b. Sensitivity analysis
    c. Delphi technique
    d. Utility theory

19. If a business venture has a 60-percent chance to earn $2 million and a 20-percent chance to lose $1.5 million, what is the expected monetary value of the venture?

    a. −$50,000
    b. $300,000
    c. $500,000
    d. $900,000

20. You are managing the construction of a highly sophisticated data center in Port Moresby, Papua New Guinea. Although this location offers significant economic advantages, the threat of typhoons has caused you to create a backup plan to operate in Manila in case the center is flooded. This plan is an example of what type of risk response?

    a. Passive avoidance
    b. Mitigation
    c. Active acceptance
    d. Deflection

21. A recent earned value analysis shows that your project is 20 percent complete, the CPI is 0.67, and the SPI is 0.87. In this situation, you should—

    a. Perform additional resource planning, add resources, and use overtime as needed to accomplish the same amount of budgeted work
    b. Rebaseline the schedule, then use Monte Carlo analysis
    c. Conduct a risk response audit to help control risk
    d. Update the risk identification and qualitative and quantitative risk analyses

22. The purpose of a numeric scale in risk management is to—

    a. Avoid high-impact risks
    b. Assign a relative value to the impact on project objectives if the risk in question occurs
    c. Rank order risks in terms of very low, low, moderate, high, and very high
    d. Test project assumptions

23. Risk score measures the—

    a. Variability of the estimate
    b. Product of the probability and impact of the risk
    c. Range of schedule and cost outcomes
    d. Reduced monetary value of the risk event

24. Which of the following is an example of recommended corrective action in risk management?

    a. Conducting a risk audit
    b. Engaging in additional risk response planning
    c. Performing the contingency plan
    d. Conducting a risk review

25. The primary advantage of using decision-tree analysis in project risk management is that it—

    a. Considers the attitude of the decision maker toward risk
    b. Forces consideration of the probability of each outcome
    c. Helps to identify and postulate risk scenarios for the project
    d. Shows how risks can occur in combination

26. Your project is using complex, unproven technology. Your team conducted a brainstorming session to identify risks. Poor allocation of project resources was the number one risk. This risk was placed on the risk register, which included at this point a—

    a. Watch list
    b. Potential risk response
    c. Known unknown
    d. List of other risks requiring additional analysis

27. When managing current projects, it is important to use lessons learned from previous projects to improve the organization's project management process. Therefore, in project closing procedures, it is important to review the—

    a. Secondary risks that occurred
    b. Checklists for identify risks
    c. WBS dictionary
    d. Fallback plan

28. Risk mitigation involves—

    a. Using performance and payment bonds
    b. Eliminating a specific threat by eliminating the cause
    c. Avoiding the schedule risk inherent in the project
    d. Reducing the probability and/or impact of an adverse risk event to an acceptable threshold

29. On a typical project, when are risks highest and impacts (amount at stake) lowest?

    a. During the concept phase
    b. At or near completion of the project
    c. During the implementation phase
    d. When the project manager is replaced

30. Two key inputs to the perform quantitative risk analysis process are the—

    a. WBS and milestone list
    b. Scope management plan and process improvement plan
    c. Schedule management plan and cost management plan
    d. Procurement management plan and quality baseline

31. The highest risk impact generally occurs during which one of the following project life-cycle phases?

    a. Concept and planning
    b. Planning and implementation
    c. Implementation and closeout
    d. Concept and closeout

32. Which one of the following statements best characterizes an activity cost or duration estimate developed with a limited amount of information?

    a. It should be part of the planning for the needed management reserve.
    b. It is an input to identify risks.
    c. It is an output from indentify risks.
    d. It must be factored into the list of prioritized project risks.

33. What is the primary difference between a risk audit and a risk reassessment?

    a. A risk reassessment is conducted at the completion of a major phase; audits are conducted after the project is complete.
    b. Project stakeholders conduct risk audits; management conducts reassessments.
    c. The project team conducts risk reassessments; those who are external to the project conduct risk audits.
    d. There is no difference; they are virtually the same.

34. Accurate and unbiased data are essential for perform qualitative risk analysis. Which one of the following should you use to examine the extent of understanding of project risk?

    a. Data quality assessment
    b. Project assumptions testing
    c. Sensitivity analysis
    d. Influence diagrams

35. Assigning more talented resources to the project to reduce time to completion or to provide better quality than originally planned are examples of which one of the following strategies?

    a. Enhance
    b. Exploit
    c. Share
    d. Contingent response

36. Which of the following is NOT an objective of a risk audit?

    a. Confirming that risk management has been practiced throughout the project life cycle
    b. Confirming that the project is well managed and that the risks are being controlled
    c. Helping to identify the deterioration of the project's value potential in its early stages
    d. Ensuring that each risk identified and deemed critical has a computed expected value

37. Contingency planning involves—

    a. Defining the steps to be taken if an identified risk event should occur
    b. Establishing a management reserve to cover unplanned expenditures
    c. Preparing a stand-alone document that is separate from the overall project plan
    d. Determining needed adjustments to make during the implementation phase of a project

38. Assume that you are working on a new product for your firm. Your CEO learned that a competitor was about to launch a new product that has similar features to those of your project. The competitor plans to launch the product on September 1. It is now March 1. Your schedule called for you to launch your product on December 1. Your CEO now has now mandated that you fast track your project so you can launch your product on August 1. This fast track schedule is an example of an—

    a. Unknown risk
    b. A risk taken to achieve a reward
    c. A response that requires sharing the risk
    d. A passive avoidance strategy

39. As head of the project management office, you need to focus on those items where risk responses can lead to better project outcomes. One way to help you make these decisions is to—

    a. Use a probability and impact matrix
    b. Assess trends in perform quantitative risk analysis results
    c. Prioritize risks and conditions
    d. Assess trends in perform qualitative risk analysis results

40. You are the project manager for the construction of an incinerator to burn refuse. Local residents and environmental groups are opposed to this project. Management agrees to move this project to a different location. This is an example of which one of the following risk responses?

    a. Passive acceptance
    b. Active acceptance
    c. Mitigation
    d. Avoidance

Answer Sheet

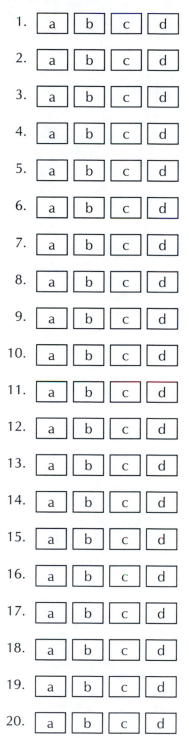

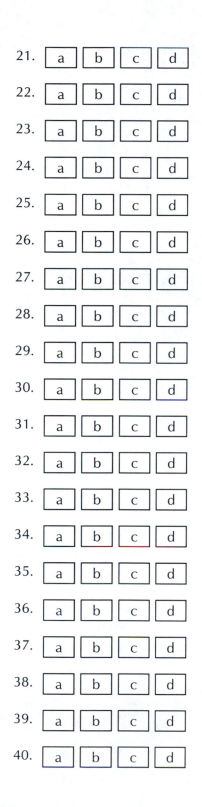

1. a b c d
2. a b c d
3. a b c d
4. a b c d
5. a b c d
6. a b c d
7. a b c d
8. a b c d
9. a b c d
10. a b c d
11. a b c d
12. a b c d
13. a b c d
14. a b c d
15. a b c d
16. a b c d
17. a b c d
18. a b c d
19. a b c d
20. a b c d

21. a b c d
22. a b c d
23. a b c d
24. a b c d
25. a b c d
26. a b c d
27. a b c d
28. a b c d
29. a b c d
30. a b c d
31. a b c d
32. a b c d
33. a b c d
34. a b c d
35. a b c d
36. a b c d
37. a b c d
38. a b c d
39. a b c d
40. a b c d

Answer Key

1. b. $44,000

$$EMV_{\text{Toyota}} = (\$50,000 \times 90\%) + (-\$10,000 \times 10\%)$$
$$= \$45,000 + (-\$1,000)$$
$$= \$44,000$$

[Planning]

PMI®, *PMBOK*® *Guide*, 2008, 299

2. c. Accept

Risk exists on every project and it is unrealistic to think it can be eliminated completely. There are certain risks that simply must be accepted because we cannot control whether or not they will occur (for example, an earthquake). Acceptance is a strategy for dealing with risk that can be used for both threats and opportunities. [Planning]

PMI®, *PMBOK*® *Guide*, 2008, 304–305

3. c. Perform qualitative risk analysis

Risks that may happen in the near-term need urgent attention. The purpose of the risk urgency assessment is to identify those risks that have a high likelihood of happening sooner rather than later. [Planning]

PMI®, *PMBOK*® *Guide*, 2008, 293

4. b. There is uncertainty in all projects

Every project has uncertainty associated with it because a project by its definition is a temporary endeavor undertaken to create a unique product, service, or result. Risks may be known or unknown. [Planning]

PMI®, *PMBOK*® *Guide*, 2008, 5 and 275

5. c. RBS

The risk breakdown structure (RBS) helps to provide framework for ensuring a comprehensive process of systematically identified risks. It is an hierarchically organized depiction of the identified risks by category and subcategory that indentifies the various areas and causes of potential risks. [Planning]

PMI®, *PMBOK*® *Guide*, 2008, 290

6. d. Brainstorming

Brainstorming is a frequently used information-gathering technique for identifying risk, because it enables the project team to develop a list of potential risks relatively quickly. Project team members, or invited experts, participate in the session. Risks are easily categorized for follow-on analysis. [Planning]

PMI®, *PMBOK® Guide*, 2008, 286

7. c. Reduce bias in the analysis and keep any one person from having undue influence on the outcome

The Delphi technique provides a means for arriving at a consensus using a panel of experts to determine a solution to a specific problem. Project risk experts are identified but participate anonymously. Each panelist answers a questionnaire. Then the responses, along with opinions and justifications, are evaluated, and statistical feedback is given to each panel member. The process continues until group responses converge toward a solution. [Planning]

PMI®, *PMBOK® Guide*, 2008, 286; Wideman 1992, C-2 and C-3

8. a. An unplanned response to a negative risk event

Used in risk monitoring and control, workarounds are risk responses that have not been defined in advance of the risk event occurring. [Monitoring and Controlling]

PMI®, *PMBOK® Guide*, 2008, 312 and 445

9. d. Monte Carlo analysis

Monte Carlo analysis supports various statistical distributions (normal, triangular, beta, uniform, and so on) used in estimating budgets, schedules, and resource allocations. [Planning]

Frame 2002, 89; PMI®, *PMBOK® Guide*, 2008, 299

10. b. 13 percent

Probability (starting activity 4 on day 6) = $(0.5)^3$ = 0.125 or 13% [Planning]

PMI®, *PMBOK® Guide*, 2008, 291

11. c. Schedule network diagram and duration estimates

When determining the likelihood of meeting the project's schedule end date through Monte Carlo, the schedule network diagram and duration estimate are used as inputs to the simulation program. Cost risk, on the other hand, uses cost estimates from the WBS. [Planning]

PMI®, *PMBOK® Guide*, 2008, 299

12. a. Use a beta or triangular probability distribution

Interviews often are used to help quantify the probability and consequences of risks on project objectives. The type of information collected during the interview depends on the type of probability distribution that is used. A beta or triangular distribution is used widely when information is gathered on the optimistic (low), pessimistic (high), and most likely scenarios. [Planning]

PMI®, *PMBOK® Guide*, 2008, 297–298

13. c. Accepts the consequences of the risk event should it occur

Accepting the consequences of the risk event is categorized as risk acceptance. With this risk response approach, the project team takes no action to reduce the probability of the risk's occurring. [Planning]

PMI®, *PMBOK® Guide*, 2008, 303–304

14. d. 56 percent

The likelihood is determined by multiplying the probability of event 1 by the probability of event 2. [Planning]

PMI®, *PMBOK® Guide*, 2008, 291; Wideman 1992, IV-7

15. a. Identifies project assumptions

Project assumptions, which should be enumerated in the project scope statement, are areas of uncertainty, and as such are potential causes of project risk. [Planning]

PMI®, *PMBOK® Guide*, 2008, 284

16. c. Watch list

Even low-priority risks must be monitored. A watch list is used to ensure such risks are tracked for continued monitoring. [Planning]

PMI®, *PMBOK® Guide*, 2008, 294

17. d. Any risks that cannot be known before they occur

There is a category of risks that is sometimes called unknown-unknowns, meaning that the risk is not knowable and, therefore, the probability of the risk is also not knowable. Your lead technical advisor becoming seriously ill, your offices being ransacked by persons engaged in industrial espionage, or one of your subcontractors winning the lottery and running off to the Cayman Islands are all examples of risks that are not known before they occur. However, such risks must be expected and a general contingency can be set aside to address the impact they leave in their wake. [Monitoring and Controlling]

PMI®, *PMBOK® Guide*, 2008, 173, 177, and 303; Pritchard 2005, 183–188

18. b. Sensitivity analysis

Sensitivity analysis, as a quantitative risk analysis and modeling technique, helps to determine the risks that have the most potential impact on the project. It examines the extent to which the uncertainty of each project element affects the objective being examined when all other uncertain elements are held at their baseline values. [Planning]

PMI®, *PMBOK® Guide*, 2008, 298; Wideman 1992, C-1 and C-2

19. d. $900,000

$EMV = (\$2M \times 60\%) + (-\$1.5M \times 20\%) =$

$(\$1.2M) + (-\$300,000) = \$900,000$

[Planning]

Frame 2002, 192; PMI®, *PMBOK® Guide*, 2008, 298

20. c. Active acceptance

Active acceptance means not only accepting the consequences of a risk, but also establishing a plan for dealing with the risk, should it occur. Organizations typically establish a contingency plan funded by a contingency reserve (of time, money, or resources) to handle known, or even sometimes potential unknown, threats or opportunities. [Planning]

PMI®, *PMBOK® Guide*, 2008, 304

21. d. Update the risk identification and qualitative and quantitative risk analyses

Earned value is used for monitoring overall project performance against a baseline plan. When a project deviates significantly from the baseline, you should update the risk identification and qualitative and quantitative risk analyses. [Monitoring and Controlling]

PMI®, *PMBOK® Guide*, 2008, 310

22. b. Assign a relative value to the impact on project objectives if the risk in question occurs

You can develop relative or numeric, well-defined scales using agreed-upon definitions by the stakeholders. When using a numeric scale, each level of impact has a specific number assigned to it. [Planning]

PMI®, *PMBOK® Guide*, 2008, 291–292

23. b. Product of the probability and impact of the risk

The risk score provides a convenient way to compare risks because comparing impacts or probabilities alone is meaningless. [Planning]

PMI®, *PMBOK® Guide*, 2008, 292

24. c. Performing the contingency plan

Corrective action in risk management is the process of making changes to bring expected performance in line with the risk management plan. Such action consists of performing either the planned risk response, such as implementing contingency plans, or a workaround. [Monitoring and Controlling]

PMI®, *PMBOK® Guide*, 2008, 312

25. b. Forces consideration of the probability of each outcome

As a graphical way to bring together information, decision-tree analysis quantifies the likelihood of failure and places a value on each decision. Usually applied to cost and time considerations, this form of risk analysis may be linked to a sensitivity analysis. [Planning]

PMI®, *PMBOK® Guide*, 2008, 298–299; Wideman 1992, C-2 and C-3

26. b. Potential risk response

The risk register is prepared first in the identify risks process. It contains a list of identified risks in as much detail as possible and a list of potential responses when they are identifiable at this time. [Planning]

PMI®, *PMBOK® Guide*, 2008, 288

27. b. Checklists for identify risks

Checklists are a tool and a technique of the identify risks process and include risks encountered on similar, previous projects identified through the lessons learned process and from other sources. The project team should review the checklist as part of the identify risks process as well as during closeout. The team should add to the list as necessary, based on its experience, to help others in the future. [Planning]

PMI®, *PMBOK® Guide*, 2008, 286

28. d. Reducing the probability and/or impact of an adverse risk event to an acceptable threshold

It is often more effective to take early action to reduce probability and/or impact of a risk occurring on a project than attempting to repair the damage after the risk has occurred. [Planning]

PMI®, *PMBOK® Guide*, 2008, 304

29. a. During the concept phase

Risks are highest at the beginning of a project because the project faces an uncertain future, and impacts are lowest at this time because investments in human and material resources are minimal. [Planning]

Frame 2002, 80; PMI®, *PMBOK® Guide*, 2008, 17;
Wideman 1992, II-1–II-5

30. c. Schedule management plan and cost management plan

The cost and schedule of a project are two areas significantly affected by risk occurrences. Information on these two areas, because of their quantitative nature, makes excellent input to the perform quantification risk process to help determine overall impact. [Planning]

PMI®, *PMBOK® Guide*, 2008, 296

31. c.   Implementation and closeout

Opportunity and risk generally remain high during the concept and planning phases. However, the amount at stake remains low because of the relatively low level of investment up to that point. During project implementation and closeout, however, risk falls to lower levels as remaining unknowns are translated into knowns. At the same time, the amount at stake rises steadily as the necessary resources are invested to complete the project. [Planning]

PMI®, *PMBOK® Guide*, 2008, 17; Wideman 1992, II-5–II-6

32. b.   It is an input to identify risks.

Much of the output from planning in other knowledge areas, such as activity cost and duration estimates, may entail risk and is reviewed during the identify risks process. This process requires an understanding of the schedule, cost, and quality management plans found in the project management plan. Estimates that are aggressive or developed with a limited amount of information are even more likely to entail risk and, therefore, must also be an input to the identify risks process. [Planning]

PMI®, *PMBOK® Guide*, 2008, 284

33. c.   The project team conducts risk reassessments; those who are external to the project conduct risk audits.

Risk reassessment is an ongoing activity by the project team. Risks should be discussed at every status meeting. Risk audits are performed during the project life cycle to examine and document the effectiveness of risk responses. [Monitoring and Controlling]

PMI®, *PMBOK® Guide*, 2008, 310

34. a.   Data quality assessment

Perform qualitative risk analysis requires accurate and unbiased data. The use of low-quality data may result in a qualitative risk analysis that is of little use to the project manager regarding understanding of the risk, data available about the risk, data quality, and data reliability and integrity. [Planning]

PMI®, *PMBOK® Guide*, 2008, 293

35. b. Exploit

Although it might have a negative connotation, exploitation is a strategy used for risks with positive impacts where the organization wants to ensure that the opportunity is realized. [Planning]

PMI®, *PMBOK® Guide*, 2008, 304

36. d. Ensuring that each risk identified and deemed critical has a computed expected value

It is not feasible or necessary to quantify every risk. Therefore, a risk audit should never have as an objective to ensure that each project risk has a computed expected value. [Monitoring and Controlling]

PMI®, *PMBOK® Guide*, 2008, 310

37. a. Defining the steps to be taken if an identified risk event should occur

For some risks it is appropriate for the project team to make a response plan that will be executed only under certain predefined conditions if it is believed that there will be sufficient warning to implement the plan. [Monitoring and Controlling]

PMI®, *PMBOK® Guide*, 2008, 308–309

38. b. A risk taken to achieve a reward

Project risk has its origin in the uncertainty that is present in all projects. Organizations and stakeholders are willing to accept varying degrees of risk, and risks that are threats to the project may be accepted if the risks are within tolerances and are in balance with the rewards to be gained. This example of adopting a fast-track schedule is a risk taken to achieve the reward created by the earlier completion date.

PMI®, *PMBOK® Guide*, 2008, 276

39. a. Use a probability and impact matrix

The probability and impact matrix can be used to classify risks according to their level of impact and to prioritize them for future quantitative analyses and responses based on their rating. Typically these risk rating rules are specified by the organization in advance of the project. The matrix specifies combinations of probability and impact that lead to rating the risks as low, moderate, or high priority. [Planning]

PMI®, *PMBOK® Guide*, 2008, 291

40. d. Avoidance

Risk avoidance involves changing the project management plan to eliminate the threat entirely. [Planning]

PMI®, *PMBOK® Guide*, 2008, 303

PROJECT PROCUREMENT MANAGEMENT

Study Hints

The Project Procurement Management questions on the PMP® certification exam tend to be more process oriented than legally focused. You do not need to know any country's specific legal code; however, some non-U.S. exam takers complain that the nature of many of the questions requires an understanding of U.S. contract law. Although an occasional question relating to the U.S. system may appear on the exam, such questions do not seem to be problematic for most exam takers. A firm understanding of the procurement process usually will help you to find the correct answer. Moreover, the questions will be worded such that the project manager or project team is the "buyer."

The exam requires you to know the basic differences between the three broad categories of contracts (fixed-price, cost-reimbursement, and time-and-materials) and the risks inherent in specific contract types for both the buyer and the seller. Several questions will also test your knowledge of the various types of contracts within each category (for example, firm-fixed-price versus fixed-price-incentive-fee contracts). A question or two may also be included on international contracting, such as the timing of foreign currency exchange and duty on goods delivered to a foreign country.

PMI® views Project Procurement Management as a four-step process comprising plan procurements, conduct procurements, administer procurements, and close procurements. See *PMBOK® Guide* Figure 12-1 for an overview of this structure. Know this chart thoroughly.

Following is a list of the major Project Procurement Management topics. Use it to help focus your study efforts on the areas most likely to appear on the exam.

Major Topics

Project procurement management overview

Plan procurements

- Make-or-buy analysis
- Procurement management plan
- Contract statement of work
- Contract categories and risks
  - Fixed-price or lump-sum
  - Cost-reimbursement
  - Time-and-materials
- Contract types and risks
  - Cost-plus-fixed-fee
  - Cost-plus-incentive-fee
  - Fixed-price-plus-incentive-fee
  - Firm-fixed-price
- Contract incentives
- Contract origination
- Evaluation criteria
- Procurement documents

Conduct procurements

- Proposals
- Qualified seller list
- Evaluating prospective sellers
  - Contract negotiation
  - Weighting system
  - Screening system
  - Independent estimates
  - Seller rating systems
  - Bidder conferences
  - Proposal evaluation techniques
  - Expert judgment
- Contract negotiation stages and tactics
  - Five stages
  - Negotiation tactics
  - Source selection output

Major Topics (continued)

Administer procurements

- Contract documentation
- Standard clauses
- Elements of a legally enforceable contract
- Changes and change control
- Undefined work
- Contract management plan

Close procurements

- Records management system
- Contract closure procedure
- Procurement audit
- Negotiated settlements
- Closed contracts

Organizing for contract management

- Centralized contracting
- Decentralized contracting

Privity of contract

Foreign currency exchange

Practice Questions

INSTRUCTIONS: Note the most suitable answer for each multiple-choice question in the appropriate space on the answer sheet.

1. What doctrine causes a party to relinquish rights under a contract because it knowingly fails to execute those rights?

    a. Assignment of claims
    b. Material breach
    c. Waiver
    d. Warranties

2. Which term describes those costs in a contract that are associated with two or more projects but are not traceable to either of them individually?

    a. Variable
    b. Direct
    c. Indirect
    d. Semivariable

3. Contract type selection is dependent on the degree of risk or uncertainty facing the project manager. From the perspective of the buyer, the preferred contract type in a low-risk situation is—

    a. Firm-fixed-price
    b. Fixed-price-incentive
    c. Cost-plus-fixed fee
    d. Cost-plus-a-percentage-of-cost

4. The buyer has negotiated a cost-plus-incentive fee contract with the seller. The contract has a target cost of $300,000, a target fee of $40,000, a share ratio of 80/20, a maximum fee of $60,000, and a minimum fee of $10,000. If the seller has actual costs of $380,000, how much fee will the buyer pay?

    a. $104,000
    b. $56,000
    c. $30,000
    d. $24,000

5. Which term describes the failure by either the buyer or the seller to perform part or all of the duties of a contract?

    a. Termination of contract
    b. Partial performance
    c. Breach of contract
    d. Contract waiver

6. In some cases, contract termination refers to—

    a. Contract closeout by mutual agreement
    b. Contract closeout by delivery of goods or services
    c. Contract closeout by successful performance
    d. Certification of receipt of final payment

7. Significant differences between the seller's price and your independent estimate may indicate all the following EXCEPT the—

    a. SOW was not adequate
    b. Seller misunderstood the SOW
    c. Marketplace has drastically changed
    d. Project team chose the wrong contract type

8. You are a contractor for a state agency. Your company recently completed a water resource management project for the state and received payment on its final invoice today. A procurement audit has been conducted. Formal notification that the contract has been closed should be provided to your company by the—

    a. State's project manager
    b. Person responsible for procurement administration
    c. Project control officer
    d. Project sponsor or owner

9. Which term describes contract costs that are traceable to or caused by a specific project work effort?

    a. Variable
    b. Fixed
    c. Indirect
    d. Direct

10. When a seller breaches a contract, the buyer cannot receive—

    a. Compensatory damages
    b. Punitive damages
    c. Liquidated damages
    d. Consequential damages

11. Which term is NOT a common name for a procurement document that solicits an offer from prospective sellers?

    a. Contractor initial response
    b. Request for information
    c. Request for quotation
    d. Invitation for negotiation

12. Because you are working under a firm-fixed-price contract, management wants you to submit the final invoice and close out the contract as soon as possible. Before final payment on the contract can be authorized, you must—

    a. Prepare a contract completion statement
    b. Audit the procurement process
    c. Update and archive contract records
    d. Settle subcontracts

13. Recent data indicate that more than 10,000 airline passengers are injured each year from baggage that falls from overhead bins. You performed a make-or-buy analysis and decided to outsource an improved bin design and manufacture. The project team needs to develop a list of qualified sources. As a general rule, which method would the project team find especially helpful?

    a. Advertising
    b. Internet
    c. Trade catalogs
    d. Relevant local associations

14. As you prepare to close out contracts on your project, you should review all the following types of documentation EXCEPT the—

    a. Contract document for the contract being closed out
    b. Procurement audit report
    c. Invoice and payment records
    d. Seller performance reports

15. You are working on a new project in your organization. You need to decide how best to staff the project and handle all its resource requirements. Your first step should be to—

    a. Conduct a make-or-buy analysis
    b. Conduct a market survey
    c. Solicit proposals from sellers using an RFP to determine whether you should outsource the project
    d. Review your procurement department's qualified-seller lists and send an RFP to selected sellers

16. Your company decided to award a contract for project management services on a pharmaceutical research project. Because your company is new to project management and does not understand the full scope of services that may be needed under the contract, it is most appropriate to award a—

    a. Lump-sum contract
    b. Fixed-price-incentive contract
    c. Cost-plus-a-percentage-of-cost contract
    d. Time-and-materials contract

17. Requirements for formal contract acceptance and closure usually are defined in the—

    a. Proposal
    b. Statement of work
    c. Contract terms and conditions
    d. Procurement audit report

18. You plan to award a contract to provide project management training for your company. You decide it is important that any prospective contractor have an association with a major university that awards master's certificates in project management. This is an example of—

    a. Setting up an independent evaluation
    b. Preparing requirements for your statement of work
    c. Establishing a weighting system
    d. Establishing a selection criteria

19. All the following elements must be evident in a written contract for it to be legally enforceable EXCEPT—

    a. Legal capacity
    b. Mutual assent
    c. Appropriate form
    d. Pricing structure

20. A purchase order is a good example of which form of contracting?

    a. Unilateral
    b. Bilateral
    c. Trilateral
    d. Severable

21. You are responsible for ensuring that your seller's performance meets contractual requirements. For effective contract administration, you should—

    a. Hold a bidders' conference
    b. Establish the appropriate contract type
    c. Implement the contract change control system
    d. Develop a statement of work

22. The primary purpose of administer procurements is to ensure that—

    a. Buyers conduct performance reviews
    b. Payment is made in a timely fashion
    c. Disagreements are handled quickly and to everyone's satisfaction
    d. Both parties meet contractual obligations and protect their legal rights

23. Buyers use a variety of methods to provide incentives to a seller to complete work early or within certain contractually specified time frames. One such incentive is the use of liquidated damages. From the seller's perspective, liquidated damages are what form of incentive?

    a. Positive
    b. Negative
    c. Nominal
    d. Risk-prone

24. The principal function of a warranty is to—

    a. Provide assurance of the level of quality to be provided
    b. Provide a way to assert claims for late payment
    c. Provide a way to allow additional time following acceptance to correct deficiencies, without additional costs
    d. Ensure that goods purchased fit the purposes for which they are to be used

25. You have decided to award a contract to a seller that has provided quality services to your company frequently in the past. Your current project, although somewhat different from previous projects, is similar to other work the seller has performed. In this situation, to minimize your risk you should award what type of contract?

    a. Fixed price with economic price adjustment
    b. Fixed-price-incentive (firm target)
    c. Firm-fixed-price
    d. Cost-plus-award-fee

26. As project manager, you need a relatively fast and informal method addressing disagreements with contractors. One such method is to submit the issue in question to an impartial third party for resolution. This process is known as—

    a. Alternative dispute resolution
    b. Problem processing
    c. Steering resolution
    d. Mediation litigation

27. A no-cost settlement sometimes is used—

    a. To close out a successful contract
    b. In lieu of formal termination procedures
    c. When buyer property has been furnished under the contract
    d. When such an arrangement is acceptable to one of the parties involved

28. When writing payment terms in your lump-sum subcontracts it is especially important to—

    a. Include incentives for outstanding performance
    b. Describe the payment process in detail to avoid confusion
    c. Link progress made to compensation paid
    d. Associate the payment to a specific time period for more efficient accounting

29. A buyer has negotiated a fixed-price-incentive contract with the seller. The contract has a target cost of $200,000, a target profit of $30,000, and a target price of $230,000. The buyer also has negotiated a ceiling price of $270,000 and a share ratio of 70/30. If the seller completes the contract with actual costs of $170,000, how much profit will the buyer pay the seller?

    a. $21,000
    b. $35,000
    c. $39,000
    d. $51,000

30. Requirements for formal deliverable acceptance are defined in the—

    a. Contract
    b. Procurement management plan
    c. Overall project management plan
    d. Specifications

31. Payment bonds are often required by the contract and require specific actions under the stated conditions. Payment bonds are specifically designed to ensure that the prime contractor provides payment of—

    a. Insurance premiums
    b. Weekly payrolls
    c. Subcontractors, laborers, and sellers of material
    d. Damages for accidents caused

32. You are working on a contract in a remote location. The contract requires you to be on site at the office on a daily basis. You were unable to get to the office for three days last month because of severe blizzard conditions. Your failure to appear at the office was excused because of a clause in the contract entitled—

    a. Non compos mentis
    b. Forjurer royalme
    c. Force majeure
    d. Force minoris dictus

33. All of the following are examples of good contract administration skills that project managers need to exercise EXCEPT—

    a. Approving invoices as the work is completed
    b. Supervising the work to be done under the terms of the contract
    c. Developing contract clauses
    d. Preparing and processing change orders

34. The least preferred method in resolving the settlement of all outstanding contract issues, claims, and disputes is using—

    a. Litigation
    b. Binding arbitration
    c. Negotiation
    d. Mediation

35. On large contracts, the contract administrator typically has a need to resolve ambiguity in the clauses that govern work performance and other issues. Assume that on your contract there is an order of precedence clause. This means that—

    a. Inconsistencies in the solicitation of the contract shall be resolved in a given order of procedure
    b. An alternative dispute resolution process is in place that shall be followed to resolve any conflicts
    c. Any ambiguities are generally interpreted against the party who drafted the document
    d. Undefinitized contractual actions cannot be authorized

36. During contract negotiations on large contracts, the negotiation process focuses on many key issues, with price being one of them. Separate negotiations can be made on price, quantity, quality, and timing, which can significantly lengthen the process. The negotiation process can be shortened, however, provided that—

    a. Planning is done for negotiations
    b. Expertise of the project management staff in the procurement process is at a high level
    c. A request for proposal is used rather than a request for quotation
    d. There is integrity in the relationship and prior history with the vendor

37. Contract negotiations are NOT required when—

    a. A company uses sealed bids
    b. There is a sole source procurement
    c. A competitive range is established
    d. A two-step process is used

38. It is critical during the proposal preparation stage that—

    a. The negotiation strategy is determined
    b. A change management strategy is developed
    c. Roles and responsibilities for the ultimate project are determined
    d. Contract terms and conditions are reviewed before the proposal is submitted to the client

39. Which of the following types of contracts has the least risk to the seller?

    a. Firm-fixed-price
    b. Cost-plus-fixed-fee
    c. Cost-plus-award-fee
    d. Fixed-price-incentive fee

40. Assume that your company has a cost-plus-fixed-fee contract. The contract value is $110,000, which consists of $100,000 of estimated costs with a 10-percent fixed fee. Assume that your company completes the work but only incurs $80,000 in actual cost. What is the total cost to the project?

    a. $80,000
    b. $90,000
    c. $10,0000
    d. $125,000

Answer Sheet

1. a b c d
2. a b c d
3. a b c d
4. a b c d
5. a b c d
6. a b c d
7. a b c d
8. a b c d
9. a b c d
10. a b c d
11. a b c d
12. a b c d
13. a b c d
14. a b c d
15. a b c d
16. a b c d
17. a b c d
18. a b c d
19. a b c d
20. a b c d

21. a b c d
22. a b c d
23. a b c d
24. a b c d
25. a b c d
26. a b c d
27. a b c d
28. a b c d
29. a b c d
30. a b c d
31. a b c d
32. a b c d
33. a b c d
34. a b c d
35. a b c d
36. a b c d
37. a b c d
38. a b c d
39. a b c d
40. a b c d

Answer Key

1. c. Waiver

Under the doctrine of waiver, a party can relinquish rights that it otherwise has under the contract. If the seller offers incomplete, defective, or late performance and the buyer's project manager knowingly accepts that performance, the buyer has waived its right to strict performance. In some circumstances, the party at fault may remain liable for provable damages, but the waiver will prevent the buyer from claiming a material breach and, thus, from terminating the contract. [Executing]

Adams et al. 1997, 275

2. c. Indirect

The nature of an indirect cost is such that it is neither possible nor practical to measure how much of the cost is attributable to a single project. These costs are allocated to the project by the performing organization as a cost of doing business. [Planning]

PMI®, *PMBOK® Guide,* 2008, 321

3. a. Firm-fixed-price

Buyers prefer the firm-fixed-price contract because it places more risk on the seller. Although the seller bears the greatest degree of risk, it also has the maximum potential for profit. Because the seller receives an agreed-upon amount regardless of its costs, it is motivated to decrease costs by efficient production. [Planning]

Adams et al. 1997, 229–231; PMI®, *PMBOK® Guide,* 2008, 321

4. d. $24,000

Comparing actual costs with the target cost shows an $80,000 overrun. The overrun is shared 80/20 (with the buyer's share always listed first). In this case 20% of $80,000 is $16,000, the seller's share, which is deducted from the $40,000 target fee. The remaining $24,000 is the fee paid to the seller. [Closing]

Garrett 2007, 123

5. c. Breach of contract

A breach of contract is a failure to perform either express or implied duties of the contract. Either the buyer or the seller can be responsible for a breach of contract. [Executing]

Adams et al. 1997, 278; Ward 2008, 45

6. a. Contract closeout by mutual agreement

A contract can end in successful performance, mutual agreement, or breach of contract. Contract closeout by mutual agreement or breach of contract is called contract termination. [Closing]

Garrett 2007, 185

7. d. Project team chose the wrong contract type

The contract type is typically dictated by the SOW and chosen by the contracting officer. [Planning]

PMI®, *PMBOK® Guide*, 2008, 332–333

8. b. Person responsible for procurement administration

The person responsible for procurement administration should provide, in writing, formal notification that the contract has been completed. Requirements for formal acceptance and closeout should be defined in the contract. [Closing]

PMI®, *PMBOK® Guide*, 2008, 344

9. d. Direct

Direct costs are always identified with the cost objectives of a specific project and include salaries, travel and living expenses, and supplies in direct support of the project. [Planning]

PMI®, *PMBOK® Guide*, 2008, 323–324

10. b. Punitive damages

Punitive damages are designed to punish a guilty party and, as such, are considered penalties. Because a breach of contract is not unlawful, punitive damages are not awarded. The other remedies listed are available to compensate the buyer's loss. [Closing]

Ward 2008, 357

11. b. Request for information

Procurement documents are used to solicit proposals from prospective sellers. A request for information is generally a tool to obtain source information. [Planning]

PMI®, *PMBOK® Guide*, 2008, 326–327

12. d. Settle subcontracts

All payments due must be settled by the seller before the contract can be closed out. The other items listed are activities performed by the buyer. [Closing]

Garrett 2007, 128–133

13. a. Advertising

Advertising in newspapers or professional journals is an excellent way to identify qualified bidders. Detailed information about specific sources may require more extensive effort, such as site visits or contact with previous customers. [Executing]

PMI®, *PMBOK® Guide*, 2008, 332

14. b. Procurement audit report

In most organizations, a procurement audit is conducted after the contract has been closed out. Therefore, the project manager would not have a procurement audit report to review. Contract document for the contract being closed out, invoice and payment records, and seller performance reports are examples of the documents that should be available to the project manager and should be reviewed at closeout. [Closing]

PMI®, *PMBOK® Guide*, 2008, 338 and 343

15. a. Conduct a make-or-buy analysis

A make-or-buy analysis is a plan procurements tool and technique used to determine whether a particular product or service can be produced or performed cost effectively by the performing organization, or should be contracted out to another organization. The analysis includes both direct and indirect costs and any administrative costs incurred to manage the contractor. [Planning]

PMI®, *PMBOK® Guide*, 2008, 321

16. d. Time-and-materials contract

A time-and-materials contract is a type of contract that provides for the acquisition of supplies or services on the basis of direct labor hours, at specified fixed hourly rates for wages, overhead, general and administrative expenses, and profit; and materials at cost, including materials-handling costs. [Planning]

PMI®, *PMBOK® Guide*, 2008, 324

17. c. Contract terms and conditions

The contract terms and conditions typically describe the procedure the buyer will employ to close the contract. [Closing]

PMI®, *PMBOK® Guide*, 2008, 341–342

18. d. Establishing a selection criteria

The selection criterion sets forth minimum requirements of performance for one or more of the evaluation criteria. [Executing]

PMI®, *PMBOK® Guide*, 2008, 326–327

19. d. Pricing structure

The following elements must be present for a contract to be legally enforceable: legal capacity, mutual assent, consideration, legality, and an appropriate contract form that follows applicable laws governing businesses. [Executing]

Adams et al. 1997, 240

20. a. Unilateral

The purchase order is a unilateral (one signature) offer that includes a promise to pay upon delivery. [Planning]

Adams et al. 1997, 231

21. c. Implement the contract change control system

Contract change control entails ensuring that contract changes are properly approved and that everyone who needs to know is made aware of such changes. [Monitoring and Controlling]

PMI®, *PMBOK® Guide*, 2008, 338

22. d. Both parties meet contractual obligations and protect their legal rights

Contracts are awarded to obtain goods and services in accordance with the buyer's stated requirements. Although there are multiple purposes in the administer procurements process, ensuring that the seller delivers what is stated in the contract is of paramount importance. [Monitoring and Controlling]

PMI®, *PMBOK® Guide*, 2008, 335

23. b. Negative

Liquidated damages are considered negative incentives because they result in a loss of revenue for the seller if it fails to perform rather than a gain in revenue if it performs well. [Closing]

Ward 2008, 251

24. a. Provide assurance of the level of quality to be provided

A warranty is one party's assurance to the other that goods will meet certain standards of quality, including condition, reliability, description, function, or performance. This assurance may be express or implied. [Executing]

Adams et al. 1997, 272

25. c. Firm-fixed-price

In a firm-fixed-price contract, the seller receives a fixed sum of money for the work performed regardless of costs. This arrangement places the greatest financial risk on the seller and encourages it to control costs. [Planning]

Adams et al.1997, 229

26. a. Alternative dispute resolution

Alternative dispute resolution, or dispute resolution, is a relatively informal way to address differences of opinion on contracts. Its purpose is to address such issues without having to seek formal legal redress through the courts. [Executing]

Ward 2008, 15–17

27. b. In lieu of formal termination procedures

A no-cost settlement can be used in lieu of formal termination procedures when the seller has indicated that such an arrangement is acceptable, no buyer property has been furnished under the contract, no payments are due the seller, no other obligations are outstanding, and the product or service can be readily obtained elsewhere. [Closing]

Garrett 2007, 191

28. c. Link progress made to compensation paid

A buyer under a lump-sum contract should pay a seller for work delivered rather than time expended. Linking payment with progress ensures that the seller will focus on results and not on effort expended. [Planning]

Garrett 2007, Chapter 8

29. c. $39,000

To calculate the fee that the buyer must pay, actual costs are compared with the target cost. If actual costs are less than the target cost, the seller will earn profit that is additional to the target profit. If actual costs are more than the target cost, the seller will lose profit from the target profit. The amount of profit is determined by the share ratio (with the buyer's share listed first). In this example, the seller is under target cost by $30,000. That amount will be split 70/30. So the buyer keeps $21,000, and the seller receives an additional $9,000 added to the target profit, which is the incentive. Total fee is $39,000. [Closing]

Garrett 2007, 123

30. a. Contract

Two important components of any contract include what the buyer wants to buy and how the buyer defines acceptance of the products or services delivered. For contract closure to occur, deliverable acceptance must be completed. [Closing]

PMI®, *PMBOK® Guide*, 2008, 344

31. c. Subcontractors, laborers, and sellers of material

Payment bonds, which are required by the buyer, are issued by guarantors to prime contractors. The buyer wants to ensure that subcontractors of the prime contractor receive payment so that work is not disrupted. [Closing]

Adams et al. 1997, 273

32. c. Force majeure

Force majeure clauses can be used to protect either party from events that are outside their control and not a result of their negligence, such as acts of nature, war, civil disobedience, or labor disruption. [Executing]

Garrett 2007, 56

33. c. Developing contract clauses

First, developing contract clauses is done during contract formation, not contract administration, which begins at contract signing. Second, contract specialists and attorneys—given their legal expertise—are typically the individuals who write contract clauses, not project managers. [Monitoring and Controlling]

Verma 1995, 63

34. a. Litigation

Litigation involves seeking remedy through the courts. It is the most expensive and time-consuming method of solving problems. [Monitoring and Controlling]

PMI®, *PMBOK® Guide*, 2008, 343

35. a. Inconsistencies in the solicitation of the contract shall be resolved in a given order of procedure

The order of precedence specifies that any inconsistency in the contract shall be resolved in a given order. This avoids confusion and debate, which could lead to litigation. [Monitoring and Controlling]

Kerzner 2006, 819

36. d. There is integrity in the relationship and prior history with the vendor

When people know and trust one another, and in particular have worked with each other before, the negotiation process can be significantly shortened. Three major factors of negotiation should be followed: compromise ability, adaptability, and good faith. [Executing]

Kerzner 2006, 808

37. a. A company uses sealed bids

When using the sealed bid method, competitive market forces determine the price, and the award goes to the lowest bidder, provided all other terms and conditions of the contract are met. [Executing]

Kerzner 2006, 808

38. d. Contract terms and conditions are reviewed before the proposal is submitted to the client

The contracts (legal) representative is responsible for the preparation of the contract portion of the proposal. Generally, contracts with the legal department are handed through or in coordination with the proposal group. Before the proposal is submitted to the client, contract terms and conditions should be reviewed and approved. [Executing]

Kerzner 2006, 823

39. b. Cost-plus-fixed-fee

On a firm-fixed-price contract, the seller absorbs 100 percent of the risks, while on a cost-type contract, the buyer carries the most risk. Cost-plus-fixed-fee contracts have less risk to sellers than cost-plus-award-fee or cost-plus-incentive-fee contracts because the fee is fixed based on costs, so the seller is guaranteed a certain level of profit. [Planning]

PMI®, *PMBOK*® *Guide*, 322–324

40. b. $90,000

In this situation the fixed-fee of $10,000 does not change but now represents a seller profit of 12.5 percent on incurred costs. This means that the total cost to the project is $90,000. [Monitoring and Controlling]

Fleming 2003, 97; PMI®, *PMBOK*® *Guide*, 323

PROFESSIONAL AND SOCIAL RESPONSIBILITY

Study Hints

Professional and Social Responsibility covers the legal, ethical, and professional behaviors of the profession.

The Professional and Social Responsibility questions on the PMP® certification exam relate directly to project managers' responsibilities to PMI®, to themselves, to the profession, *and* to their organizations. They cover the legal, ethical, and professional behaviors of the profession.

You should anticipate a host of situational questions in this area, yet most exam takers do not find these questions difficult. When considering ethical issues, always select the answer that represents the most ethical choice, even if another answer would be deemed acceptable in your experience.

Professional and Social Responsibility is not covered as a specific knowledge area in the *PMBOK® Guide*; therefore, you must refer to publications such as the following:

- *Doing Business Internationally: The Guide to Cross-Cultural Success* by Terence Brake et al.

- *Global Literacies: Lesson on Business Leadership and National Cultures* by Robert Rosen et al.

- *The Cultural Dimension of International Business* by Gary P. Ferraro

PMI® publications that address professional and social responsibility include—

- PMI® Code of Ethics and Professional Conduct

- *Project Management Experience and Knowledge Self-Assessment Manual*

See page 237 for a list of the major Professional and Social Responsibility topics you will see on the exam. Use it to help focus your study efforts on the areas most likely to appear on the exam.

Major Topics

Ensure individual integrity and professionalism

- Legal requirements
- Ethical standards
- Social norms
- Community and stakeholder values
- Communication techniques

Contribute to the project management knowledge base

- Knowledge base in project management
- Techniques for transferring knowledge
- Research strategies
- Effective communication techniques

Enhance individual competence

- Personal strengths and weaknesses
- Instructional methods and tools
- Appropriate professional competencies
- Self-assessment strategies
- Training options

Interact in a professional and cooperative manner

- Interpersonal techniques
- Ethnic and cultural norms of team members and stakeholders
- Stakeholders' and team members' communication techniques
- Community and stakeholder values
- Team motivation strategies

Practice Questions

INSTRUCTIONS: Note the most suitable answer for each multiple-choice question in the appropriate space on the answer sheet.

1. You just learned that the European Union has issued a new regulation for handling toxic waste. You recommend to management that your company undertake a project to develop guidelines in response to this regulation. This recommendation demonstrates the importance of—

   a. Adhering to legal requirements and ethical standards
   b. Continually searching for new and more effective methods of doing your work
   c. Using legal requirements as the basis for all project selection decisions
   d. The limited time frame in which projects must be completed

2. Your company is bidding on an international project with a requirement to perform an environmental impact study before beginning construction. The requirement to perform such a study represents—

   a. The impact that demonstrations can have on international affairs
   b. A project constraint
   c. A factor that needs to be taken into consideration as part of the bid-no bid decision
   d. An example of complying with international law

3. Your contract requires you to submit a final report in one month. The project sponsor has asked you to complete the project with incomplete data. The final report must be submitted to receive the monies due. In this situation, you should—

   a. Prepare a rough estimate based on your knowledge of the subject, and complete the project
   b. Explain in writing and in your oral presentation that you cannot complete the project because of the incomplete data
   c. Use the results of research prepared by another organization as the basis for your effort data
   d. Inform management that you need additional time, and ask for a formal extension

4. You are managing a project team that is preparing a comprehensive set of food processing regulations. At a recent industry meeting, one of the manufacturers presented you with a free gift. In this situation, you should probably—

   a. Not accept this gift because it could be interpreted as being for personal gain
   b. Determine whether the manufacturer gave the certificate to everyone else attending the meeting and, if so, accept it
   c. Accept the gift, and then inform your project sponsor when you return to your job
   d. Accept the gift to avoid embarrassing the provider

5. You are managing an international construction project. You know the city expects some form of "unofficial" compensation for approving the issuance of licenses and permits. Your best approach is to—

   a. Follow local customs explicitly, even if this means that you must make "payments" to local officials
   b. Abide by the laws, regulations, and requirements of your own country and follow them explicitly in this situation
   c. Refrain from knowingly engaging in professional misconduct
   d. Recognize the need for government involvement in the project and do whatever is required for success

6. Your manager allegedly violated PMI®'s intellectual property policy guidelines when he reproduced and distributed portions of the *PMBOK® Guide* without first requesting permission from PMI®. Yesterday, a PMI® Ethics Review Committee member asked you a series of questions related to your manager's alleged misdeeds. In this situation, you have—

   a. No involvement because you are not a party to the ethics proceedings
   b. A responsibility to cooperate with PMI® concerning ethics violations and the collection of related information
   c. No responsibility because you were not a PMI® member at the time this alleged misuse took place
   d. No obligation to provide PMI® with any information because you have no firsthand knowledge of the extant case

7. Your company is submitting a proposal for a government contract, and you are the proposal manager. One of the requirements is that the project manager must be a PMP®. Your proposed project manager, Katrina, is not a PMP®, but will be taking the exam soon. Another PMP®, Rikard, works for the company, but he is managing another project. In preparing your proposal you should—

   a. Submit Rikard's resume as the project manager; after the contract award, replace him with Katrina, provided the client agrees to the substitution
   b. Submit Katrina's resume and state she is a PMP® because you know she will pass the exam and obtain the certification
   c. Disclose Katrina's status concerning PMP® certification in your proposal and submit her resume as the project manager
   d. Request that the government change its requirement for PMP® status

8. You need to build another facility for your company and have prepared an invitation for bid (IFB) package. You probably will not conduct negotiations with the sellers; however, you may or may not award the contract to the lowest-bidding seller, which has been made clear in the IFB. In this situation, you should be prepared to—

   a. Prohibit sellers from attending the bid opening because you will need time to decide to whom to award the contract
   b. Document your award decision as completely as possible to all sellers
   c. Inform the seller who won the bid and indicate to the others that no further discussion will take place on this issue
   d. Limit the sellers who will receive the IFB to reduce conflict

9. As part of your proposal to provide project management services to Arktic Research Laboratories, you must provide information about previous experience. Your firm recently completed a contract for one of Arktic's key competitors, Polar Investigations, Ltd., for similar services. The contract requires you to keep the client information confidential for one year. Arktic has discovered that you worked with Polar and is asking for a reference at Polar with whom it can discuss your work. In this case you should—

   a. Give Arktic the Polar reference. After all, Arktic learned of your Polar work from an outside source; therefore, you are released from the terms of the contract's confidentiality clause.
   b. Include Polar as a reference, assuming that the confidentiality agreement is unnecessarily restrictive of trade
   c. Contact Polar and let it know that if you can use it as a reference you will let it know the type of work you will be doing for Arktic so that no one is at a competitive disadvantage
   d. Contact Polar and ask for permission to list it as a reference in your proposal

10. You were part of a team that worked with one of the company's most successful project managers who left to work for a competitor. Several months after he left he asked you to send him a copy of the charter he used on the MCCAW project to compare to his current assignment. In this situation you should—

    a. Send him the update because he developed the original charter and basically knows what it includes
    b. Not send him the update; invite him to the office where he can review it in your cubicle
    c. Send him the update along with a confidentiality agreement to sign
    d. Not send him the update; he does not have a legitimate need to know the contents of the document

11. You are submitting a proposal on a contract but are concerned that your labor rates may be too high based on industry standards. You have been asked to look for ways to reduce costs. Which one of the following recommendations should you make to management?

    a. Reduce existing labor rates so that they are similar to those of the competition, and, if selected, pay each person on the project extra money out of another project's account
    b. Use your existing labor rates combined with a value engineering approach as a way to lower overall cost
    c. Put resumes from the existing staff in the proposal, but plan to hire new people at a lower labor rate
    d. Use a parametric model, and submit a different type of cost proposal using lump sum pricing

12. To support the future use and improvement of your organization's risk management process, you establish a lessons learned program. The basis of a risk lessons learned program is to—

    a. Document the results of risk response audits
    b. Capture meeting minutes from project risk reviews
    c. Provide updates to risk identification checklists
    d. Establish a risk register

13. On your last project, one client wanted you to use a different material than you normally use for laying a foundation, which reduced the actual construction time by 20 percent. At the end of the project, you realized that its continued use would lead to significant improvement in your construction practices. Your next step should be to—

    a. Document the lessons learned and share them within the company
    b. Adjust the schedule baseline to note the reduction in time
    c. Calculate the savings based on the schedule reduction and pass the savings on to the client
    d. Issue a new methodology and mandate that it be followed

14. During the past four years, you have awarded 10 different contracts of various types and the project is finally coming to an end. As you close out these contracts, you should—

    a. Provide each contractor with formal written notice that the project is complete
    b. Prepare a complete set of indexed records and contractual files for future reference
    c. Conduct a variance analysis
    d. Conduct a procurement audit

15. Yesterday, you called a team meeting and explained your new project's objectives to the team, which included a description of the project's quality management plan. You explained that the objective of any quality management plan is to—

    a. Ensure that all regulations governing the use of biological agents will be followed
    b. Ensure that process adjustments are made in a timely fashion
    c. Improve quality in every aspect of project performance
    d. Ensure that the scope management plan is followed

16. You have a practice of conducting not one, but multiple, quality audits on a project to ensure adherence to the quality management plan. Which one of the following types of audits is not an example of a quality audit?

    a. Internal
    b. System
    c. Baseline
    d. Prospective

17. You recently completed a major environmental remediation project for which your company has been paid. In working on a new project that happens to be located at the same site, you have discovered a possible flaw in the disposal system that was delivered for the earlier project. The drawings for the project are incomplete. In this situation, you should—

    a. Do nothing because the project is complete and the customer accepted the work based on its own independent inspection
    b. Alert your management to the situation, both orally and in writing, and request that someone else confirm your findings
    c. Contact the customer directly and inform it of the potential problem so that it can modify your contract to correct the problem
    d. Enhance your quality assurance and project review system immediately for future projects

18. After completing a systems upgrade, you and your team performed a lessons learned review that uncovered the uneven use of resources causing a 25-percent cost overrun. Now you are moving on to the next company project. When starting this new project, you should—

    a. Have an outside audit team periodically review your project to provide ideas and insight for midcourse correction
    b. Use automated software cost estimating techniques
    c. Implement a structured approach to risk management
    d. Read the qualifications of the people joining your team

19. Your recent project required extensive overtime by the project team to meet a demanding schedule. You are managing the company's next project and want to avoid a similar situation. Therefore, you should—

    a. Ensure that all work efforts are traced back to the scope statement for scope verification
    b. Use project management software that includes resource histograms and resource leveling
    c. Ensure that the WBS is detailed enough and that all the activities are defined in sufficient detail
    d. Use critical chain scheduling to account for possible unplanned events with its emphasis on buffers

20. A project management maturity review revealed that no one shares information, and that people are managing projects the same way they were managed three generations ago. To promote better sharing of information, a consultant suggests that the company support which one of the following?

    a. Project team meetings
    b. In-progress customer review sessions
    c. Kickoff meetings
    d. Benchmarking forums

21. You recently were assigned to a project in Australia. Coming from Japan, you are excited about the opportunity to visit the Outback, tour Sydney Harbor, and travel to the Great Barrier Reef. To make the transition as easy as possible, your company should do which of the following first?

    a. Hire a consultant who knows the country to brief you on what to expect in Australia
    b. Give you a tourist's guide to Australia to read on the plane to your new assignment
    c. Send you to Australia for a couple of weeks before the assignment so that you get to know the place and to meet your new teammates
    d. Arrange a meeting at the Australian embassy in Tokyo so that you can meet Australian nationals and they can explain what it is like for a Japanese person to live there

22. You have been selected to manage an international project headquartered overseas. As you list the pros and cons of accepting the assignment, there is one question that you must answer honestly before saying "yes" or "no." That question is—

    a. What common ground exists between the people with whom I will be working and me?
    b. How do I translate my cultural awareness and knowledge into functional skills that I can use on the project?
    c. How can I continue to refine my skills and to develop my level of cultural competence and adaptability?
    d. How adaptable am I?

23. You are working on a joint venture with a Korean firm. During a conversation with the company president, you mention that you know how to spell several words in Hangul. Which one of the following traits best identifies the disclosure of your knowledge of his language?

    a. Confident humility
    b. Authentic flexibility
    c. Aggressive insight
    d. Positive aggrandizement

24. A person's negotiating behavior is influenced by his or her culture. Over time, an individual who is living in a culture that is different from his or her own may take on characteristics of the new culture and may behave from a new frame of reference. With respect to negotiation, this illustrates the importance of—

    a. Always looking at those with whom you are negotiating as members of a particular cultural group
    b. Moving beyond cultural stereotyping and seeing people as individuals with unique personality traits and experiences
    c. Recognizing that cultural stereotyping should be used as a starting point for all international negotiations
    d. Becoming overly dependent on cultural knowledge as the cornerstone for all negotiations

25. You are ready to enter a negotiating session with people from another country who have earned a reputation as tough negotiators. To earn your yearly bonus, you must not be at a disadvantage in your negotiations with them. Therefore, you must concentrate on—

    a. Seating arrangements in the negotiating room
    b. Ingratiating yourself to the most powerful negotiator on the other side of the negotiating table to earn his or her trust
    c. Active listening
    d. Setting and following strict time limits at each step of the negotiating process

26. You are meeting with several project stakeholders, including the customer. Everyone is irritated, hot, and in violent disagreement regarding the best way to proceed with the project. In general, disagreements among stakeholders should be resolved in favor of the—

    a. Sponsor
    b. Senior management
    c. Performing organization
    d. Customer

27. You are managing the construction of luxury condominiums. The client is focused on timely performance and has provided contract incentives if the job is completed early. An environmental group is concerned about adverse impacts on water drainage and is considering suing. You need to—

    a. Find appropriate resolutions to resolve differences between or among stakeholders
    b. Put the owner's requirements at the top of the list as you resolve stakeholder differences
    c. Carefully manage all communication and make status information available only on a need-to-know basis
    d. Build the condominiums according to the specifications and not worry about any other stakeholder

28. Certain members have been arguing about which project management software will work best for the project. You conduct a meeting to see whether they can reach consensus by identifying common points of agreement and striving for fair resolution. Which style of conflict resolution will you employ?

    a. Withdrawal
    b. Smoothing
    c. Problem solving
    d. Compromise

29. None of the people on your 15-person project team have worked together before, and it really shows. Each meeting is characterized by disagreements and debates. You need to get this situation under control quickly. Therefore, the first action you should take is to—

    a. Hold periodic group meetings
    b. Use a group facilitator at the next meeting
    c. Perform careful project planning
    d. Enforce strict rules about meeting behavior

30. Conflict can slow project completion. Although each conflict situation is unique, the project manager's goal remains the same: to achieve a win-win solution for everyone involved. The method most often used by project managers to resolve conflict is—

    a. Compromise
    b. Confrontation
    c. Smoothing
    d. Negotiation

31. You are managing a project whose team members are located in eight different countries. English is the lingua franca of your company. The single best way to be an effective communicator in this situation is to—

    a. Learn and use the local language
    b. Rely on interpreters
    c. Focus primarily on formal, written communication
    d. Use gestures and other forms of nonverbal communication to make your point

32. Metacommunication, paralinguistics, second-order messages, and the hidden dimension of communication all refer to—

    a. Communication skills
    b. Communication requirements
    c. Ways to exercise tolerance and compromise
    d. Nonverbal communication

33. Some people believe that to have an effective conversation, a distance of about 20 inches (51 centimeters) between the two parties involved is required. In certain cultural groups, however, the normal conversational distance is in the range of 14 to 15 inches (36 to 38 centimeters); and some groups say 9 to 10 inches (23 to 25 centimeters) is ideal. This area of nonverbal communication is important for cross-cultural communication. It is known as—

    a. Proxemics
    b. Personal space dynamics
    c. Posturing
    d. Linguistics

34. A person who believes in the inherent superiority and naturalness of his or her own culture is defined as being—

    a. Racist
    b. Ethnocentric
    c. Imperialistic
    d. Jingoistic

35. After working on various projects around the world, you have come to expect people, at times, to put other people into categories. You know that many people categorize those from your country as "brash" and "boorish." In fact, you think your current project team has categorized you as a brash person. Therefore, you should—

    a. Treat the other team members according to their country stereotypes
    b. Focus on the personalities involved
    c. Take a passive view and ignore the situation
    d. Behave in a manner that contradicts their expectations

36. Maximizing one's influence facilitates communication. This involves building and sustaining credibility. Which of the following is not a behavior that can help in this regard?

    a. Being flexible and open to differences
    b. Being respectful
    c. Exhibiting expertise by the answers you give
    d. Being reliable and committed

37. You have been sent abroad to conduct negotiations for a large telecommunications project. You arrive at the office promptly at 8:00 a.m.; however, at least 45 minutes of talk about families and weekend adventures goes by before anyone mentions business. Given their business approach, your hosts' culture is noted for which one of the following characteristics?

    a. High context
    b. Low context
    c. Friendliness
    d. Expressiveness

38. You are meeting with your diverse project team, represented by different nationalities, levels of experience, and positions in the company hierarchy. Everyone is encouraged to state their opinion, which is considered by the group. This team exhibits which of the following characteristics?

    a. Integrate others' worlds into your own
    b. Look globally for new ideas
    c. Be open to change
    d. Understand and value others

39. All professional organizations and their members have a code of ethics by which individuals may be guided to the correct behavior in professional dealings with others. This means that the code of ethics—

    a. Cannot overlap with the law of the country in which the professional organization is located
    b. Can never conflict with the law
    c. Can never conflict with the accepted norm of professional conduct when applied to individuals in different countries
    d. Cannot overlap with the law of the community

40. When dealing with customers, a code of ethics can be used to—

    a. Describe project roles and responsibilities
    b. Establish relationships
    c. Serve as a statement as to what can be expected
    d. Describe what is to be done in all situations

Answer Sheet

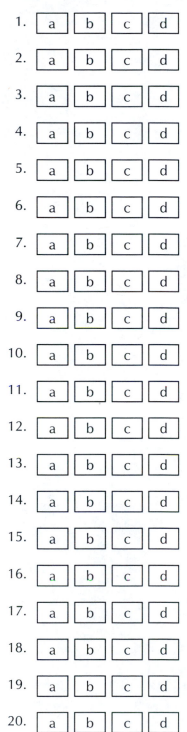

1. a b c d
2. a b c d
3. a b c d
4. a b c d
5. a b c d
6. a b c d
7. a b c d
8. a b c d
9. a b c d
10. a b c d
11. a b c d
12. a b c d
13. a b c d
14. a b c d
15. a b c d
16. a b c d
17. a b c d
18. a b c d
19. a b c d
20. a b c d

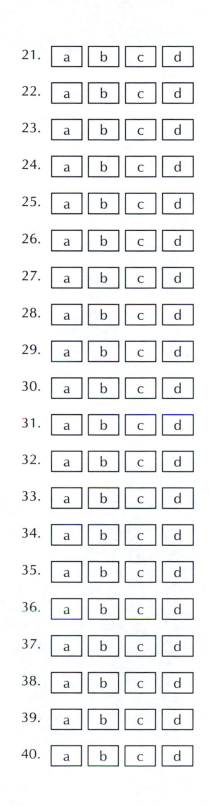

21. a b c d
22. a b c d
23. a b c d
24. a b c d
25. a b c d
26. a b c d
27. a b c d
28. a b c d
29. a b c d
30. a b c d
31. a b c d
32. a b c d
33. a b c d
34. a b c d
35. a b c d
36. a b c d
37. a b c d
38. a b c d
39. a b c d
40. a b c d

Answer Key

1. a. Adhering to legal requirements and ethical standards

As part of one's professional and social responsibility in project management, legal requirements and ethical standards must be adhered to in order to protect the community and all project stakeholders.

PMI®, *PMP® Examination Specification*, 2005, 29–30

2. b. A project constraint

Constraints are factors that limit the project management team's options. A requirement that the product of the project be socially, economically, and environmentally sustainable also will have an effect on the project scope, staffing, and schedule.

PMI®, *PMBOK® Guide*, 2008, 29

3. b. Explain in writing and in your oral presentation that you cannot complete the project because of the incomplete data

Deliverables are an output from the direct and manage project execution process. In this situation, however, you cannot complete the assigned deliverable because of the incomplete data. You must ensure individual integrity and professionalism by explaining the situation both in writing and orally—even though it means you cannot complete the assigned tasks.

PMI®, *Project Management Professional (PMP)^SM Credential Handbook*, 2009, 33–37; PMI®, *PMP® Examination Specification*, 2005, 29–30

4. a. Not accept this gift because it could be interpreted as being for personal gain

As a PMP®, you have a responsibility to refrain from offering or accepting inappropriate payments, gifts, or other forms of compensation for personal gain unless the giving or receiving of those things conforms to applicable laws and customs of the country where project management services are being provided.

PMI®, *Project Management Professional (PMP)^SM Credential Handbook*, 2009, 33–37

5. c. Refrain from knowingly engaging in professional misconduct

Although it is important to understand politics, bribing local officials to resolve problems regarding constraints and requisite business contacts raises a question of ethics. As a PMP®, you should abide by the laws, regulations, and requirements of communities and nations and not knowingly engage or assist in any activities that have negative implications.

PMI®, *Project Management Professional (PMP)^{SM} Credential Handbook*, 2009, 33–37; Verma 1997, 90–91

6. b. A responsibility to cooperate with PMI® concerning ethics violations and the collection of related information

According to PMI®'s ethical standards, PMI® members must cooperate with the Institute concerning the review of possible ethics violations and other PMI® matters.

PMI®, *Project Management Professional (PMP)^{SM} Credential Handbook*, 2009, 33–37; PMI®, *PMP® Examination Specification*, 2005, 29–30

7. c. Disclose Katrina's status concerning PMP® certification in your proposal and submit her resume as the project manager

As a PMI® member, you must provide customers, clients, and employers with fair, honest, complete, and accurate information concerning qualifications, professional services, and the preparation of estimates concerning costs, services, and expected results.

PMI®, *Project Management Professional (PMP)^{SM} Credential Handbook*, 2009, 33–37; PMI®, *PMP® Examination Specification*, 2005, 29–30

8. b. Document your award decision as completely as possible to all sellers

In an IFB, all bids are open at a specific time, and sellers are allowed to attend the bid opening. Most of the time bids are open and read aloud for those who are present. Usually the contract award goes to the lowest-bidding seller that also is financially responsible and capable of doing the work. On occasion, however, the buyer also will consider quality and time when selecting a seller. Professional judgment is critical. If the contract is not awarded to the lowest seller, it is important to document the reasons carefully. This type of contracting method is open to fraud, collusion, and other dishonest conduct. Therefore, project managers and contracting personnel must practice carefully defined, ethical business procedures.

Adams et al. 1997, 240–243

9. d. Contact Polar and ask for permission to list it as a reference in your proposal

PMI® members must honor and maintain the confidentiality and privacy of customers, clients, and employers with regard to identities, assignments undertaken, product knowledge, and other information obtained throughout the course of a professional relationship unless the customer, client, or employer grants you permission to do otherwise.

PMI®, *Project Management Professional (PMP)^SM Credential Handbook*, 2009, 33–37; PMI®, *PMP® Examination Specification*, 2005, 29–30

10. d. Not send him the update; he does not have a legitimate need to know the contents of the document

As part of PMI®'s code of professional conduct and ethical standards, you are responsible for maintaining and respecting the confidentiality of sensitive information obtained in the course of professional activities.

PMI®, *Project Management Professional (PMP)^SM Credential Handbook*, 2009, 33–37; PMI®, *PMP® Examination Specification*, 2005, 29–30

11. b. Use your existing labor rates combined with a value engineering approach as a way to lower overall cost

PMI® members are responsible for providing accurate and truthful representations to the public when preparing estimates concerning costs, services, and expected results. Use value engineering when there is a more effective and less expensive way to achieve the same result.

PMI®, *Project Management Professional (PMP)ᔆᴹ Credential Handbook*, 2009, 33–37; PMI®, *PMP® Examination Specification*, 2005, 29–30; Ward 2008, 461

12. d. Establish a risk register

The risk register enumerates the project's key risks and the plan for dealing with them. The risk register is produced based on the results of the qualitative and quantitative risk analyses, as well as the risk response planning process. Use of the risk register will assist in managing risk throughout the organization and, over time, will form the basis of a risk lessons learned program. This will contribute to the project management knowledge base.

PMI®, *PMBOK® Guide*, 2008, 288; PMI®, *PMP® Examination Specification*, 2005, 29–30

13. a. Document the lessons learned and share them within the company

It is important to contribute to the project management knowledge base by sharing lessons learned and best practices for improving the quality of project management services. Lessons learned from scope control should be shared so that they become part of the database for the current project and other projects in the organization.

PMI®, *PMBOK® Guide*, 2008, 100, 429

14. d. Conduct a procurement audit

The procurement audit is a structured review of the procurement processes on a project to identify successes and failures. Each insight gained can be transferred to other procurements on the project or other projects in the performing organization. This can contribute to the project management knowledge base and improve the quality of project management services. A procurement audit should be conducted as part of the contract closure process.

PMI®, *PMBOK® Guide*, 2008, 343

15. c. Improve quality in every aspect of project performance

The quality management plan increases the effectiveness and efficiency of the project and provides added benefits to the project stakeholders. Improving the quality of project management services also is a key aspect of a project manager's professional responsibilities.

PMI®, *PMBOK® Guide*, 2008, 200; PMI®, *PMP® Examination Specification*, 2005, 29–30

16. d. Prospective

Prospective is not a term used in the quality discipline to describe an audit. Quality audits should be viewed as a system of audits. Types of quality audits include internal and external; system, product, process, location, and organization; baseline and regular; and special and comprehensive. Quality audits also are one way to improve the quality of project management services because their results will contribute to the project management knowledge base and the sharing of best practices.

PMI®, *PMBOK® Guide*, 2008, 204; PMI®, *PMP® Examination Specification*, 2005, 29–30

17. b. Alert your management to the situation, both orally and in writing, and request that someone else confirm your findings

In this situation, there is a potential, yet unconfirmed, problem with a deliverable that has been completed and accepted by the customer. The project is closed; however, further action is required. Personal and professional conduct, work-related conduct, community responsibility, and client relations are issues that must be considered when working as a professional in the project management business.

PMI®, *Project Management Professional (PMP)*SM *Credential Handbook*, 2009, 33–37; PMI®, *PMP® Examination Specification*, 2005, 29–30

18. c. Implement a structured approach to risk management

This situation shows the possibility of poor scheduling and inadequate risk identification and response planning. Delays in using these programmers could have been identified early as a possible project management risk. Typically, project management risks include items such as poor allocation of time and resources, inadequate quality of the project plan, and poor use of project management disciplines.

PMI®, *PMBOK® Guide*, 2008, 275–276

19. c. Ensure that the WBS is detailed enough and that all the activities are defined in sufficient detail

The purpose of the WBS is to organize and define the total scope of the project. Work not described in the WBS is outside the scope of the project. Therefore, it is important to develop a WBS that is complete and that defines all activities with appropriate detail to facilitate clear responsibility assignments.

PMI®, *Practice Standard for the Work Breakdown Structure*, 2006, 6

20. d. Benchmarking forums

Benchmarking is one way to foster learning about best practices and opportunities for process improvements. Forums in which companies meet and discuss best practices provide a standard by which to measure performance and enable experiences to be shared.

Brake, et al. 2002, 156–157

21. a. Hire a consultant who knows the country to brief you on what to expect in Australia

Cultural competence is no longer a nice skill to have; it is an economic necessity. It begins with open attitudes, which facilitate self-development and an awareness of others' differences. One must be grounded in cultural knowledge to be able to develop cross-cultural skills.

Brake, et al. 2002, 74–75

22. d. How adaptable am I?

Other self-awareness questions include the following: What are my primary cultural orientations? How do they affect the way I do business? How do I differ from my mainstream culture and mainstream business culture?

Brake, et al. 2002, 33–34

23. c. Aggressive insight

Response to this situation demonstrates aggressive insight because it is proactive. Leaders who understand their strengths and their weaknesses will question assumptions and ask for feedback from others. This constant self-examination allows a person to improve his or her work performance.

Rosen, et al. 2000, 156–157

24. b. Moving beyond cultural stereotyping and seeing people as individuals with unique personality traits and experiences

Never assume that all members of a particular cultural group will act the same way. Although success in any aspect of international business is related directly to one's knowledge of the cultural environment in which one is operating, it is inadvisable to depend on this knowledge too much.

Ferraro 1998, 121

25. c. Active listening

The best negotiator is a well-informed negotiator. Active listening is absolutely essential for understanding the other side's positions and interests. The understanding that comes from your active listening can have a positive persuasive effect on your negotiating partners because it can convince them that you are knowledgeable and also that you have made the effort to really hear what they are saying. This can enhance both rapport and trust.

Ferraro 1998, 125

26. d. Customer

Customer requirements must be satisfied. However, because the needs and expectations of other stakeholders cannot be disregarded, finding appropriate resolutions to disagreements among stakeholders can be a major project management challenge and is part of one's responsibility as a PMP®.

PMI®, *PMP® Examination Specification*, 2005, 29–30

27. a. Find appropriate resolutions to resolve differences between or among stakeholders

The project manager must balance stakeholder interests by recommending approaches that strive for fair resolution to satisfy competing needs and objectives. Stakeholders often have different, conflicting objectives. The first step is to identify the stakeholders, determine their requirements, and then manage and influence those requirements. Finding appropriate solutions to differences can be one of the major challenges of project management.

PMI®, *PMP® Examination Specification*, 2005, 29–30

28. b. Smoothing

Smoothing is a style of conflict resolution that deemphasizes differences and emphasizes commonalities regarding conflict issues. It keeps the atmosphere friendly. As a PMP®, you should recommend approaches that strive for fair resolution to satisfy competing needs and objectives.

PMI®, *PMBOK® Guide*, 2008, 239–240; Verma 1996, 118 and 120

29. c. Perform careful project planning

Careful and early project planning can reduce conflict later in the project life cycle. Skill in resolving conflicts and striving for fair resolution to satisfy competing needs and objectives is part of one's professional and social responsibility as a project professional.

PMI®, *PMBOK® Guide*, 2008, 239–240

30. b. Confrontation

Although all the methods listed are useful in resolving conflict, the one project managers use most often is confrontation (also called problem solving), in which two parties work together toward a win-win solution. This type of conflict resolution is particularly effective in project management because problems are solved as they surface, preventing any accumulation of problems during the project life cycle.

PMI®, *PMBOK® Guide*, 2008, 239–240; Verma 1996, 118 and 120

31. a. Learn and use the local language

Communication skills must be assessed in terms of language competency, motivation to learn another language, and willingness to use it in professional and personal situations.

Ferraro 1998, 147

32. d. Nonverbal communication

Nonverbal communication is as important as the language used to send and receive messages because it helps us interpret the linguistic messages being sent. In the international business environment, successful communication requires not only an understanding of other languages but also an understanding of the nonverbal aspects of those languages. In cross-cultural situations, people will rely more heavily on nonverbal cues when they are not from the same speech community.

Ferraro 1998, 65

33. a. Proxemics

How people use personal space in their interactions with others is another "silent language" that must be understood to achieve clear communication across cultures. How close a person gets to another in normal conversation depends on the nature of the social interaction and cultural norms.

Ferraro 1998, 78–80

34. b. Ethnocentric

Ethnocentrism is a basic human response, and through it we rate others according to our standards and ways of doing things. It can be highly destructive because it closes off our ability to relate to others and leads to hasty evaluations and derogatory remarks. It is important to recognize this tendency and try to avoid it.

Brake, et al. 2002, 169–170

35. d. Behave in a manner that contradicts their expectations

If you believe you are being stereotyped, behave in a manner that contradicts the expectations and, if necessary, allude to the differences between yourself and the stereotype. Try not to become defensive because that will only cause the situation to degenerate. Focus on the problem, not on the personalities.

Brake, et al. 2002, 171

36. c. Exhibiting expertise by the answers you give

Establishing credibility is an important task—one that requires you to be knowledgeable about your business and the current developments in your field. Ask questions that show the level of your understanding. Demonstrate credibility by the questions you ask, rather than by the answers you give.

Brake, et al. 2002, 179

37. a. High context

High-context cultures are relationship centered, that is, a great deal of broad contextual information is needed about an individual or company before the specific business at hand can be transacted. A significant amount of time may be spent on "small talk," and information may not be communicated in a linear form.

Brake, et al. 2002, 54–55

38. d. Understand and value others

You must be confident and clear about your own identity and express the best of your country. The natural next step is to understand and value others. By developing the capacity to see the world from another perspective, you open yourself to learning what the other country has to offer.

Rosen, et al. 2000, 174

39. b. Can never conflict with the law

Codes of ethics guide professional behavior on the basis of obligations to others and typically complement, but do not conflict with, applicable law. While the code of ethics may overlap the law of the country or community, it can never conflict with the law The scope statement describes the project's major objectives. Based on those objectives, the project team can then identify the major deliverables that need to be completed to satisfy the objectives and the resources required to complete the project. There are many tools that can be used to identify the deliverables, including expert judgment.

Cleland and Ireland 2007, 479–481

40. c. Serve as a statement as to what can be expected

A code of ethics can serve as a statement to clients, employees, and others that "this is what you can expect from us." Violations or perceived violations of the code often erode confidence in the person whose actions are questionable

Cleland and Ireland 2007, 479–481

Practice Test

This practice test is designed to simulate PMI®'s 200-question PMP® certification exam.

INSTRUCTIONS: Note the most suitable answer for each multiple-choice question in the appropriate space on the answer sheet.

1. Because your project is slated to last five years, you believe rolling wave planning is appropriate. It provides information about the work to be done—

    a. Throughout all project phases
    b. For successful completion of the current project phase
    c. For successful completion of the current and subsequent near-term project phases
    d. In the next project phase

2. In the initial stage of the project life cycle, the project's technical objectives are apt to be understood only in a general sense. A major component of project conflict during this stage of the project is—

    a. Concerns over priorities and procedures
    b. Concerns about technical issues
    c. Schedules
    d. Confusion of establishing a project in the matrix management environment

3. The PMI® Code of Ethics and Professional Conduct includes two types of standards, those that you strive to uphold as practitioners and those that establish firm requirements and may limit behavior. PMI® refers to these two types (respectively) as—

    a. Expected and required
    b. Desired and mandatory
    c. Aspirational and mandatory
    d. Aspirational and required

4. Requirements typically are classified into product requirements and project requirements. Capturing and managing both types of requirements is important for project success, so you and your team decided to follow this classification system on your project to modernize all the telecommunications equipment in your company. During such an approach, all the following are examples of product requirements EXCEPT—

   a. Delivery requirements
   b. Technical requirements
   c. Security requirements
   d. Performance requirements

5. Risk registers, planned risk responses, and defined risk impacts are examples of which of the following in the develop project management plan process:

   a. Enterprise environmental factors
   b. Organizational process assets
   c. Part of the project's risk management plan, which as a subsidiary plan will be part of the project management plan
   d. Project documents that are included as configuration items and are part of the configuration management plan

6. You are managing a project that has five subcontractors. You must monitor contract performance, make payments, and manage provider interface. One subcontractor submitted a change request to expand the scope of its work. You decided to award a contract modification based on a review of this request. All these activities are part of—

   a. Administer procurements
   b. Conduct procurements
   c. Form contract
   d. Resolve disputes

7. Although the project charter serves to state the project manager's authority and responsibility on the project, the project manager further requires which type of power in order to be an effective leader?

   a. Expert
   b. Legitimate
   c. Position
   d. Referent

8. The performance measurement baseline consists of all the following EXCEPT—

   a. Scope baseline
   b. Quality baseline
   c. Schedule baseline
   d. Cost baseline

9. While working as the project manager on a new project to improve overall ease of use in the development of a railroad switching station, you have decided to add a subject matter expert who specializes in ergonomics to your team. She has decided to observe the existing approach as you and your team work to define requirements for the new system. This method is also called—

   a. Mentoring
   b. Coaching
   c. Job shadowing
   d. User experimentation

10. In addition to providing support to the project, quality assurance also provides an umbrella for—

    a. Plan-do-check-act
    b. Continuous process improvement
    c. Project management maturity
    d. Work performance information

11. As a PMP®, you are bound by a code of ethics to do project work without misrepresenting the truth and validity of the information. As a project manager, you are resourceful and skilled in gathering, assessing, compiling, and documenting information. All the following tasks associated with professional and social responsibility involve this skill EXCEPT—

    a. Ensure personal integrity and professionalism by adhering to legal requirements, ethical standards, and social norms to protect the community and all stakeholders and to create a healthy working environment
    b. Contribute to the project management knowledge base by sharing lessons learned, best practices, and research
    c. Enhance personal professional competency
    d. Promote interaction among team members and stakeholders by respecting personal and cultural differences

12. Assume that your company is working under a fixed-price-incentive contract. It has a target cost of $100,000, a target profit of 10%, a price ceiling of $120,000, and a share formula of 80/20. Assume that your company completes all of the work but has actual costs of $110,000. What is the final value of this procurement?

    a. $120,000
    b. $132,000
    c. $118,000
    d. $110,000

13. If you apply the configuration management system along with change control processes project wide, you will achieve all but which following objective?

    a. Establish an evolutionary method to continuously identify and request changes to established baselines and to assess the value and effectiveness of those changes.
    b. Provide an opportunity to continuously validate and improve the project by considering the impact of each change.
    c. Document the specific responsibilities of each stakeholder in the perform integrated change control process.
    d. Provide the mechanism for the project team to consistently communicate all changes to the stakeholders.

14. You need to outsource the testing function of your project. Your subcontracts department informed you that the following document must be prepared before conducting the procurement:

    a. Statement of work
    b. Procurement management plan
    c. Evaluation methodology
    d. Contract terms and conditions

15. Constraints common to projects include—

    a. Scope, quality, schedule, budget, and risk
    b. Scope, teaming, planning, and resources
    c. Scope
    d. Practice, practice, and practice

16. You are developing a project charter and want to ensure that any changes that may occur after the project begins will be controlled rigorously. You have consulted your company's configuration management knowledge base, and it contains versions and baselines of all the following official company documents EXCEPT—

    a. Standards
    b. Strategic plans
    c. Policies
    d. Procedures

17. To identify inefficient and ineffective policies, processes, and procedures in use on a project, you should conduct—

    a. An inspection
    b. A process analysis
    c. Benchmarking
    d. A quality audit

18. Your project management office implemented a project management methodology that emphasizes the importance of integrated change control. It states that change requests can occur in all the following forms EXCEPT—

    a. Indirect
    b. Legally mandated
    c. Informal
    d. Internally initiated

19. Configuration management describes procedures for applying technical and administrative direction and surveillance. Which one of the following tasks is NOT performed in configuration management?

    a. Identifying functional and physical characteristics of an item or system
    b. Controlling changes to characteristics
    c. Performing an audit to verify conformance to requirements
    d. Allowing automatic approval of changes

20. A number of tools and techniques are helpful in the perform integrated change control process. If you want to implement an integrated change control process, you should use—

    a. Configuration management software
    b. A project management information system
    c. Project status review meetings
    d. Change control meetings

21. Having worked previously as a software project manager, you were pleased to be appointed as the project manager for a new systems integration project designed to replace the existing air traffic control system in your country. You found a requirements traceability matrix to be helpful on software projects, so you decided to use it on this systems integration project. Using such a matrix helps to ensure that each requirement—

    a. Adds quality and supports the organization's quality policy
    b. Adds business value as it links to business and project objectives
    c. Sets forth the level of service, performance, safety, security, and compliance
    d. Shows the impact to other organizational areas and to entities outside of the performing organization

22. During the closing phase of the project, the top-ranked source of conflict is—

    a. Schedule
    b. Administrative procedures
    c. Cost
    d. Human resources

23. Which of the following ensures that requested changes to both product scope and project scope are thoroughly considered before they are processed through the perform integrated change control process?

    a. Scope change control system
    b. Configuration management system
    c. Change control board
    d. Configuration status audits

24. Which following tool is used in process analysis to determine the underlying causes of defects?

    a. Root cause analysis
    b. Assumptions analysis
    c. Cost-benefit analysis
    d. Quality metrics

25. All the following statements concerning scope verification and quality control are true EXCEPT—

    a. The processes can be performed in parallel
    b. Both processes use inspection as a tool and technique
    c. Scope verification is concerned with the acceptance of deliverables, and quality control is concerned with meeting quality requirements for the deliverables
    d. Scope verification typically precedes quality control

26. Consider a company that sells products to consumers. As one product begins the deterioration and death phases of its life cycle (or the divestment phase of a system), new products or projects must be established. This means that—

    a. The company requires a continuous stream of projects to survive
    b. The company is not at a high level of maturity
    c. The company is in a period of overall decline
    d. The company definitely lacks a balanced portfolio

27. You are in the process of performing quality assurance on your product and find that some requirements are not as complete as they should be, which causes rework and adds costs to your overall project. The term for all costs incurred over the life of the product by investing in appraising and inspecting the product for conformance and nonconformance to requirements is called—

    a. Life-cycle costs
    b. Expected value
    c. Cost of conformances
    d. Cost of quality

28. The project scope baseline should be used in the identify risks process because it—

    a. Identifies project assumptions
    b. Identifies all work that must be done ;therefore, it includes all risks on the project
    c. Helps organize all work that must be done on the project
    d. Contains information on risks from prior projects

29. Although there are various tools and techniques to consider as you collect requirements on your project, one approach that supports the concept of progressive elaboration is—

    a. Idea/mind mapping
    b. Affinity diagrams
    c. Prototypes
    d. Joint Application Design® sessions

30. Tools and techniques used to perform quality assurance include—

    a. Tools from perform quality control and plan quality
    b. Tools from perform quality control
    c. Variance analysis
    d. Direct and manage project execution

31. An approach to provide insight into the health of the project and to identify any areas that require special attention is to—

    a. Conduct periodic status reviews
    b. Prepare regular status and progress reports
    c. Prepare forecasts of the project's future
    d. Continuously monitor the project

32. Although your company's project life cycle does not mandate when a project review should be conducted, you believe it is important to review performance at the conclusion of each phase. The objective of such a review is to—

    a. Determine how many resources are required to complete the project according to the project baseline
    b. Adjust the schedule and cost baselines based on past performance
    c. Obtain customer acceptance of project deliverables
    d. Determine whether the project should continue to the next phase

33. The key management skills required during the adjourning stage of team development include all but which one of the following?

    a. Evaluating
    b. Reviewing
    c. Celebrating
    d. Improving

34. Assume that your actual costs are $800; your planned value is $1,200; and your earned value is $1,000. Based on these data, what can be determined regarding your schedule variance?

    a. At +$200, the situation is favorable as physical progress is being accomplished ahead of your plan.
    b. At -$200, the physical progress is being accomplished at a slower rate than is planned, indicating an unfavorable situation.
    c. At +$400, the situation is favorable as physical progress is being accomplished at a lower cost than was forecasted.
    d. At -$200, you have a behind-schedule condition, and your critical path has slipped.

35. Fairness is a PMP® duty; therefore, as a member of the PMP® community, you should act impartially and objectively. To demonstrate this duty, you should do all the following EXCEPT—

    a. Demonstrate transparency in decision making
    b. Document impartiality at the beginning of the project
    c. Provide equal access to information (for those who are authorized)
    d. Always be vigilant in looking for potential conflict-of-interest situations

36. The CPI on your project is 0.84. This means that you should—

    a. Place emphasis on improving the timeliness of the physical progress
    b. Reassess the life-cycle costs of your product, including the length of the life-cycle phase
    c. Recognize that your original estimates were fundamentally flawed and your project is in an atypical situation
    d. Place emphasis on improving the productivity by which work was being performed

37. Project deliverables are the outputs that include the product, service, or result of the project as well as ancillary results. These ancillary results should be in the—

    a. Requirements management plan
    b. Scope management plan
    c. Project scope statement
    d. Project acceptance criteria

38. Which of the following tools and techniques is used in the close project or phase process?

    a. Project management methodology
    b. Work performance information
    c. Expert judgment
    d. Project management information system

39. After the project scope statement is complete, it may be necessary to update other project documents. All the following are examples of a document that may require updates EXCEPT—

    a. Project charter
    b. Stakeholder register
    c. Requirements documentation
    d. Requirements traceability matrix

40. A challenge of earned value management is predicting percent complete. The simplest formula to use to calculate EV is—

    a. 0/100 rule
    b. 50/50 rule
    c. (Percent complete) (budget at completion)
    d. Milestone method

41. While managing a large project in your organization, you realize that your project team requires training in contract administration because you will be awarding several major subcontracts. After you analyze your project requirements and assess the expertise of your team members, you decide that your team will need a one-week class in contract administration. This training should—

    a. Commence as scheduled and stated in the staffing management plan
    b. Commence as scheduled and stated as part of the procurement management plan
    c. Be scheduled if necessary after performance assessments are prepared and after each team member has had an opportunity to serve in the contract administrator role
    d. Commence as scheduled and stated in the team development plan

42. Assume that on your project, you are using earned value management. Your project is one that has extremely long work packages. Therefore, the method you should use to calculate EV is—

    a. 0/100 rule
    b. Milestone method
    c. Equivalent effort
    d. Apportioned effort

43. Your project sponsor has asked you, "What do we now expect the total job to cost?" Given that you are using earned value, you should calculate the—

    a. To-complete performance index
    b. Estimate to complete
    c. Estimate at completion
    d. Budget at completion

44. One key reason that the develop project charter process is so important is that it—

    a. Documents the boundaries of the project
    b. States the methods for acceptance of the project's deliverables
    c. Describes the project's characteristics
    d. Links the project to the ongoing work of the organization

45. Your company is preparing a proposal for project management consulting services for the government. You are a member of the proposal writing team and are PMP® certified. Both a technical and a financial proposal must be submitted, but your company realizes that low cost will win the contract, and it needs a win to achieve its profit targets for the year. Although your company has won several government contracts in the past, and has had its rates audited, the chief financial officer has decided that if it uses nonaudited overhead rates, the firm can submit a competitive bid. You learned of this decision today. Your next step should be to—

    a. Continue to prepare your part of the proposal
    b. Tell your CEO that this action by your company constitutes a violation of the PMI® Code of Ethics and Professional Conduct in the section titled: "Conflict of Interest Situations and Other Prohibited Professional Conduct"
    c. Tell your CEO that this action by your company constitutes a violation of the PMI® Code of Ethics and Professional Conduct in the section titled: "Qualifications, Experience, and Performance of Professional Services"
    d. Tell your CEO that this action by your company constitutes a violation of the PMI® Code of Ethics and Professional Conduct in the section titled: "Candidate/Certificant Practice"

46. Your organization has a miserable project completion rate. In reviewing the lessons learned database to determine the root cause of these problems, you should be looking at all the following information EXCEPT—

    a. New or revised activity duration estimates
    b. Modified activity sequences
    c. Analysis of alternative schedules
    d. Schedule updates

47. Consider the data in the table below. Assume that your project consists only of these three activities. Your estimate at completion is $4,400.00. This means you are calculating your EAC by using which of the following formulas?

Activity	% Complete	PV	EV	AC
A	100	2,000	2,000	2,200
B	50	1,000	500	700
C	0	1,000	0	0

a. EAC = AC / EV x BAC
b. EAC = AC / EV x [work completed and in progress] + [actual (or revised) cost of work packages that have not started]
c. EAC = [Actual to date] + [all remaining work to be done at the planned cost including remaining work in progress]
d. EAC = % complete x BAC

48. Rolling wave planning in the WBS process refers to situations in which—

a. Certain deliverables or subprojects will be accomplished far into the future
b. Additional work is added to the project after the scope baseline has been established; therefore, additional decomposition is required
c. Identification codes for the WBS elements cannot be determined until the schedule activity list is complete in case revisions are required
d. Subprojects are developed by external organizations and then become part of the WBS for the entire project

49. The lessons learned documentation is an output from the—

a. Identify stakeholders process
b. Develop project plan process
c. Distribute information process
d. Plan communications process

50. Your experience has taught you that inappropriate responses to cost variances can produce quality or schedule problems or unacceptable project risk. When leading a team meeting to discuss the importance of cost control, you note that cost control is concerned with—

    a. Influencing the factors that create change to the cost performance baseline to ensure that the change is beneficial
    b. Developing an approximation of the costs of the resources needed to complete the project
    c. Allocating the overall cost estimate to individual work items
    d. Establishing a cost performance baseline

51. Leadership has been portrayed as a relationship with four major variables: the characteristics of the leader; the attitudes, needs, and other personal characteristics of the followers; the characteristics of the organization; and the social, economic, and political milieu. This view is attributable to—

    a. Peter Drucker
    b. Douglas McGregor
    c. Chris Argyris
    d. Rensis Likert

52. The WBS represents all product and project work, including project management. It is sometimes called the—

    a. Control account level
    b. 100% rule
    c. integration of scope, cost, and schedule for comparison to the earned value
    d. The code of accounts

53. Your company is in the project management training business. In addition, the company publishes several exam study aids for the PMP® and CAPM® exam. You are fairly new to the organization and lack the experience to actually qualify to take the PMP®, but you had the required experience for the CAPM® and took and passed it three months ago. Today, you were contacted by someone at PMI® headquarters to see if you would like to be part of a CAPM® Exam item writing session. You should—

    a. Accept the invitation so you can contribute to the profession
    b. Ask your supervisor if it is acceptable to be on this committee
    c. Decline the invitation since it is a conflict of interest
    d. Decline the invitation because you are not PMP® certified

54. You are trying to determine whether or not to conduct 100% final system tests of 500 ground-based radar units at the factory. The historical radar field failure rate is 4%; the cost to test each unit in the factory is $10,000; the cost to reassemble each passed unit after the factory test is $2,000; the cost to repair and reassemble each failed unit after factory test is $23,000; and the cost to repair and reinstall each failed unit in the field is $350,000. Using decision tree analysis, what is the expected value if you decide to conduct these tests?

    a. $5.5 million
    b. $5.96 million
    c. $6.42 million
    d. $7 million

55. Motivation is dynamic and complex. The statement, "Motivation is an intrinsic phenomenon. Extrinsic satisfaction only leads to movements, not motivation" is attributed to which of the leading theories of motivation?

    a. Maslow's Hierarchy of Needs Theory
    b. Herzberg's Motivator-Hygiene Theory
    c. Morse and Lorsch's Contingency Theory
    d. McGregor's Theory X/Theory Y

56. Each time you meet with your project sponsor, she emphasizes the need for cost control. To address her concerns, you should provide—

    a. Work performance measurements
    b. Cost baseline updates
    c. Resource productivity analyses
    d. Trend analysis statistics

57. One output of the control costs process is work performance measurements, which is when—

    a. Modifications are made to the cost information used to manage the project
    b. The project team needs to prepare a change request and process it through the perform integrated change control process
    c. A budget update is required and communicated to all stakeholders
    d. The calculated CV, SV, CPI, and SPI values for WBS components are documented and communicated to stakeholders

58. You work for an electrical utility company and will be managing a project to build a new substation that will serve a new industrial park. This project was authorized because of a—

    a. Business need
    b. Market demand
    c. Technological advance
    d. Customer request

59. A final project report is a recommended best practice. Although this report can be organized in a variety of ways, how should each item that is covered in the report be addressed?

    a. A recommendation for changing current practice should be made and defended.
    b. The focus should be solely on items that did not work well on the project.
    c. Individuals who did not contribute successfully as team members should be noted.
    d. An earned value discussion is warranted.

60. At the time the risk register is first prepared, it should contain all the following entries EXCEPT—

    a. Root causes of risk
    b. Updated risk categories
    c. List of risks requiring near-term responses
    d. List of potential responses

61. Which of the following theorists stated that people generally are motivated according to the strength of their desire either to achieve high levels of performance or to exceed in competitive situations?

    a. David McGregor
    b. David McClelland
    c. Victor Vroom
    d. B. F. Skinner

62. If when developing a project schedule, you want to define a distribution of probable results for each schedule activity and use it to calculate a distribution of probable results for the total project, the most common technique to use is—

    a. PERT
    b. Monte Carlo analysis
    c. Linear programming
    d. Concurrent engineering

63. Project execution must be compared and deviations must be measured for management control according to the—

   a. Scope baseline
   b. Performance measurement baseline
   c. Schedule baseline
   d. Control system

64. A number of items may be part of the schedule data for the project. The amount of additional detail will vary, but the data should include all the following items EXCEPT—

   a. Schedule activities
   b. Activity attributes
   c. Identified assumptions
   d. Resource breakdown structure

65. If a team member, when facing schedule delays and cost overruns, develops several alternatives for completing the project successfully on schedule and within budget and asks questions such as, "Can we do it?," "If we do it what are the consequences?," and "Is it really worth the effort involved?," he or she is primarily motivated by the—

   a. Contingency Theory
   b. Expectancy Theory
   c. Reinforcement Theory
   d. Equity Theory

66. Which tool or technique is NOT used for schedule control?

   a. Variance analysis
   b. Project management software
   c. Work performance information
   d. Schedule change control system

67. All the following are examples of lessons learned EXCEPT—

   a. Position descriptions
   b. Ground rules
   c. Recognition events
   d. Project performance appraisals

68. Recording and reporting information regarding when appropriate configuration information should be provided and regarding the status of proposed and approved changes effectively is done through—

    a. Configuration status accounting
    b. Configuration verification and auditing
    c. Project management methodology
    d. A project management information system (PMIS)

69. Decomposition is a technique used for both WBS development and activity definition. Which statement best describes the role decomposition plays in activity definition as compared to creating the WBS?

    a. Final output of activity definition is described in terms of work packages in the WBS.
    b. Final output of activity definition is described as deliverables or tangible items.
    c. Final output of activity definition is described as schedule activities.
    d. Decomposition is used the same way in scope definition and activity definition.

70. The schedule management plan is a key document. It is—

    a. An output of the develop schedule process
    b. A tool and technique used in the develop schedule process
    c. A separate planning effort completed before the time management processes
    d. A separate planning effort completed in conjunction with the time management processes

71. Activity attributes are used to extend the description of the activity and to identify its multiple components. In the early stages of the project, an example of an activity attribute is—

    a. Activity codes
    b. Activity description
    c. Predecessor and successor activities
    d. Activity name

72. You are working on a new project in your city to construct an environmentally friendly landfill. The existing site is so undesirable that many residents have moved to other neighboring cities because of their proximity to it. However, even though the project has the support of the public, you need to have a number of hearings of the city's government before you are authorized to begin work. As you are in the planning phase of the project, you are waiting for these hearings to be scheduled and held before you can begin site preparation. These hearings are an example of—

   a. A milestone
   b. An external dependency
   c. An item to be scheduled as a fragnet
   d. A mandatory dependency

73. You are working on a project and want to know how many activities in the previous month were completed with significant variances. You should use a(n)—

   a. Control chart
   b. Inspection
   c. Scatter diagram
   d. Run chart

74. Your project has a budget of $1.5 million for the first year, $3 million for the second year, $2.2 million for the third year, and $800,000 for the fourth year. Most of the project budget will be spent during—

   a. Starting the project
   b. Organizing and preparing
   c. Carrying out the work
   d. Closing the project

75. If you decide to follow an open subordination approach to resolving conflict, you are using which style of conflict resolution?

   a. Avoiding
   b. Accommodating
   c. Compromising
   d. Collaborating

76. Typically, the seller receives formal written notice that the contract has been completed by the—

   a. Project manager
   b. Authorized procurement administrator
   c. Member of the project management team responsible for daily contract administration
   d. Purchasing department head

77. Assume that you were recently elected to be on the board of your local PMI® chapter. You are friends with the vice president of membership for the chapter, Kim, as you both worked for the same manufacturing company in project management. Kim, a PMP®, left the manufacturing company six months ago and now works for a project management training and consulting company in your city. Today at work, another member of the local chapter showed you some unsolicited mail she had received from Kim's company concerning their services. She was surprised this company had her name and address. In this situation, you should—

    a. Tell her you have no idea how Kim's company received her name and address and take no further action.
    b. Confront Kim and ask her whether she provided her management with the local chapter's membership list.
    c. Report Kim to PMI® because this is obviously a conflict of interest.
    d. Convene a meeting of the PMI® Board to discuss this potential conflict of interest with them before taking further action.

78. You are beginning a new project staffed with a virtual team that is located in five countries. To help avoid conflict in work priorities among your team and the functional managers, you ask the project sponsor to prepare a—

    a. Memo to team members informing them that they work for you now
    b. Project charter
    c. Memo to functional managers informing them that you have authority to direct their employees
    d. Human resource management plan

79. To anticipate and help develop approaches to deal with potential quality problems on your project, you want to use a variety of root-cause analysis techniques including all the following approaches EXCEPT—

    a. Fishbone diagrams
    b. Ishikawa diagrams
    c. System or process flowcharts
    d. Checklists

80. All of the following are examples of ways to generate options for mutual gain during negotiations EXCEPT—

    a. Separating inventing from deciding
    b. Options broadening
    c. Zero-sum game analysis
    d. Multiplying options by shuttling between the specific and the general

81. Recently, your company introduced a new processing system for its products. You were the project manager for this system and now have been asked to lead a team to implement needed changes to increase efficiency and productivity. To help you analyze the process outputs, you and your team have decided to use which following technique?

    a. System flowcharts
    b. Design of experiments
    c. Pareto analysis
    d. Control charts

82. Effective leadership is one key to successful project management. There are several theories of leadership. One model is Hershey and Blanchard's situational leadership model that describes directive behavior and supportive behavior. Of the following, which one is NOT a key word for supportive behavior?

    a. Listen
    b. Structure
    c. Praise
    d. Facilitate

83. Based on quality control measurements on your manufacturing project, management realizes that immediate corrective action is required to the material requirements planning (MRP) system to minimize rework. To implement the necessary changes you should follow—

    a. The organization's quality policy
    b. The quality management plan
    c. Established operational definitions and procedures
    d. A defined integrated change control process

84. You are the project manager on a project to improve traffic flow in the company's parking garage. You decide to use flowcharting to—

    a. Help anticipate how problems occur
    b. Show dependencies between tasks
    c. Show the results of a process
    d. Forecast future outcomes

85. Successful project management involves both project leadership as well as project management skills. Several different leadership styles are appropriate in different phases of the project life cycle. Assume that you are working on a project, and it is in the execution phase. The leadership style that is most appropriate should consist of a blend of all but which one of the following?

    a. Change master
    b. Decision maker
    c. Team and synergy
    d. Trustworthiness

86. Schedule control is one important way to avoid delays. While planning and executing schedule recovery, one tool available to you for control schedules is—

    a. Making unpopular decisions
    b. Immediately rebaselining
    c. Adjusting leads and lags
    d. Resource leveling

87. You have been studying for the PMP® certification exam for some time and are scheduled to take the exam in one month. You further plan to attend a boot camp the week before the exam. You feel you definitely will pass because of your extensive preparations. Your company is bidding on a government contract, which has required that the project manager must be PMP® certified. You know the technical area and the prospective client well and really want to manage this project. Today, your company learned that it is on the "short list" of possible contractors. The government has asked for the resume of the person who will be your company's project manager. Your manager wants to give them your name as the contract will not be awarded, at the earliest, until two weeks after you take the exam, and because he knows you want the job. You should tell your manager—

    a. To submit your resume even though you do not have your certification because you are sure you will pass the exam
    b. To submit your resume now; if for some reason you do not pass the exam, your manager can then substitute someone who is PMP® certified
    c. That while you want to manage this project, your resume cannot be submitted at this time
    d. That he can submit your resume because you are not yet a member of PMI® so you have no conflicts at this time

88. You are a personnel management specialist recently assigned to a project team working on a team-based reward and recognition system. The other team members also work in the human resources department. The project charter should be issued by—

    a. The project manager
    b. The client
    c. A manager at the level appropriate to funding the project
    d. A member of the program management office (PMO) who has jurisdiction over human resources

89. In which of the following methods of resolving conflict will the conflict typically reappear again in another form?

    a. Smoothing
    b. Compromising
    c. Collaborating
    d. Confronting

90. Statistical sampling is a method in perform quality control to determine the conformance to requirements for some component or product of a project. Its greatest advantage is that it—

    a. Does not require a large expenditure of resources
    b. Is accurate enough with a sampling of less than 1%
    c. Does not require 100% inspection of the components to achieve a satisfactory inference of the population
    d. Needs to be conducted only when a problem is discovered with the end product or when the customer has some rejects

91. Your project sponsor wants to know whether process variables are within acceptable limits. To answer this question, you should—

    a. Conduct a process analysis
    b. Conduct a root cause analysis
    c. Use a control chart
    d. Use a run chart

92. All but which one of the following is true about the grassroots estimate?

    a. It has an accuracy rate of from -5% to +10%.
    b. It is also called an engineering estimate.
    c. It is used primarily for Level 1 of the WBS.
    d. It may take months to prepare.

93. When you review cost performance data on your project, different responses are required depending on the degree of variance from the baseline. For example, a variance of 10% might not require immediate action, whereas a variance of 100% will require investigation. A process description of how you plan to manage cost variances should be included in the—

    a. Cost management plan
    b. Change management plan
    c. Performance measurement plan
    d. Variance management plan

94. Assume that you are managing a project team. Your team is one in which its members confront issues rather than people, establish procedures collectively, and is team oriented. As the project manager, which of the following represents your team's stage of development and the approach you should use during this time?

    a. Storming; high directive and supportive approach
    b. Norming; high directive and low supportive approach
    c. Norming; high supportive and low directive approach
    d. Performing; low directive and supportive approach

95. You are finalizing all the contracts and ensuring that they are closed. The close procurements process involves all the following administrative actions EXCEPT—

    a. The procurement administrator is reassigned
    b. Finalizing open claims
    c. Updating the project records to show the final contract results
    d. Archiving the contracts and contract records for future use

96. You are working on a project and want to identify the cause of problems in a process by the shape and width of the distribution of the process variables. You should use a—

    a. Histogram
    b. Pareto chart
    c. Scatter diagram
    d. Trend analysis

97. You are working on a construction project in a city different from your headquarters' location. You and your team have not worked in this city, City B, previously, and you lack knowledge of the local building codes. You had a team member review the codes and he said they were in far greater detail than those in your city, City A. When you asked him how much time he would need to spend to gain a complete understanding of these codes, he estimated that at least five weeks would be needed. You then decided it would be more cost effective to hire a local person from City B who specializes in this area. As a result, as you prepare your schedule and estimate your resource requirements for this project, you should coordinate this work closely with which of the following processes:

    a. Estimate costs
    b. Define activities
    c. Determine budgets
    d. Develop schedule

98. Assume that you were the first person in your company to be PMP® certified and also that you earned a doctorate in project management. People throughout the organization admired your achievements. Based on your success in managing projects, your company now has adopted a management-by-projects philosophy. You have been appointed head of your company's project management office to lead the organization as it transitions to this new way of working. So far, people seem to willingly comply with your demands and requests. In this situation, you are using which type of power?

    a. Legitimate
    b. Expert
    c. Contacts
    d. Referent

99. The nature of project work is such that it inevitably causes stress. Project managers thus need to learn how to cope with and manage stress and understand what stress is and why it is created. Project managers need to note that it can be a positive experience depending on how people perceive stress and should work to mentor team members accordingly. As you strive to become more aware of stress, which one of the following is NOT considered a stress-creating factor that is related to the project environment?

    a. Role ambiguity
    b. Corporate politics
    c. Career development
    d. Selection of team members

100. A member of PMI® is obligated to follow the association's member code of ethics, the purpose of which is to—

    a. Earn and maintain the confidence of team members, colleagues, employees, employers, customers/clients, the public, and the global community
    b. Describe the obligations and expectations associated with membership in PMI®
    c. Set forth one's professional obligations and also one's obligations to PMI®
    d. Describe responsibilities to the profession, to customers, and the public, along with administration of the code of conduct for all those who are certified as project management professionals

101. You are in the early stages of a project to manufacture disposable medical devices. You need a number of engineers including ones with specialties in mechanical, environmental, and systems engineering. In the early stages of this project, your resource pool includes a large number of both junior and senior engineers in the various specialty areas. However, as the project progresses—

    a. Fewer systems engineers will be needed
    b. The resource pool can be limited to those people who are knowledgeable about the project
    c. To complete the project on time, you will continue to require access to a large number of engineers in their specialty areas
    d. You will only need junior level engineers as the senior level people can be used early in the project to mentor and train them

102. A number of approaches can be helpful when estimating resource requirements for activities on a project. Assume you are managing a project and you have already prepared your WBS. When you decomposed your WBS, it has 45 work packages. You then prepared an activity list. Now, you are preparing your schedule and determining your resource requirements. You found there were about 30 activities that you could not estimate with a reasonable degree of confidence, so you and your team decided to use which one of the following approaches to help with these activity resource estimates:

    a. Resource breakdown structure
    b. Published estimating data
    c. Alternatives analysis
    d. Bottom-up estimating

103. To practice effective schedule control, your project team must be alert to any issues that may cause problems in the future. To best accomplish effective schedule control, the team should—

    a. Review work performance information
    b. Allow no changes to the schedule
    c. Update the schedule management plan on a continuous basis
    d. Hold status reviews

104. Functional managers play a vital role in ensuring project success. Since most projects operate in a matrix environment, there is shared authority between project managers and functional managers. Functional managers tend to focus on—

    a. Who will do the task
    b. Why the project manager needs resources
    c. How much time and money is available for the task
    d. Why will the task be done

105. You are a member of the project selection committee using the discounted cash-flow approach. Using this approach, the project is acceptable is the—

    a. Sum of the net present value of all estimated cash flow during the life of the project equals the profit
    b. Net present value of the inflow is greater than the net present value of the outflow by a specified amount or percentage
    c. Gross present value of all future expected cash flow divided by the initial cash investment is greater than one
    d. Payback period occurs by the second year of the project

106. A watch list of low priority risks is documented in the—

    a. Work performance information
    b. Risk register
    c. Fallback plans
    d. Risk response plan

107. You are project manager for a systems integration effort and need to procure the hardware components from external sources. Your subcontracts administrator has told you to prepare a product description, which is referenced in a—

    a. Project statement of work
    b. Contract scope statement
    c. Request for proposal
    d. Contract

108. It often is advantageous to appoint a termination manager in the closing phase of the project and release the project manager so that he or she is available to work on another project. If this is the case, the termination manager should focus attention on all but which one of the following?

    a. Ensuring that documentation is complete
    b. Ascertaining any product support requirements
    c. Receiving formal acceptance of the project from the client
    d. Preparing personnel performance evaluations

109. You are working on a project to upgrade the existing fiber-optic cables in your province. You have determined that a resource can install 25 meters of cable per hour, so the duration required to install 1,000 meters would be 40 hours. This means you are using—

    a. Productivity efficiency factors
    b. Parametric estimating
    c. Analogous estimating
    d. PERT

110. During the stages of team development, your team is in which stage when there is problem solving and interdependence along with achievement and synergy?

    a. Storming
    b. Forming
    c. Norming
    d. Performing

111. When you are about to close a contract, the one place to look for specific procedures for contract closure is in the—

    a. Statement of work in the contract
    b. Terms and conditions in the contract
    c. Procurement management plan
    d. Organizational process assets

112. Today, the primary cause of why projects are not completed on time and within cost and are terminated early is due to—

    a. Contractual issues
    b. Complexity of the project
    c. An increase in the allocated time
    d. Behavioral-oriented reasons

113. Life-cycle phase definitions are different in different industries. For example, all of the following are terms that could be used in the closing phase of a project EXCEPT—

    a. Testing and commissioning
    b. Conversion
    c. Implementation
    d. Final audit

114. Your company is embarking on a project to eliminate defects in its products. You are the project manager for this project, and you have just finished the concept phase. A deliverable for this phase is the—

    a. Project management plan
    b. Statement of work
    c. Project charter
    d. Resource spreadsheet

115. Behavior roles of team members influence the team's process, behavior, and effectiveness. An example of a task-oriented role to perform is that of a(n)—

    a. Harmonizer
    b. Initiator
    c. Devil's advocate
    d. Group observer

116. You are managing a project in which your team members all work in the same geographic location and have worked together previously on many projects. Everyone is aware of the various strengths and weaknesses of the individual team members and their key areas of expertise. As a result—

    a. A kickoff meeting is recommended
    b. Team-building activities will not be needed on your project
    c. You should expect minimal conflicts and changes to occur
    d. Rewards and recognition will be handled smoothly throughout the project

117. Team building should be ongoing throughout the project life cycle. However, it is hard to maintain momentum and morale, especially on large, complex projects that span several years. One guideline to follow to promote team building is to—

    a. Consider every meeting a team meeting, not the project manager's meeting
    b. Conduct team building at specific times during the project through off-site meetings
    c. Engage the services of a full-time facilitator before any team-building initiatives are conducted
    d. Develop the project schedule using the services of a project control officer and then issue it immediately to the team

118. You have been assigned as the project manager for a major project in your company where the customer and key supplier are located in another country. Recently, you traveled to this country, and at the conclusion of a critical design review meeting, which was highly successful, your customer's point of contact gave you an upgrade to a first-class ticket for your trip home since it is a 17-hour flight. Although your company's code of ethics states that gifts cannot be accepted, you know it is common practice in this country to give and to accept gifts, and you do not wish to offend your customer. Furthermore, your supplier also was rewarded for her company's outstanding performance to date at this meeting, and your customer's representative gave her an envelope that contained some extra cash. In this situation—

    a. You can accept the upgrade to first class since it is a common practice to give and accept gifts in this country.
    b. It is acceptable for the supplier to accept the gift since she also lives in the same country.
    c. You and your supplier should decline the gifts since gifts are not permitted by your organization's code of ethics, and your company is the prime contractor.
    d. You should explain to the customer that your company does not allow you to accept the gift, but you will do so this one time as you are building a relationship, but cannot accept gifts in the future.

119. You are leading a team to establish a project selection and prioritization method. The team is considering many different management concerns, including financial return, market share, and public perception. The most important criterion for building a project selection model is—

    a. Capability
    b. Realism
    c. Ease of use
    d. Cost

120. Because risk management is relatively new on projects in your company, you decide to examine and document the effectiveness of risk responses in dealing with identified risks and their root causes. You therefore—

    a. Conduct a risk audit
    b. Hold a risk status meeting
    c. Ensure that risk is an agenda item at regularly scheduled staff meetings
    d. Reassess identified risks on a periodic basis

121. Thinking back to lessons that your company learned from experiences with its legacy information systems during the Y2K dilemma, you finally convinced management to consider systems maintenance from the beginning of the project. However, maintenance should—

    a. Always be included as an activity to be performed during the closeout phase
    b. Have a separate phase in the life cycle for information systems project because 60% to 70% of computer systems' life-cycle costs generally are devoted to maintenance
    c. Not be viewed as part of the project life cycle
    d. Be viewed as a separate project

122. On your systems development project, you noted during a review that the system had less functionality than planned at the critical design review. This note suggests that during the monitor and control risks process you used which following tools and techniques?

    a. Risk reassessment
    b. Variance analysis
    c. Technical performance measurement
    d. Reserve analysis

123. The workaround that you used to deal with a risk that occurred should be documented and included in which following processes?

    a. Report performance and monitor and control risks
    b. Verify scope and perform quality assurance
    c. Direct and manage project execution and perform integrated change control
    d. Direct and manage project execution and monitor and control risks

124. Contested changes are requested changes when the buyer and seller cannot agree on compensation for the change. They are also known as all but which one of the following?

    a. Disputes
    b. Demands
    c. Appeals
    d. Claims

125. A structured review of the seller's progress to deliver project scope and quality within cost and schedule is known as a(n)—

    a. Procurement performance review
    b. Procurement audit
    c. Inspection
    d. Status review meeting

126. Within your company's portfolio, your project is ranked in the top five in terms of importance of the 60 projects under way; however, the number of resources available to you is still limited. You have decided to pilot test the use of critical chain on your project. You have calculated your critical path. You want to ensure that your target finish date does not slip in the critical chain method. To do so you should—

    a. Add a project buffer
    b. Put in three feeding buffers
    c. Determine the drum resource
    d. Manage the total float of the network paths

127. The greatest degree of uncertainty is encountered during which phase of the project life cycle?

    a. Concept
    b. Planning
    c. Implementation
    d. Closeout

128. A team-building approach that facilitates concurrent engineering is—

    a. Matrix management
    b. Fast-tracking
    c. Tight matrix
    d. Task force

129. A number of different decision-making styles can be used in a team environment. When quality and acceptance are both important, which of the following styles should be used?

    a. Command
    b. Consultation
    c. Consensus
    d. Coin flip

130. Historical information is used—

    a. To compare current performance with prospective lessons learned
    b. To prepare the stakeholder management plan
    c. To evaluate the skills and competencies of prospective team members
    d. As an input to develop project charter

131. You are managing a new product development project for a leading pharmaceutical company. Even though he had a nondisclosure agreement in place for two years, your brother recently left a rival firm and told you that his company had to abandon a similar product development project, as it lacked the ability to obtain a key compound. You realize that your company will need this compound to proceed further in its development initiatives. You also realize that, if you are successful in the development of this new product in a timely manner, and if it then is approved quickly by the Food and Drug Administration, then you will be assured of a vice president position in your firm. It is very important to you to be successful on this project. You should therefore—

    a. Use your brother's information and obtain the needed compound immediately
    b. Recognize that this is an example of an inappropriate connection and disclose it immediately to your company's executive management
    c. Suggest that your company hire your brother so that he can make this critical information known to everyone on the team
    d. Realize that while your company does have a code of ethics that it can be interpreted broadly and has no affect on your actual behavior

132. Two team members on your current construction project are engaged in a major argument concerning the selection of project management software. They refuse to listen to each other. The most appropriate conflict resolution approach for you to use in this situation is—

    a. Accommodating
    b. Compromising
    c. Collaborating
    d. Forcing

133. As you use the critical chain method in lieu of the critical path method in developing your schedule, assume you have determined the buffer schedule activities. Your planned activities are scheduled to their latest possible planed start and end dates. Therefore, you are focusing on—

    a. Managing the free float of each network path
    b. Managing the total float of the network paths
    c. Managing remaining buffer durations against the remaining durations of task chains
    d. Managing the total buffer durations against the durations of the task chains

134. A key member of your project has deep technical skills and many years of experience in the company. Although she is not a manager, people respect her and do what she suggests. Of the following types of power, which one does she have?

    a. Legitimate
    b. Reward
    c. Referent
    d. Expert

135. You have been placed in charge of a group of people that is selecting one of three possible projects. The project is to develop an antidote to prickly heat. As you gather in the conference room, many team members already have decided which project selection technique to use. Some prefer IRR, and others argue for BCR. In deciding which method to use, your first step should be to—

    a. Compare and contrast selection techniques and identify the advantages and disadvantage of each
    b. Identify the technique used most often in the company and determine if it is appropriate for this project
    c. Select the method for which most team members have knowledge
    d. Determine the philosophy and wishes of management

136. Before considering a project closed, what document should be reviewed to ensure that project scope has been satisfied?

    a. Project scope statement
    b. Project management plan
    c. Project closeout checklists
    d. Scope management plan

137. There are a number of different earned value rules of performance measurement that can be established as part of the cost management plan. Which one of the following is NOT an example of such a rule?

    a. Code of accounts allocation provision
    b. Formulas to determine the ETC
    c. Earned value credit criteria
    d. Definition of the WBS level

138. All the following elements are organizational process asset updates, resulting from closing a project or phase EXCEPT—

    a. Project files
    b. Project or phase closure documents
    c. Historical information
    d. Final product, service, or result transition

139. You have a conflict on your team but have enough time to resolve it, and you want to maintain future relationships. Thankfully, there is mutual trust, respect, and confidence among the parties involved. You decide to use confronting to resolve this conflict. In using this approach, your first step should be to—

    a. Separate people from the problem
    b. Acknowledge that conflict exists
    c. Establish ground rules
    d. Explore alternatives

140. One way to evaluate the project schedule performance is to—

    a. Use the project management information system (PMIS)
    b. Determine the percent complete of in-progress schedule activities
    c. Establish a schedule change control system
    d. Determine the total float variance

141. Verify scope works hand-in-hand with quality control and generally follows quality control. The tool most commonly used with verifying scope is—

    a. Requirements traceability matrix
    b. Inspection
    c. Project document updates
    d. Variance analysis

142. Research has shown that during the execution phase of the project, the majority of conflicts involve—

    a. Personalities
    b. Project priorities
    c. Cost
    d. Schedule

143. You are a goal-oriented project manager who is more interested in work accomplishment than relationship building. This indicates that you tend to resolve conflicts primarily through the use of—

    a. Smoothing
    b. Compromising
    c. Collaborating
    d. Forcing

144. You are working on a long-term project that has a number of benefits to its customers and users. Therefore, as the project manager, one of your first steps was to identify the stakeholders that were critical to project success. Because this project will need long-term support by your organization once it is completed, key stakeholders are—

    a. Operations managers
    b. Functional managers
    c. Sellers
    d. Business partners

145. Effective communication occurs in groups as well as between individuals and is made up of several key components, such as the purpose of the message, the audience that you are delivering the message to, and the content of the message itself. One important area to consider when working with information distribution is—

    a. The choice of media
    b. How often to distribute the information
    c. The communications plan
    d. The project performance report structure

146. A conflict resolution approach that is NOT considered to be very effective when more than a few players are involved and their viewpoints are mutually exclusive is—

    a. Forcing
    b. Avoiding
    c. Compromising
    d. Collaborating

147. The key output of identify stakeholders that documents identification information, assessment information, and classification is the—

    a. Stakeholder management plan
    b. Communications plan
    c. Stakeholder register
    d. Communications log

148. Improvement to the processes and the product is a goal of project quality management. Assume that after completing a quality audit, you have discovered some gaps/shortcomings in the way that the project team is completing one deliverable. As an output to your perform quality assurance, you would create which following item that feeds directly into the perform integrated change control processes?

    a. Project management plan updates
    b. Risk register
    c. Change requests
    d. Project document updates

149. All the following outputs are from the estimate costs process EXCEPT—

    a. Activity cost estimates
    b. Basis of estimates
    c. Risk register updates
    d. Cost performance baseline

150. As part of your project, you are conducting a major conference. You need to find the most appropriate conference facility. You visit five sites. The most expensive location has said that if you chose them, they will give you free vouchers for your family at one of their resorts. The next lowest-priced site has not offered you any extras; however, the location is fine for your conference. You find yourself in a situation that is an example of—

    a. An inappropriate connection
    b. A conflict of interest
    c. An opportunity to take advantage of a good deal
    d. An illegal action

151. As you prepare to close your project, you know there are inputs to the process of closing a project or phase. Which of the following is an input to the close project or phase process?

    a. Work performance information
    b. Expert judgment
    c. Accepted deliverables
    d. Change requests

152. Managing change to the scope baseline is the main objective of the process of control scope. The scope baseline consists of the following components EXCEPT—

    a. Project scope statement
    b. WBS
    c. WBS dictionary
    d. Scope management plan

153. Unfortunately, your project has produced less-than-expected results. To ensure this doesn't happen again, you conducted a thorough lessons-learned session. You did so because—

    a. You considered it to be a good idea
    b. It is a professional obligation of every project manager to do so
    c. Your organization's project management methodology requires you to do one
    d. It is a best practice used by many organizations

154. Procurement documents are used in the identify stakeholder process because they—

    a. Are an enterprise environmental factor and an input to the process
    b. Are an organizational process asset and an input to the process
    c. Note key stakeholders as parties in the contract
    d. Serve as a way to prioritize and classify stakeholders

155. You completed your stakeholder analysis. How do you want to manage those stakeholders that have a high interest in your project and high power over decisions affecting your project?

    a. Manage them closely
    b. Keep them satisfied
    c. Keep them informed
    d. Monitor them occasionally

156. Change requests include a group of potential changes to a project. Other types of change requests used in projects include all the following EXCEPT—

    a. Preventive actions
    b. Defect repairs
    c. Corrective actions
    d. Preventive requests

157. You are working on a project that needs approval from your City Council and the courts, because the project is one with significant environmental and social impacts. Although many consumer groups are advocates of this project, others are opposed to it. Hearings are scheduled to resolve these issues and to obtain the needed permits to proceed. In preparing your human resource plan, you decide to designate a person as the court liaison, which is an example of a—

    a. Role
    b. Responsibility
    c. Required competency
    d. Ability of the team member to make appropriate decisions

158. The key to successfully managing an international project is to build an effective project team in spite of different cultural backgrounds. This is accomplished by—

    a. Recognizing that people are different
    b. Aligning the personal inputs of different project participants
    c. Establishing the project culture during the executing stage of the project
    d. Identifying basic cultural characteristics and selecting one to follow

159. As a project manager, you recognize the importance of actively engaging key project stakeholders on a project. You have prepared an analysis of your stakeholders early in your project and classified them according to their interest, influence, and involvement in your project. Now that this analysis is complete, you are able to—

    a. Focus on relationships necessary to ensure success
    b. Assess stakeholder legitimacy
    c. Determine the urgency that each stakeholder requires when he or she requests information about the project
    d. Focus on each stakeholder's power relevant to the project

160. Which of the following quality "gurus" noted that when the per-unit costs for prevention and appraisal were less expensive than the costs of nonconformance, resources should be assigned to prevention and appraisal; however, when these costs begin to increase the per unit cost of quality, then a policy should be to maintain quality?

    a. Deming
    b. Shewhart
    c. Juran
    d. Taguchi

161. Benchmarking is a technique used in—

    a. Inspections
    b. Root cause analysis
    c. Plan quality
    d. Perform quality control

162. You are managing a major international project, and your contract requires you to prepare both a project plan and a quality management plan. Your core team is preparing a project quality management plan. The first step in developing this plan is to—

    a. Determine specific metrics to use in quality management
    b. Identify the quality standards for the project
    c. Assess the organization's quality policy and its impact on the project
    d. Identify specific quality management roles and responsibilities for the project

163. You are working on a project that management has decided to terminate early, because the product was rendered obsolete by the introduction of new technology by a competitor. You have awarded a contract for part of the project that will be terminated, and fortunately have a clause that enables you to terminate it for convenience at any time. This means that—

    a. Your contractual obligations are complete once you issue the termination for convenience
    b. You may need to compensate the seller for seller preparations and for any completed or accepted work
    c. You need to compensate the seller only for accepted work that was completed prior to the termination order
    d. Specific rights and responsibilities are determined once the termination order is issued

164. Of the following, which one is NOT true concerning a contract?

    a. It is a legal relationship subject to remedy in the courts.
    b. It can take the form of a complex document or a simple purchase order.
    c. It is a mutually binding legal relationship that obligates the seller to provide specific products, services, or results and obligates the buyer to pay the seller.
    d. It includes a specific contract management plan.

165. All of the following can be used in lieu of the term "bidders conferences" EXCEPT—

    a. Contractor conferences
    b. Prebid conferences
    c. Vendor conferences
    d. Project review meetings

166. During postnegotiation analysis, a negotiation agreement is prepared in the form of a—

    a. Purchase order
    b. Bill of lading
    c. Contract or memorandum of understanding
    d. Revised SOW

167. Your role in the project includes helping to resolve problems; making recommendations regarding priorities; accelerating activities to meet the target schedule; promoting communications among project team members; and helping management monitor the project's progress on a regular basis. Most of the people working on your project are scientists or technical experts. You are working in which of the following types of organizational structures?

    a. Task force
    b. Balanced matrix
    c. Project expeditor
    d. Project coordinator

168. In order for a matrix organizational approach to be successful, the two-boss situation should be resolved. To overcome the two-boss problem, it is important to—

    a. Have the project manager and the functional manager work together to complete performance evaluations
    b. Prepare a responsibility chart to define responsibilities
    c. Guarantee a balance of power between the functional manager and the project manager
    d. Promote interface relationship management

169. The project team directory is an output of which following process?

    a. Develop project team
    b. Acquire project team
    c. Develop human resource plan
    d. Manage project team

170. Documented, authorized directions to reduce the probability of negative consequences associated with project risks are—

    a. Approved preventive actions
    b. Approved corrective actions
    c. Implemented change requests
    d. Work performance information

171. Close procurements is a process that involves—

    a. Customer acceptance and final payment
    b. Administrative closure and archiving records
    c. Final contractor payment and lessons learned
    d. Product verification and acceptance of deliverables

172. As a project manager, not only must you be a leader, but you also must be responsible for the management, administrative, and technical aspects of the project. Which following skill is NOT representative of the skills needed for project leadership/interpersonal relations?

    a. Influencing the organization by sharing power and getting others to cooperate toward common goals
    b. Creating an environment to meet project objectives while offering maximum self-satisfaction related to what people value the most
    c. Helping a group of people bound by a common sense of purpose to work interdependently with each other
    d. Understanding of policies, operating procedures, and regulations of external stakeholder organizations

173. All the following are acceptable forms of change requests EXCEPT—

    a. Direct or indirect
    b. Externally or internally initiated
    c. Vertical or horizontal
    d. Optional or legally/contractually mandated

174. One way to help mitigate personnel risks that may occur during the end of the project is to—

    a. Meet individually with each team member
    b. Provide specific recognition to each team member who has worked on the project
    c. Prepare a staff release plan
    d. Document the time each person is to work on the project in a resource calendar

175. You are conducting a stakeholder analysis on your project. After identifying potential stakeholders, the next step in the process is to—

    a. Determine their desired level of participation
    b. Provide detailed contact information for each identified stakeholder
    c. Perform an assessment to see how each stakeholder might react in certain situations
    d. Identify each stakeholder's impact or support and classify them

176. If a negotiator is away from the known and familiar and is faced with differing customs and ways of doing things, the result may be—

    a. Culture shock
    b. Ethnocentrism
    c. High probability of project failure
    d. Duplicity

177. Although there is no single best method for dealing with conflict, research has shown that the least effective style is—

    a. Competing
    b. Smoothing
    c. Forcing
    d. Withdrawal

178. You are conducting a stakeholder analysis on your project. Your organization uses an approach to classify stakeholders based on their level of authority and their active involvement in the project. This approach is known as—

    a. A power/interest grid
    b. A power/influence grid
    c. An influence/impact grid
    d. A salience model

179. When managing current projects, it is important to use lessons learned from previous projects to improve the organization's project management process. Therefore, in project closing procedures, it is important to review the—

    a. Secondary risks that occurred
    b. Checklists for risk identification
    c. WBS dictionary
    d. Team members' curriculum vitae

180. The basic approach to quality management in projects is to be compatible with which of the following:

    a. Only the nonproprietary methods, such as Six-Sigma, failure mode and effect analysis (FMEA), and total quality management
    b. Only the International Organization for Standardization (ISO)
    c. Proprietary methods, such as those recommended by Deming, Juran, and Crosby
    d. The ISO, proprietary, and nonproprietary methods

181. During a bidders conference, it is important that—

    a. Only qualified sellers participate
    b. All potential sellers are given equal standing
    c. The evaluation criteria for the proposal is used to determine participation
    d. Responses to questions be provided solely to the prospective seller that asked the question

182. One key interpersonal skill used to manage stakeholder expectations is—

    a. Negotiation skills
    b. Building trust
    c. Compromise
    d. Conversation

183. You are the project manager for the construction of an incinerator to burn refuse. Local residents and environmental groups are opposed to this project. Management agrees to move this project to a different location. This is an example of which of the following risk responses?

    a. Passive acceptance
    b. Active acceptance
    c. Mitigation
    d. Avoidance

184. All the following are processes in project procurement management EXCEPT—

    a. Terminate procurements
    b. Administer procurements
    c. Plan procurements
    d. Close procurements

185. Working in the systems integration field, you are primarily responsible for coordinating the work of numerous subcontractors. Your current project is coming to an end. You have 15 major subcontractors as well as a variety of other sellers. Now that you are closing contracts (procurements), you should—

    a. Conduct a trend analysis
    b. Use earned value to assess lessons learned
    c. Ask each contractor to meet with you individually at its own expense
    d. Conduct a procurement audit

186. The risk urgency assessment is a tool and technique used for—

    a. Plan risk responses
    b. Identify risks
    c. Perform qualitative risk analysis
    d. Perform quantitative risk analysis

187. You are working on identifying possible risks to your project to develop a nutritional supplement. You want to develop a comprehensive list of risks that can be addressed later through qualitative and quantitative risk analysis. Although a number of possible techniques can be used, a key information gathering technique used to identify risks is—

    a. Documentation reviews
    b. Probability/impact analysis
    c. Checklist analysis
    d. Brainstorming

188. To identify the success or failure of procurement contracts on your project or on other projects in your organization, you should—

    a. Conduct a procurement audit
    b. Establish a records management system
    c. Use the quality audit in your quality assurance process
    d. Use lessons learned documentation

189. A weighting system can be used for all but which one of the following reasons?

    a. To select a single seller that will be asked to sign a standard contract
    b. To establish a negotiating sequence by ranking all proposals by the weighted evaluation scores that have been assigned
    c. To quantify qualitative data to minimize possible bias
    d. To establish minimum requirements of performance for one or more of the evaluation criteria

190. Research has shown that there are seven major cultural elements that affect projects. In terms of the impact on the project, the cultural element that determines technical and personnel constraints is—

    a. Social organization
    b. Material culture
    c. Political life
    d. Language

191. Your firm specializes in roller-coaster construction. It recently received an RFP to build the world's most "death-defying" roller coaster. You know that such a roller coaster has never been built before and that this would be a high-risk project. Accordingly, what type of contract would you want to be awarded for this project?

    a. Firm-fixed-price
    b. Time-and-materials
    c. Cost-plus-a-percentage-of-cost
    d. Cost-plus-fixed fee

192. Close procurements and close project or phase are similar in that they both require—

    a. That someone other than the project manager manage the activities involved
    b. Verification that no errors occurred at any time while the work was being performed
    c. That a WBS be prepared
    d. Verification that the work and deliverables were transferred and accepted

193. One source of relevant information in the conduct procurements process is seller performance evaluation documentation. This is generated in the—

    a. Close procurements process
    b. Administer procurements process
    c. Conduct procurements process
    d. Plan procurements process

194. For complex procurement items, often contract negotiation can be an independent process. An example of an input if such a process is used is—

    a. Open items list
    b. Approved changes
    c. Documented decisions
    d. Expert judgment

195. Marketplace conditions are an input to which one of the following processes?

    a. Plan procurements
    b. Conduct procurements
    c. Administer procurements
    d. Close procurements

196. Each project can benefit from stakeholder involvement; however, it is in both the project manager's and the team's best interest to ensure that all project stakeholders have positive attitudes toward the project and its goals and objectives. Working as a project manager, you have a number of key stakeholders on your project. The stakeholder that reviews the project for its return on investment, its value, risks, and other attributes is the–

    a. Sponsor
    b. Portfolio manager or the portfolio review board
    c. Director of the project management office
    d. Chief Operating Officer

197. While many different techniques can be used to rate or score proposals, all will use—

    a. A screening system
    b. A weighting system in conjunction with a screening system
    c. Expert judgment and some form of evaluation criteria
    d. Quality ratings and contractual compliance

198. When determining the message that you will deliver to stakeholders, knowing both the content (what you want to say) and your audience is important. Which of the following helps you to understand how others may interpret your message?

    a. Sender-receiver models
    b. Facilitation techniques used in delivery
    c. Negotiation skills
    d. Presentation skills used in the development of the message

199. One of the reasons why it is challenging to work on a virtual team is that e-mail is the primary form of communications. However, words alone typically comprise what percent of the total impact of any message?

    a. 7 percent
    b. 15 percent
    c. 38 percent
    d. 55 percent

200. If any of the ingredients or elements of the communications process are defective in any way, clarity of meaning and understanding will be reduced. An example of a communication macro barrier is—

a. Cultural differences
b. Perceptions
c. Message competition
d. Project jargon and terminology

Answer Sheet

1.	a	b	c	d		26.	a	b	c	d
2.	a	b	c	d		27.	a	b	c	d
3.	a	b	c	d		28.	a	b	c	d
4.	a	b	c	d		29.	a	b	c	d
5.	a	b	c	d		30.	a	b	c	d
6.	a	b	c	d		31.	a	b	c	d
7.	a	b	c	d		32.	a	b	c	d
8.	a	b	c	d		33.	a	b	c	d
9.	a	b	c	d		34.	a	b	c	d
10.	a	b	c	d		35.	a	b	c	d
11.	a	b	c	d		36.	a	b	c	d
12.	a	b	c	d		37.	a	b	c	d
13.	a	b	c	d		38.	a	b	c	d
14.	a	b	c	d		39.	a	b	c	d
15.	a	b	c	d		40.	a	b	c	d
16.	a	b	c	d		41.	a	b	c	d
17.	a	b	c	d		42.	a	b	c	d
18.	a	b	c	d		43.	a	b	c	d
19.	a	b	c	d		44.	a	b	c	d
20.	a	b	c	d		45.	a	b	c	d
21.	a	b	c	d		46.	a	b	c	d
22.	a	b	c	d		47.	a	b	c	d
23.	a	b	c	d		48.	a	b	c	d
24.	a	b	c	d		49.	a	b	c	d
25.	a	b	c	d		50.	a	b	c	d

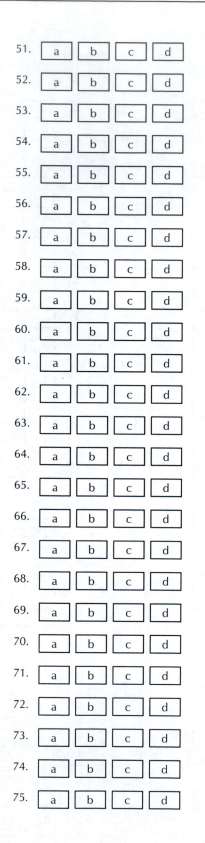

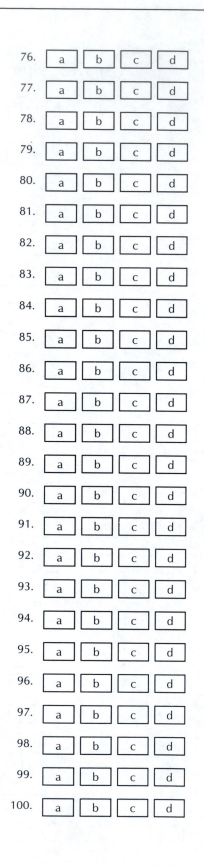

51. a b c d
52. a b c d
53. a b c d
54. a b c d
55. a b c d
56. a b c d
57. a b c d
58. a b c d
59. a b c d
60. a b c d
61. a b c d
62. a b c d
63. a b c d
64. a b c d
65. a b c d
66. a b c d
67. a b c d
68. a b c d
69. a b c d
70. a b c d
71. a b c d
72. a b c d
73. a b c d
74. a b c d
75. a b c d

76. a b c d
77. a b c d
78. a b c d
79. a b c d
80. a b c d
81. a b c d
82. a b c d
83. a b c d
84. a b c d
85. a b c d
86. a b c d
87. a b c d
88. a b c d
89. a b c d
90. a b c d
91. a b c d
92. a b c d
93. a b c d
94. a b c d
95. a b c d
96. a b c d
97. a b c d
98. a b c d
99. a b c d
100. a b c d

101. a b c d   126. a b c d
102. a b c d   127. a b c d
103. a b c d   128. a b c d
104. a b c d   129. a b c d
105. a b c d   130. a b c d
106. a b c d   131. a b c d
107. a b c d   132. a b c d
108. a b c d   133. a b c d
109. a b c d   134. a b c d
110. a b c d   135. a b c d
111. a b c d   136. a b c d
112. a b c d   137. a b c d
113. a b c d   138. a b c d
114. a b c d   139. a b c d
115. a b c d   140. a b c d
116. a b c d   141. a b c d
117. a b c d   142. a b c d
118. a b c d   143. a b c d
119. a b c d   144. a b c d
120. a b c d   145. a b c d
121. a b c d   146. a b c d
122. a b c d   147. a b c d
123. a b c d   148. a b c d
124. a b c d   149. a b c d
125. a b c d   150. a b c d

151.	a	b	c	d
152.	a	b	c	d
153.	a	b	c	d
154.	a	b	c	d
155.	a	b	c	d
156.	a	b	c	d
157.	a	b	c	d
158.	a	b	c	d
159.	a	b	c	d
160.	a	b	c	d
161.	a	b	c	d
162.	a	b	c	d
163.	a	b	c	d
164.	a	b	c	d
165.	a	b	c	d
166.	a	b	c	d
167.	a	b	c	d
168.	a	b	c	d
169.	a	b	c	d
170.	a	b	c	d
171.	a	b	c	d
172.	a	b	c	d
173.	a	b	c	d
174.	a	b	c	d
175.	a	b	c	d

176.	a	b	c	d
177.	a	b	c	d
178.	a	b	c	d
179.	a	b	c	d
180.	a	b	c	d
181.	a	b	c	d
182.	a	b	c	d
183.	a	b	c	d
184.	a	b	c	d
185.	a	b	c	d
186.	a	b	c	d
187.	a	b	c	d
188.	a	b	c	d
189.	a	b	c	d
190.	a	b	c	d
191.	a	b	c	d
192.	a	b	c	d
193.	a	b	c	d
194.	a	b	c	d
195.	a	b	c	d
196.	a	b	c	d
197.	a	b	c	d
198.	a	b	c	d
199.	a	b	c	d
200.	a	b	c	d

Answer Key

1. c. For successful completion of the current and subsequent near-term project phases

Rolling wave planning provides progressive detailing of the work to be accomplished throughout the life of the project. [Planning]

PMI®, *PMBOK® Guide*, 2008, 135

2. d. Confusion of establishing a project in the matrix management environment

During project formation, there is always an element of confusion or lack of clarity regarding the balance of power between the project manager and functional managers. If not resolved, such confusion manifests itself in conflicts regarding technical decisions, resource allocation, and scheduling later in the project. [Executing]

Meredith and Mantel 2009, 220

3. c. Aspirational and mandatory

Aspirational standards are those that we strive to uphold as practitioners and mandatory standards are those that establish firm requirements and may limit behavior. [Professional and Social Responsibility]

PMI®, Code of Ethics and Professional Conduct, Chapter 1

4. a. Delivery requirements

Such classification systems are helpful in both defining and documenting stakeholder needs to meet project objectives. Delivery requirements, along with business requirements and project management requirements, are examples of project requirements. [Planning]

PMI®, *PMBOK® Guide*, 2008, 105

5. b. Organizational process assets

Organizational process assets include formal and informal plans, policies, procedures, and guidelines. As an input to the develop project management plan process, they include project files from past projects such as risk registers, planned response actions, and desired risk impacts. [Planning]

PMI®, *PMBOK® Guide*, 2008, 80

6. a. Administer procurements

The purpose of administer procurements is to ensure that the contractual requirements are met by the seller. This objective is accomplished by monitoring contract performance and performing associated activities. [Monitoring and Controlling]

PMI®, *PMBOK® Guide*, 2008, 335–337

7. a. Expert

Expert power is a function of knowledge, skills, and reputation possessed by the project manager. In such situations, project personnel will do what the project manager wants because they believe he or she knows best and they trust and respect the project manager. [Executing]

Adams et al. 1997, 174–180; Verma 2005, 54

8. b. Quality baseline

The scope, schedule, and cost baselines may be combined into a performance measurement baseline. It then is used as an overall project baseline against which integrated performance is measured. It also is used for earned value measurements. [Planning]

PMI®, *PMBOK® Guide*, 2008, 82

9. c. Job shadowing

Observations are a tool and technique in the collect requirements process. They provide a way to view individuals in their environment and to see how they perform their jobs or tasks and carry out processes. Another term for this approach is job shadowing and usually is done by an observer viewing the user performing his or her job. [Planning]

PMI®, *PMBOK® Guide*, 2008, 109

10. b. Continuous process improvement

Continuous process improvement provides an iterative means for improving the quality of all processes and is part of the definition of quality assurance. Its objective is to reduce waste and eliminate non–value-added activities. [Executing]

PMI®, *PMBOK® Guide*, 2008, 202

11. c. Enhance personal professional competency

According to the skills breakout in the *PMP® Examination Specification*, the skill of gathering, assessing, compiling and documenting information shows up in all tasks but Task 3: enhance personal professional competency. [Professional and Social Responsibility]

PMI, *PMP® Examination Specification*, 2005, 29–30

12. c. $118,000

In this situation, there is a $10,000 overrun from the target costs. Applying the 80/20 share ratio, the seller's share of the overrun is 20% of $10,000 or a minus $2,000 in earned fee. The final value of this procurement is $110,000 in costs plus a seller fee of $10,000 less $2,000 or $8,000 for a final price of $118,000. [Monitoring and Controlling]

Fleming 2003, 92

13. c. Document the specific responsibilities of each stakeholder in the perform integrated change control process.

Configuration management is an integral part of the perform integrated change control process. It is necessary because projects by their nature involve changes. The integrity of baselines must be maintained by releasing only approved changes for incorporation into the project's products or services and by maintaining their related configuration and planning documentation. [Monitoring and Controlling]

PMI®, *PMBOK® Guide*, 2008, 93

14. b. Procurement management plan

The procurement management plan describes how all aspects of the procurement process—from developing the contract SOW to describing closeout procedures—will be managed. This includes the type of contracts to be used, preparation of independent estimates, actions to be taken by the procurement department and the project management team, location of standardized procurement documents, management of multiple providers, and coordination of the procurement with other aspects of the project. [Planning]

PMI®, *PMBOK® Guide*, 2008, 324

15. a. Scope, quality, schedule, budget, and risk

The constraints include, but are not limited to scope, budget (cost), quality, resources, and risk. [Monitoring and Controlling]

PMI®, *PMBOK® Guide*, 2008, 6

16. b. Strategic plans

The configuration management knowledge base is part of the organizational corporate knowledge base for storing and retrieving information. It contains the versions and baselines of all company policies, practices, procedures, and standards, as well as pertinent project documents. [Initiating]

PMI®, *PMBOK® Guide*, 2008, 98

17. d. A quality audit

A quality audit is a tool and technique for the perform quality assurance process. It is primarily used to determine whether the project team is complying with organizational and project policies, processes, and procedures. [Executing]

PMI®, *PMBOK® Guide*, 2008, 204

18. c. Informal

Requested changes are an input to the perform integrated change control process. Although occurring in many forms, they must be formal requests developed within the context of a change control system consisting of documented procedures. [Monitoring and Controlling]

PMI®, *PMBOK® Guide*, 2008, 93–95

19. d. Allowing automatic approval of changes

Allowing for automatic approval of defined changes is a function of the change control system, not configuration management. Configuration management ensures that the description of the project product is correct and complete. [Monitoring and Controlling]

PMI®, *PMBOK® Guide*, 2008, 95

20. d.   Change control meetings

The project management methodology is a key tool and technique for integrated change control to aid the team in implementing this process for the project. [Monitoring and Controlling]

PMI®, *PMBOK® Guide*, 2008, 98

21. b.   Adds business value as it links to business and project objectives

The requirements traceability matrix is a table that links requirements to their origin and traces them throughout the life cycle. This approach helps to ensure that each requirement adds value as it links to the business and project objectives. It also tracks requirements during the life cycle to help ensure that the requirements listed in the requirements document are delivered at the end of the project. [Planning]

PMI®, *PMBOK® Guide*, 2008, 111

22. a.   Schedule

In many projects, there is a rush to finish due to schedule slippages that develop in the execution/implementation phase. Delays in schedules become cumulative and impact the project most severely in the final stages of the project. While there are other sources of conflict, such as personalities and cost, attempting to finish on time is always on everyone's mind. [Closing]

Verma 1996, 103 and105

23. b.   Configuration management system

The formal configuration management system is an important tool and technique for scope control and is part of the project management information system for the project. [Monitoring and Controlling]

PMI®, *PMBOK® Guide*, 2008, 94–95

24. a.   Root cause analysis

Determining the root cause of the problem means to determine the origin of the problem. What may appear to be the problem on the surface is often revealed, after further analysis, not to be the real cause of the problem. One technique used in root cause analysis is to ask "why" five times. [Executing]

PMI®, *PMBOK® Guide*, 2008, 208

25. d. Scope verification typically precedes quality control

Scope verification focuses on accepting project deliverables, and to be accepted, they must meet the requirements. Quality control is one way to ensure that the requirements have been met, which is why quality control typically is done before scope verification. [Monitoring and Controlling]

PMI®, *PMBOK® Guide*, 2008, 123

26. a. The company requires a continuous stream of projects to survive

Organizations that rely on products for their revenue must constantly be introducing new products into the marketplace as old products are removed. Ideally, this should be an overlapping process to maintain balanced or increasing revenue over time. The closure phase evaluates the efforts of the total system and serves as input to the conceptual phase for new projects and systems. It also has an impact on other ongoing projects with regard to identifying priorities. [Closing]

Kerzner 2006, 67–69

27. d. Cost of quality

The term cost of quality deals with conformance costs (money spent to avoid failures) and nonconformance costs (money spent because of failures). [Executing]

PMI®, *PMBOK® Guide*, 2008, 195

28. a. Identifies project assumptions

Project assumptions, which should be enumerated in the project scope baseline, are areas of uncertainty, and therefore, potential causes of project risk. [Planning]

PMI®, *PMBOK® Guide*, 2008, 284

29. c. Prototypes

Prototypes are used to obtain early feedback on requirements by providing a working model of the expected product before it is built. Stakeholders then can experiment with this model rather than discussing abstract representations of requirements. This approach supports progressive elaboration, because it is used in iterative cycles of mock-up creation, user experimentation, feedback generation, and prototype revision. [Planning]

PMI®, *PMBOK® Guide*, 2008, 109

30. a. Tools from perform quality control and plan quality

The tools used within project quality management are used across all three processes: plan quality, perform quality assurance, and perform quality control. [Executing]

PMI®, *PMBOK® Guide*, 2008, 204

31. d. Continuously monitor the project

The monitor and control project work process is performed throughout the project and includes collecting, measuring, and disseminating performance information and assessing measurements and trends to effect process improvement. Continuous monitoring is important because it provides insight into the project's health, highlighting areas requiring special attention. [Monitoring and Controlling]

PMI®, *PMBOK® Guide*, 2008, 89

32. d. Determine whether the project should continue to the next phase

The review at the end of a project phase is called a phase-end review. The purpose of this review is to determine whether the project should continue to the next phase for detecting and correcting errors while they are still manageable and for ensuring that the project remains focused on the business need it was undertaken to address. [Initiating]

PMI®, *PMBOK® Guide*, 2008, 78

33. c. Celebrating

During the adjourning stage of team development, the emphasis is on tasks and relationships that promote closure and celebration. There is recognition and satisfaction as the theme is moving on and separation. Management skills involve evaluating, reviewing, and improving, while leadership qualities are celebrating and bringing closure. [Executing]

Verma 1997, 40

34. b. At –$200, the physical progress is being accomplished at a slower rate than is planned, indicating an unfavorable situation.

Schedule variance is calculated: EV – PV or $1,000 – $1,200 = –$200. Because the SV is negative, physical progress is being accomplished at a slower rate than planned. [Monitoring and Controlling]

Kerzner 2006, 616

35. b. Document impartiality at the beginning of the project

A PMP® must *continuously* review his or her impartiality and objectivity, not just at the beginning of the project. Furthermore, a PMP® does not need to document impartiality because it is an inherent part of the PMI® Code of Ethics and Professional Conduct. [Professional and Social Responsibility]

PMI®, Code of Ethics and Professional Conduct, Chapter 4

36. d. Place emphasis on improving the productivity by which work was being performed

CPI = EV / AC and measures the efficiency of the physical progress accomplished compared to the baseline. A CPI of 0.84 means that for every dollar spent, you're only receiving 84 cents of progress. Therefore, you should focus on improving the productivity by which work is being performed. [Monitoring and Controlling]

Kerzner 2006, 618

37. c. Project scope statement

The project scope statement describes in detail the deliverables and what work must be done to prepare them. Ancillary results are also considered deliverables and are included in the project scope statement. They include items such as project management reports and documentation. Deliverables in the project scope statement may be described at a summary level or in a detailed way. [Planning]

PMI®, *PMBOK® Guide*, 2008, 115

38. c. Expert judgment

According to the *PMBOK® Guide*, the only tool and technique listed for close project or phase is expert judgment. [Closing]

PMI®, *PMBOK® Guide*, 2008, 101

39. a. Project charter

Outputs of the define scope project are the project scope statement and project document updates that include updates to the stakeholder register, requirements documentation, and the requirements traceability matrix. [Planning]

PMI®, *PMBOK® Guide*, 2008, 116–117

40. c. (Percent complete) (budget at completion)

Multiplying the percent complete by the budget at completion, or the total budget for the project, is the simplest formula to use. The 50/50 rule, or the more conservative 0/100 rule, can eliminate the necessity for the continuous determination of percent complete. After the percent complete is determined, it can be plotted against time expended. [Monitoring and Controlling]

Kerzner 2006, 623–624

41. a. Commence as scheduled and stated in the staffing management plan

Training is a tool and technique for the develop project team process. The requirements and schedule for the develop project team process should be stated in the staffing management plan. Project team members' skills can be developed as part of the project activities. [Executing]

PMI®, *PMBOK® Guide*, 2008, 232

42. b. Milestone method

The milestone method is especially helpful for work packages of long duration that have interim milestones or a functional group of activities with a milestone established at specific control points. In the EV system, value is earned when the milestone is completed. In such cases, a budget is assigned to the milestone rather than to the work packages. [Monitoring and Controlling]

Kerzner 2006, 623–624

43. c. Estimate at completion

EAC is the total amount of money estimated to be spent on the project. It can be calculated several different ways. However, the basic approach is to add the actual costs to date plus the estimate to complete. [Monitoring and Controlling]

Kerzner 2006, 626

44. d. Links the project to the ongoing work of the organization

The project charter not only authorizes a project, it shows how the project is linked to the strategic plan of the organization. Among other things, the project charter documents the business need for the project and describes the current understanding of the customer's requirements. [Initiating]

PMI®, *PMBOK® Guide*, 2008, 77

45. c. Tell your CEO that this action by your company constitutes a violation of the PMI® Code of Ethics and Professional Conduct in the section titled: "Qualifications, Experience, and Performance of Professional Services"

The PMI® Code of Ethics and Professional Conduct specifically states that a PMP® is responsible for providing accurate and truthful representation to the public. This obligation applies to the preparation of estimates concerning costs, services, and expected results. Therefore, such an action in terms of not using the audited overhead rates would violate this responsibility. [Professional and Social Responsibility]

PMI®, Code of Ethics and Professional Conduct, Chapter1

46. d. Schedule updates

An output from schedule control, project management plan updates (including updates to the schedule baseline and schedule management plan) occur after the prospective changes have been analyzed and the appropriate changes have been selected and processed through the change control system. Reviewing lessons learned and analyzing prospective changes can help improve the quality of project management services. [Professional and Social Responsibility]

PMI®, Code of Ethics and Professional Conduct, Chapter 1

47. c. EAC = [Actual to date] + [all remaining work to be done at the planned cost including remaining work in progress]

This formula assumes that all of the remaining work is independent of the burn rate incurred thus far. AC is $2,900 + [$500 + $1,000]. The $500 is from Activity B, and the $1,000 is from Activity C. [Monitoring and Controlling]

Kerzner 2006, 629

48. a. Certain deliverables or subprojects will be accomplished far into the future

Many projects involve deliverables or subprojects that will be accomplished far into the future and cannot be specified in detail at the current time. In these situations, the project management team typically waits until the deliverable or subproject is clarified so that details for that portion of the WBS can be developed. Then a rolling wave planning approach can be used. [Planning]

PMI®, PMBOK® Guide, 2008, 120

49. c. Distribute information process

The lessons learned process is an output of the distribute information process. It is an element of the organizational process assets updates. It describes the importance of lessons learned sessions throughout the project life cycle with the project team and key stakeholders by identifying lessons learned and compiling, formalizing, and storing them throughout the project's duration. [Executing]

PMI®, *PMBOK® Guide*, 2008, 261

50. a. Influencing the factors that create change to the cost performance baseline to ensure that the change is beneficial

The control costs process is also concerned with ensuring that requested changes have been acted upon and with managing actual changes if and when they occur. [Monitoring and Controlling]

PMI®, *PMBOK® Guide*, 2008, 179

51. b. Douglas McGregor

Douglas McGregor's (Theory X & Y) views illustrate that leadership is not the property of a single individual factor, but is a complex relationship among these variables. [Executing

Cleland and Ireland 2006, 383

52. b. 100% rule

The WBS is a deliverable-oriented, hierarchical decomposition of work to be done by the project team. Sometimes called the 100% rule, it shows the total of the work at the lowest levels must roll up to the higher levels so that nothing is left out and no extra work is done. [Planning]

PMI®, *PMBOK® Guide*, 2008, 121

53. c. Decline the invitation since it is a conflict of interest

By participating in a CAPM® exam writing session, you would know which questions would be on the exam. Given your organization helps people prepare for the exam, your knowledge, if used in your training materials, would give your company an unfair advantage. [Professional and Social Responsibility]

PMI®, Conflict of Interest Policy, 2; PMI®, Code of Ethics and Professional Conduct, Chapter 1

54. c. $6.42 million

Test: $5M + $960K + $460K = $6.42M; Don't Test: $7M. [Planning]

PMI®, *PMBOK® Guide*, 2008, 299

55. b. Herzberg's Motivator-Hygiene Theory

Frederick Herzberg's Motivator-Hygiene Theory asserts that some job factors lead to satisfaction, whereas others can only prevent dissatisfaction. There are two types of factors associated to the motivation process: hygiene factors, which relate to the work environment, and motivators, which relate to the work itself. Hygiene factors, if provided appropriately, can prevent dissatisfaction, while motivating factors can increase job satisfaction and are more permanent. [Executing]

Verma 1996, 56, 64–65

56. a. Work performance measurements

The project's work performance measurements should document and communicate the CV, SV, CPI, and SPI for the WBS components of specific work packages and control accounts. [Monitoring and Controlling]

PMI®, *PMBOK® Guide*, 2008, 181–183

57. d. The calculated CV, SV, CPI, and SPI values for WBS components are documented and communicated to stakeholders

Performance measurements involve calculating CV, SV, CPI, and SPI values for WBS components. These values show critical project performance information that must be documented and communicated, most typically through performance reports. [Monitoring and Controlling]

PMI®, *PMBOK® Guide*, 2008, 187

58. d. Customer request

Projects can be authorized as a result of a market demand, organizational need, customer request, technological advance, legal requirement, ecological impact, or a social need. The new industrial park is an example of a project authorized because of a customer request. [Initiating]

PMI®, *PMBOK® Guide*, 2008, 76–77

59. a. A recommendation for changing current practice should be made and defended.

It is important to capture lessons learned, which then can be used on subsequent projects. The more detailed the lessons the better. However, when it comes to personnel lessons learned, the information should be handled in a confidential manner. [Closing]

Meredith and Mantel 2009, 566–568

60. c. List of risks requiring near-term responses

The primary outputs from identify risks are initial entries into the risk register. It ultimately contains outcomes of other risk management processes as they are conducted. As an output of identify risks, the risk register should contain a list of identified risks, a list of potential responses, root causes that gave rise to the identified risks, and updated risk categories. [Planning]

PMI®, *PMBOK® Guide*, 2008, 288

61. b. David McClelland

According to David McClelland, there are three relevant motives or needs in work situations: the need for achievement, power, and affiliation or association. This theory supports the view that there is a high correlation between achievement, affiliation, and power motives and the overall motivation and performance achieved in a project. [Executing]

Verma 1996, 68

62. b. Monte Carlo analysis

Simulation is a tool and technique for develop schedule by which multiple project durations with different sets of activity assumptions are calculated. Monte Carlo analysis is the most commonly used simulation technique. [Planning]

PMI®, *PMBOK® Guide*, 2008, 156

63. b. Performance measurement baseline

The PMB is a time-phased budget plan used to measure performance. It is formed by the budgets assigned to schedule cost accounts and the applicable indirect accounts. It typically integrates scope, schedule, and cost parameters of the project, but it may also include technical and quality parameters. [Monitoring and Controlling]

PMI®, *PMBOK® Guide*, 2008, 178

64. d. Resource breakdown structure

Schedule data for the project schedule may include a number of items, but at a minimum it should include the schedule milestones, schedule activities, activity attributes, and documentation of all identified assumptions and constraints. [Planning]

PMI®, *PMBOK® Guide*, 2008, 159

65. b. Expectancy Theory

Developed by Victor Vroom, Expectancy Theory asserts that people think seriously about how much effort they should put into a task before doing it. Motivation is linked to an expectation of a favorable outcome. It is based on the concept that people choose behaviors that they believe will lead to desired rewards and outcomes. [Executing]

Verma 1996, 73

66. c. Work performance information

Work performance information is an input to control schedule. [Planning]

PMI®, *PMBOK® Guide*, 2008, 161

67. d. Project performance appraisals

Lessons learned during the manage project team process can include project organization charts, position descriptions, staffing management plans, ground rules, conflict management techniques, and recognition events that were particularly useful. Performance appraisals document and record an individual project team member's contribution to the project measured against what was expected of him or her, and are a tool and technique used in this process. [Monitoring and Controlling]

PMI®, *PMBOK® Guide*, 2008, 241

68. a. Configuration status accounting

Configuration status accounting captures, stores, and accesses the needed configuration information to manage products and product information effectively. [Monitoring and Controlling]

PMI®, *PMBOK® Guide*, 2008, 93

69. c. Final output of activity definition is described as schedule activities.

In the create WBS process, final output is described as deliverables or tangible items. [Planning]

PMI®, *PMBOK® Guide*, 2008, 121–122

70. c. A separate planning effort completed before the time management processes

The work involved in performing the six time management processes is preceded by a separate planning effort during the develop project management plan process, in which the schedule management plan is prepared. It is a subsidiary plan to the project management plan. [Planning]

PMI®, *PMBOK® Guide*, 2008, 130

71. d. Activity name

The components for each activity evolve over time. In the initial stages of the project, they include the activity ID, WBS ID, and the activity name. Later, additional information is added as other time management processes are performed. [Planning]

PMI®, *PMBOK® Guide*, 2008, 130

72. b. An external dependency

Some dependencies are external ones, and they involve a relationship between project activities and nonproject activities. In sequencing activities, the project management team must determine which dependencies are external as they are usually outside of the team's control. [Planning]

PMI®, *PMBOK® Guide*, 2008, 140

73. d. Run chart

A run chart shows the history and pattern of process variation. It shows trends, variation, declines, or improvements in a process over time. One benefit of using a run chart is it provides data that is usable in trend analysis. [Monitoring and Controlling]

PMI®, *PMBOK® Guide*, 2008, 211–212

74. **c. Carrying out the work**

The implementation phase (carrying out the work) is when all interfaces affecting the project must be coordinated and when the product or service of the project is created. In most projects, this phase is also when most of the project budget is spent. [Executing]

PMI®, *PMBOK® Guide*, 2008, 17

75. **b. Accommodating**

Open subordination is much like an accommodating style of conflict management in which negotiators are more concerned about positive relationships than about substantive outcomes. It can dampen hostility, increase support and cooperation, and foster more interdependent relationships. This is an effective style for project managers to use with support staff. [Executing]

Verma 1996, 157

76. **b. Authorized procurement administrator**

The buyer, through its authorized procurement administrator, is responsible for providing the seller with formal written notice of contract completion. The procurement administrator does so when the seller has met all contractual requirements as articulated in the contract. [Closing]

PMI®, *PMBOK® Guide*, 2008, 344

77. **b. Confront Kim and ask her whether she provided her management with the local chapter's membership list.**

While it seems possible that Kim may be using the membership list to assist her company, you cannot be certain until you talk with Kim and obtain additional information. This should be your first step. In your discussion, you should point out the need to take responsibility for one's actions and the importance of maintaining high standards of integrity and professional conduct. Once Kim explains whether or not she has used the membership list inappropriately, you can then determine whether other actions are warranted. [Professional and Social Responsibility]

PMI®, Code of Ethics and Professional Conduct, Chapter 1

78. b. Project charter

Although the project charter cannot stop conflicts from arising, it can provide a framework to help resolve them because it describes the project manager's authority to apply organizational resources to project activities. [Initiating]

Meredith and Mantel, 2009, 164; PMI®, *PMBOK® Guide*, 2008, 77–78

79. d. Checklists

Checklists are used to verify that a set of required steps has been performed during the plan quality process. [Monitoring and Controlling]

PMI®, *PMBOK® Guide*, 2008, 201 and 207

80. c. Zero-sum game analysis

Achieving mutual gain during negotiations means that each party benefits by the decisions made. A zero-sum game is where one side wins at the expense of the other. [Executing]

Ward 2008, 474

81. d. Control charts

Control charts help determine whether or not a process is stable or has predictable performance. This function of control charts is achieved through the graphical display of results over time to determine whether differences in the results are created by random variations or are unusual events. In a manufacturing environment, such charts are used to track repetitive actions such as manufactured lots. In a project management environment, they can be used to monitor processes such as cost and schedule variances, number requirements, and errors in project documents. [Monitoring and Controlling]

PMI®, *PMBOK® Guide*, 2008, 209

82. b. Structure

Supportive behavior is relationship oriented and is the extent to which the leader engages in two-way communication, listens, provides support and encouragement, facilitates interaction, and involves the followers in decision making. Structure connotes a certain level of rigidity and inflexibility and is not a term associated with supportive behavior. [Executing]

Verma 1996, 216–217

83. d. A defined integrated change control process

If the recommended corrective or preventive actions require a change to any of the project's baselines, a change request should be prepared in conformance with the perform integrated change control process. [Monitoring and Controlling]

PMI®, *PMBOK® Guide*, 2008, 213–214

84. a. Help anticipate how problems occur

Flowcharts depict the interrelationship of a system's components and show the relationships among process steps. All process flowcharts show activities, decision points, and the order of processing. As such, they aid the team in anticipating where quality problems might occur, which helps in developing approaches for dealing with these potential problems. [Monitoring and Controlling]

PMI®, *PMBOK® Guide*, 2008, 198 and 210

85. a. Change master

During the execution stage, the major attributes and emphasis is on realignment. The leadership style/blend that is most appropriate is one who is a decision maker, balances work and fun, is trustworthy, and promotes the team concept and synergy. [Executing]

Verma 1996, 225

86. c. Adjusting leads and lags

Corrective action is anything that brings expected future schedule performance in line with the project plan. Adjusting leads and lags is one of many tools available to identify the cause of variation. [Monitoring and Controlling]

PMI®, *PMBOK® Guide*, 2008, 163

87. c. That while you want to manage this project, your resume cannot be submitted at this time

According to the PMI® Code Ethics and of Professional Conduct, you are responsible for providing accurate, truthful advertising and representations concerning qualifications, experience, and performance of services. This also applies in terms of responsibilities to customer and the public. Your resume, therefore, should not be submitted. [Professional and Social Responsibility]

PMI®, Code of Ethics and Professional Conduct, Chapter 1

88. c. A manager at a level appropriate to funding the project

Projects are authorized by someone external to the project. A project initiator or sponsor at a level appropriate to funding the project should issue the project charter. Because the project charter provides the project manager with the authority to apply organizational resources to project activities, it should not be issued by the project manager. Functional managers should have approval authority. [Initiating]

PMI®, *PMBOK® Guide*, 2008, 74

89. a. Smoothing

Smoothing emphasizes areas of agreement while avoiding points of disagreement. It tends to keep peace only in the short term. [Executing]

Adams et al. 1997, 181–189; Verma 1996, 118

90. c. Does not require 100% inspection of the components to achieve a satisfactory inference of the population

The application of the statistical concept of probability has proven, over many years in many applications, that an entire population of products need not be inspected, if the sample selected conforms to a normal distribution of possible outcomes (the "bell" curve). [Monitoring and Controlling]

PMI®, *PMBOK® Guide*, 2008, 198 and 212

91. c. Use a control chart

A control chart is one of the seven basic tools of quality control that determines whether or not a process is stable or has predictable performance. It also illustrates how a process behaves over time. When a process is within acceptable limits, it need not be adjusted; when it is outside acceptable limits, an analysis should be conducted to determine the reasons why. [Monitoring and Controlling]

PMI®, *PMBOK® Guide*, 2008, 209

92. c. It is used primarily for Level 1 of the WBS.

Estimates are categorized according to accuracy and the time to prepare them. Grassroots or engineering-type estimates are definite estimates and are prepared when detailed information about the project is available. These estimates would use the work package level of the WBS. [Planning]

Kerzner 2006, 542

93. a. Cost management plan

The management and control of costs focuses on variances. Certain variances are acceptable and others, usually those falling outside a particular range, are unacceptable. The actions taken by the project manager for all variances are described in the cost management plan. [Planning]

PMI®, *PMBOK® Guide*, 2008, 166

94. c. Norming; high supportive and low directive approach

There are four stages of team development: forming, storming, norming, and performing. Different leadership styles in terms of the amount of required supportive and directive behavior are appropriate when a team is in a certain development stage. At the norming stage, the third stage in team development, leaders provide high support and low direction. [Executing]

Verma 1996, 227

95. a. The procurement administrator is reassigned

The close procurements process looks at the administration of the contract and not the people responsible or involved with the contract. [Closing]

PMI®, *PMBOK® Guide*, 2008, 341

96. a. Histogram

In a histogram, or bar chart, each column represents an attribute or characteristic of a problem or situation. The height of each column represents the relative frequency of the characteristic. [Monitoring and Controlling]

PMI®, *PMBOK® Guide*, 2008, 210

97. a. Estimate costs

The estimate activity resource process involves estimating the type and quantities of material, people, equipment, and supplies needed to perform each activity. This means close coordination with the estimate costs process is needed. [Planning]

PMI®, *PMBOK® Guide*, 2008, 141–142

98. a. Legitimate

Legitimate power is formal authority based on a person's position within the organization. It comes with the right to give orders or make requests. [Executing]

Adams et al. 1997, 174–180; Verma 1996, 233

99. a. Role ambiguity

The main sources of stress are grouped into four categories of stress-creating factors: those related to roles and relationships, those related to the job environment, personal factors, and factors related to the project environment or climate. Role ambiguity is an example of factors related to roles and responsibilities. It occurs when an individual is not clear about his or her job responsibilities. [Monitoring and Controlling]

Verma 1996, 180, 183–184

100. a. Earn and maintain the confidence of team members, colleagues, employees, employers, customers/clients, the public, and the global community

PMI® is dedicated to the development and promotion of the field of project management. Accordingly, it has a member code of ethics, which defines and clarifies ethical responsibilities for all PMI® members, present and future. PMI® members pledge to: maintain high standards of integrity and professional conduct, accept responsibility for one's actions, enhance professional capabilities, practice with fairness and honesty, and encourage others in the profession to act in an ethical and professional manner. [Professional and Social Responsibility]

PMI®, Code of Ethics and Professional Conduct, Chapter 1

101. b. The resource pool can be limited to those people who are knowledgeable about the project

Resource calendars are an input to the estimate activity resource process. They are used to estimate resource use. Early in a project, the resource pool might include people at different levels of expertise in large numbers, but as the project progresses, the resource pool then can be limited to those people who are knowledgeable about the project because of their work on it. [Planning]

PMI®, PMBOK® Guide, 2008, 143

102. d. Bottom-up estimating

When an activity cannot be estimated with a reasonable degree of confidence, the work then needs to be decomposed into more detail. The estimates then are aggregated into a total quantity for each of the activity's resources through a bottom-up approach. These activities may or may not have dependencies between them. However, when dependencies exist, this pattern of use of resources then is documented in the estimated requirements for each activity. [Planning]

PMI®, *PMBOK® Guide*, 2008, 144

103. a. Review work performance information

Performance reports provide information on schedule performance, such as which planned dates have been met and which have been missed, thereby alerting the team to problems that may arise in the future. [Monitoring and Controlling]

PMI®, *PMBOK® Guide*, 2008, 161–162

104. a. Who will do the task

In a matrix environment, project resources (that is, people) come from the functional departments. Therefore, it is the functional manager's job to identify who will work on specific project tasks. [Executing]

Verma 1995, 56–57

105. b. Net present value of the inflow is greater than the net present value of the outflow by a specified amount or percentage

The discounted cash-flow approach—or the present value method—determines the net present value of all cash flow by discounting it by the required rate of return. The impact of inflation can be considered. Early in the life of a project, net cash flow is likely to be negative because the major outflow is the initial investment in the project. If the project is successful, cash flow will become positive. [Initiating]

Meredith and Mantel 2009, 47

106. b. Risk register

The monitor and control risks process includes keeping track of those risks on the watch list. Low-priority risks are inputs to the monitor and control risks process and are documented in the risk register. Other inputs that are part of the risk register include identified risks and risk owners, agreed-upon risk responses, specific implementation actions, symptoms and warning signs of risk, residual and secondary risks, and the time and cost contingency reserves. [Monitoring and Controlling]

PMI®, *PMBOK® Guide*, 2008, 309

107. a. Project statement of work

The project statement of work describes in a narrative form the products or services that the project will deliver. It references the product scope description as well as the business need and strategic plan. [Initiating]

PMI®, *PMBOK® Guide*, 2008, 75

108. d. Preparing personnel performance evaluations

The project manager, or whoever supervised the work of each individual team member, should prepare the personnel evaluations because they have an intimate understanding of the work performed by the team members. The termination manager focuses instead on the administrative requirements of termination and the environment within which the project will be operating if it is continued in any way. [Closing]

Meredith and Mantel 2009, 565–566

109. b. Parametric estimating

Parametric estimating uses statistical relationships between historical data and other variables to calculate an estimate for activity parameters such as cost, budget, and duration. The activity durations then are determined quantitatively by multiplying the quantity of work to be performed by the labor hours per unit of work. This technique can produce higher levels of accuracy depending on the reliability of the data in the model. [Planning]

PMI®, *PMBOK® Guide*, 2008, 150

110. d. Performing

The performing stage of team development is noted by a theme of productivity. Management skills involve consensus building, problem solving, decision making, and rewarding, with leadership shown through management by walking around, stewardship delegation, mentoring, being a futurist, and being a cheerleader/champion. [Executing]

Verma 1997, 40

111. b. Terms and conditions in the contract

The terms and conditions can prescribe specific procedures for the various ways that a contract could be terminated. [Closing]

PMI®, *PMBOK® Guide*, 2008, 341

112. d. Behavioral-oriented reasons

Behavioral reasons, rather than quantitative reasons, account for more project terminations because it is much more difficult to manage people than things. Issues such as poor morale, poor human relations, poor labor productivity, and no commitment from those involved in the project combine to thwart project success in many industries. [Closing]

Kerzner 2006, 432

113. c. Implementation

Regardless of the many terms used across many industries, implementation would be considered a term used in the executing phase. [Closing]

Kerzner 2006, 69–71; PMI®, *PMBOK® Guide*, 16–17

114. c. Project charter

This document signifies official sanction by top management and starts the planning, or development, phase. The project charter formally recognizes the existence of the project and provides the project manager with the authority to apply organizational resources to project activities. [Initiating]

PMI®, *PMBOK® Guide*, 2008, 77–78

115. b. Initiator

To initiate something means to get it started. In the project environment, that typically means a task. [Executing]

Verma 1997, 78–79

116. a. A kickoff meeting is recommended

Even if team members already know one another, a kickoff meeting should still be held because the meeting always includes more than meeting team members. Specific expectations for the project can be discussed as well as other important administrative details. It also gives people an opportunity to express their commitment to the project's objectives. [Executing]

Verma 1997, 135

117. a. Consider every meeting a team meeting, not the project manager's meeting

Team building should be made as important a part of every project activity as possible. Given that there are many meetings on projects, each team member should be made to feel that it is his or her meeting and not just the project manager's meeting. This will foster greater contribution by each team member. [Executing]

Verma 1997, 137

118. c. You and your supplier should decline the gifts since gifts are not permitted by your organization's code of ethics, and your company is the prime contractor.

Many companies have written policies addressing gift acceptance. Regardless of company policy and the country in which one is working, it is usually advisable to avoid all gifts. [Professional and Social Responsibility]

Kerzner 2006, 335

119. b. Realism

The model should reflect the objectives of the company and its managers; consider the realities of the organization's limitations on facilities, capital, and personnel; and include factors for risk—the technical risks of performance, cost, and time and the market risk of customer rejection. [Initiating]

Meredith and Mantel 2009, 41

120. a. Conduct a risk audit

The risk audit is a tool and technique in the monitor and control risks process with two purposes: to assess the effectiveness of risk responses and to evaluate the effectiveness of the risk management process. [Monitoring and Controlling]

PMI®, *PMBOK® Guide*, 2008, 310

121. c. Not be viewed as part of the project life cycle

Projects are efforts that occur within a finite period of time with clearly defined beginnings and ends. Maintenance is ongoing and of an indefinite duration. A maintenance activity, such as revision of an organization's purchasing guidelines, may be viewed as a project but is a separate and distinct undertaking from the initial project that generated it. [Initiating]

Frame 2003, 16–17

122. c. Technical performance measurement

Technical performance measurement compares technical accomplishments to date to the project plan's schedule of technical achievement. Deviation, such as less functionality than planned at a key milestone, can help to forecast the degree of success in achieving the project scope. [Monitoring and Controlling]

PMI®, *PMBOK® Guide*, 2008, 311

123. d. Direct and manage project execution and monitor and control risks

A workaround is a form of corrective action, which is an output of the monitor and control risks processes. [Monitoring and Controlling]

PMI®, *PMBOK® Guide*, 2008, 312

124. b. Demands

Claims administration is a tool and technique in the administer procurements process. When the buyer and seller can't agree, this is also called claims, disputes, or appeals and should be documented, processed, monitored, and managed throughout the contract life cycle. [Monitoring and Controlling]

PMI®, *PMBOK® Guide*, 2008, 339

125. a. Procurement performance review

Such a review is a tool and technique of the administer procurements process, which can include a review of seller-prepared documentation and buyer inspections. It seeks to identify performance successes or failures, progress with respect to the contract statement of work and contract noncompliance. [Monitoring and Controlling]

PMI®, *PMBOK® Guide*, 2008, 338

126. a. Add a project buffer

After the critical path is identified using the critical chain method, resource availability is entered and a resource-limited schedule results. This schedule may have an altered critical path that is known as the critical chain. The critical chain method adds duration buffers that are nonwork schedule activities to manage uncertainty. To protect the target finish date from slippage on the critical chain, a project buffer is placed at the end of the critical chain. [Planning]

PMI®, *PMBOK® Guide*, 2008, 155

127. a. Concept

The greatest degree of uncertainty about the future is encountered during the concept phase, or at the start of the project. The direction of the project is determined in this phase, and the decisions made have the greatest influence on scope, quality, time, and cost of the project. [Initiating]

Wideman 1992, II-1; PMI®, *PMBOK® Guide*, 2008, 17

128. c. Tight matrix

A "tight" matrix refers to team members working in close proximity to one another. Studies have demonstrated that such a team approach facilitates concurrent engineering by having designers working next to manufacturing engineers to help ensure that the project is designed in such a manner that it is also cost-effective to manufacture. [Executing]

Verma 1997, 169

129. b. Consultation

Project managers tend to use four basic decision styles: command, consultation, consensus, and coin flip or random. If acceptance and quality are both important, the consultation style is preferred. It allows for some involvement of team members but allows project managers to maintain control over the final decision. In this style, team members are free to express their opinions, but the project manager makes the final decision. [Executing]

Verma 1997, 178

130. d. As an input to develop project charter

Historical information is an organizational process access in the develop project charter process. Reviewing past projects often helps a person to prepare cost and schedule estimates and a risk management plan for the current project. [Initiating]

PMI®, *PMBOK® Guide*, 2008, 78

131. b. Recognize that this is an example of an inappropriate connection and disclose it immediately to your company's executive management

Connections with family or friends may be able to provide you with information or influence by which you could gain personally in a business situation. Examples include receiving insider information, receiving privileged information, or opening doors that you could not open by yourself, at least without difficulty. As a project manager, one should abide by the PMI® Code of Ethics and Professional Conduct and conduct oneself in an ethical manner. [Professional and Social Responsibility]

Kerzner 2006, 335

132. d. Forcing

Forcing, using power or dominance, implies the use of position power to resolve conflict. It involves imposing one viewpoint at the expense of another. Project managers may use it when time is of the essence, when an issue is vital to the project's well-being, or when they think they are right based on available information. Although this approach is appropriate when quick decisions are required or when unpopular issues are an essential part of the project, it puts project managers at risk. [Executing]

Adams et al. 1997, 181–189; Verma 1996, 157

133. **c.** **Managing remaining buffer durations against the remaining durations of task chains**

The purpose of the critical chain method is to modify the project schedule to account for limited resources. The schedule is built using duration estimates with required dependencies and defined constraints as inputs. Then, the critical path is calculated and resource availability is entered, which means there is a resource-limited schedule with an altered critical path. Buffers protect the critical chain from slippage and the size of each buffer accounts for the uncertainty in the duration of the chain of dependent tasks that lead up to the buffer. This method then focuses on managing the remaining buffer durations against the remaining duration of task chains. [Planning]

PMI®, *PMBOK® Guide*, 2008, 155

134. **d.** **Expert**

Expert power is earned/personal power when project personnel admire an individual's skills and want to follow him or her as a role model. In such situations, people willingly comply with the demands of such a person. [Executing]

Adams et al. 1997, 174–180; PMI®, *PMBOK® Guide*, 2008, 409–413

135. **d.** **Determine the philosophy and wishes of management**

Any selection technique must be evaluated based on the degree to which it will meet the organization's objective for the project. Management generally establishes the organization's objective; therefore, management's wishes must be identified first. Then the most appropriate model to support management's wishes should be selected. [Initiating]

Meredith and Mantel 2009, 43

136. **b.** **Project management plan**

Project scope is measured against the project management plan. The project scope statement and scope baseline are subsets of the project management plan. However, the whole plan and all the baselines (cost and schedule) need to be met in addition to part of the scope. [Closing]

PMI®, *PMBOK® Guide*, 2008, 99

137. a. Code of accounts allocation provision

Three recognized earned value rules of performance measurement are to (1) determine the ETC calculation to be used on the project, (2) establish how EV credit will be determined (for example, 0–100, 0–50–100, and so on), and (3) define the WBS level at which the earned value analysis will be performed. [Planning]

PMI®, *PMBOK® Guide*, 2008, 166

138. d. Final product, service, or result transition

All the elements are outputs of the close project or phase processes, but the final product, service, or result transition is not part of the organizational process assets. It is an output on its own and speaks for the product that the project was created to produce. [Closing]

PMI®, *PMBOK® Guide*, 2008, 101–102

139. b. Acknowledge that conflict exists

In order to address conflict, people must recognize and acknowledge that conflict exists. Next, it is important to establish common ground or shared goals and then to separate people from the problem. [Executing]

Verma 1996, 126

140. d. Determine the total float variance

Variance analysis is a common tool and technique in the control schedule process and involves comparing target schedule dates with actual/forecast start and finish dates. After the variance is known, the project team can take corrective action to bring performance in line with the plan. [Monitoring and Controlling]

PMI®, *PMBOK® Guide*, 2008, 162

141. b. Inspection

Inspection includes activities associated with measuring, examining, and verifying whether work and deliverables meet requirements. The requirements traceability matrix is an input of the verify scope process, the project document updates are an output of the verify scope process, and the variance analysis is a tool of the control scope process. [Monitoring and Controlling]

PMI®, *PMBOK® Guide*, 2008, 162

142. d. Schedule

In a study of sources of conflict by project life-cycle phase, seven different causes of conflict were identified. In the execution phase, the highest-ranking sources of conflict were schedules, technical issues, and manpower, in this order, followed by priorities, administrative procedures, cost, and personalities. [Executing]

Verma 1996, 103–104

143. d. Forcing

Forcing and majority rule are represented by a strong desire to satisfy oneself rather than to satisfy others. It involves imposing one viewpoint at the expense of another and is characterized by a win-lose outcome in which one party overwhelms the other. [Executing]

Adams et al. 1997, 181–189; Verma 1996, 118 and 120

144. a. Operations managers

Operations managers are stakeholders on many projects. They deal with producing and managing the products and services of the organization. On many projects, they are responsible after the project is complete and has been formally handed off to them for incorporating the project into normal operations and providing long-term support for the product. [Initiating]

PMI®, *PMBOK® Guide*, 2008, 27

145. a. The choice of media

The choice of media, or the way you deliver the information is as important as what you say. [Executing]

PMI®, *PMBOK® Guide*, 2008, 258

146. d. Collaborating

Collaborating involves bringing people with opposing views together to reach a solution. When there are too many people involved, it is more difficult to reach a solution, given the multiplicity of perspectives. When the parties involved have mutually exclusive views, forcing or compromise must be used. [Executing]

Adams et al. 1997, 181–189; Verma 1996, 119

147. c. Stakeholder register

The stakeholder register is the main output of identifying stakeholders and contains all the details related to the stakeholders. [Initiating]

PMI®, *PMBOK® Guide*, 2008, 250

148. c. Change requests

Quality improvements to processes and procedures as well as the project and product will result in a change request that will be reviewed and evaluated using the perform integrated change control process. [Executing]

PMI®, *PMBOK® Guide*, 2008, 205

149. d. Cost performance baseline

Cost performance baseline is an output from the determine budget process. [Planning]

PMI®, *PMBOK® Guide*, 2008, 173–174

150. b. A conflict of interest

A conflict of interest is a situation where an individual is placed in a compromising position where the individual can gain personally based upon the decisions that are made. As project managers, one is expected to abide by the PMI® Code of Ethics and Professional Conduct, which makes it clear that project managers should conduct themselves in an ethical manner. [Professional and Social Responsibility]

Kerzner 2006, 334–335

151. c. Accepted deliverables

Accepted deliverables is an input to the close project or phase. The other selections are inputs or tools/techniques for other processes. [Closing]

PMI®, *PMBOK® Guide*, 2008, 341

152. d. Scope management plan

The scope management plan is not part of the scope baseline. However, both the scope baseline and the scope management plan are a part of the larger project management plan. [Monitoring and Controlling]

PMI®, *PMBOK® Guide*, 2008, 122 and 125

153. b. It is a professional obligation of every project manager to do so

Lessons learned should be conducted on all projects. However, to ensure that failure or less-than-expected results are minimized on subsequent projects, PMI® asserts that every project manager is professionally obligated to do so. [Professional and Social Responsibility]

PMI®, Code of Ethics and Professional Conduct, Chapter 2

154. c. Note key stakeholders as parties in the contract

Procurement documents are an input to the identify stakeholder process. If the project results from a procurement activity or is based on an established contract, the parties in the contract are key project stakeholders. Others, such as suppliers, are also stakeholders and should be added to the stakeholder list. [Initiating]

PMI®, *PMBOK® Guide*, 2008, 247

155. a. Manage them closely

You must manage them closely. High-power/high-interest stakeholders who do not support your project could have a devastating effect on your project. [Initiating]

PMI®, *PMBOK® Guide*, 2008, 249

156. b. Defect repairs

Defect repairs are the approved change requests that have been implemented by the project team during project execution. [Executing]

PMI®, *PMBOK® Guide*, 2008, 92

157. a. Role

The human resource plan documents roles and responsibilities on the project. A role is the portion of the project for which a person is responsible. The court liaison is an example of such a role on a project. [Planning]

PMI®, *PMBOK® Guide*, 2008, 222

158. b. Aligning the personal inputs of different project participants

Intercultural team building is a major challenge on an international project. To align the personal inputs of the different project participants, a project manager must be aware of and appreciate cross-cultural differences and create an intercultural environment to capitalize on these differences. [Professional and Social Responsibility]

Verma 1997, 105

159. a. Focus on relationships necessary to ensure success

The project manager has limited time on a project and his or her time should be used as efficiently and effectively as possible. Therefore, after classifying stakeholders in terms of their interest, influence, and involvement on the project, the project manager can focus on relationships necessary to ensure project success through the development of a stakeholder management strategy. [Initiating]

PMI®, *PMBOK® Guide*, 2008, 246

160. c. Juran

This concept is attributed to Joseph Juran. The implication here is that zero defects may not be a practical solution since the total cost of quality would not be minimized. [Planning]

Kerzner 2006, 839

161. c. Plan quality

The other tools and techniques used during plan quality are cost-benefit analysis, cost of quality, control charts, benchmarking design of experiments, statistical sampling, flowcharting, proprietary quality methodologies, and additional quality planning tools (brainstorming, affinity diagrams, force field analysis, nominal group technique, matrix diagrams, and prioritization matrixes). [Planning]

PMI®, *PMBOK® Guide*, 2008, 197

162. c. Assess the organization's quality policy and its impact on the project

The quality policy includes the overall intentions and direction of the organization with regard to quality, as formally expressed by top management. When the performing organization lacks a formal quality policy or if the project involves multiple performing organizations, as in a joint venture, the project management team must develop a quality policy for the project as an input to its quality planning. [Planning]

PMI®, *PMBOK® Guide*, 2008, 194

163. b. You may need to compensate the seller for seller preparations and for any completed or accepted work

Early termination of a contract is a special case of procurement closure. The rights and responsibilities of the parties are contained in a termination clause of the contract. Typically such a clause allows the buyer to terminate the whole contract or a portion of it for cause or convenience at any time. In doing so, the buyer may need to compensate the seller for seller's preparations and for any completed and accepted work related to the terminated part of the contract. [Executing]

PMI®, *PMBOK® Guide*, 2008, 342

164. d. It includes a specific contract management plan.

A contract management plan is not part of a contract. It is used to identify how the contract will be administered. [Executing]

PMI®, *PMBOK® Guide*, 2008, 333

165. d. Project review meetings

Bidders conferences are meetings with prospective sellers prior to the preparation of a bid or proposal to answer questions and clarify issues. They are a tool and technique in the conduct procurements process. Project review meetings are conducted to assess project performance and status. [Executing]

PMI®, *PMBOK® Guide*, 2008, 331

166. c. Contract or memorandum of understanding

Upon completion of negotiations, a final contract or memorandum of understanding is prepared and signed by all parties. [Professional and Social Responsibility]

Verma 1996, 153

167. c. Project expeditor

A variation of the weak matrix organizational structure, the project expeditor has no formal authority to make or enforce decisions. Nonetheless, the project expeditor must be able to persuade those in authority to maintain the project's visibility so that resources will be allocated as needed to meet the project's schedule, budget, and quality constraints. This approach is considered to be effective in high-technology and research and development environments. [Planning]

Verma 1995, 153–154

168. a. Have the project manager and the functional manager work together to complete performance evaluations

In a matrix environment, project team members have two bosses: the project manager and their functional line manager. People often are unclear as to which manager is their "real" boss, as there may be a continual shifting balance of power. To avoid confusion regarding performance issues, it is a good idea to have the project manager and functional line manager complete the individual's performance evaluations. Also, greater weight should be given to the project manager's assessment for the time the individual actually worked on the project. [Planning]

Verma 1995, 178

169. b. Acquire project team

The project team directory is part of project staff assignments, an output from the acquire project team process. Other outputs are resource availability and updates to the staffing management plan. [Planning]

PMI®, *PMBOK® Guide*, 2008, 229

170. a. Approved preventive actions

As a specific subset of change requests, approved preventive actions are an input to the direct and manage project execution process. Such actions reduce the probability of negative consequences associated with project risks. Approved corrective actions, on the other hand, focus on ensuring that future performance will conform to the project management plan. [Executing]

PMI®, *PMBOK® Guide*, 2008, 87

171. d. Product verification and acceptance of deliverables

This process supports the close project or phase process. It involves completing and settling each contract, including resolving open items, and closing each contract. It involves verifying that all work and deliverables were acceptable. [Closing]

PMI®, *PMBOK*® *Guide*, 2008, 341

172. d. Understanding of policies, operating procedures, and regulations of external stakeholder organizations

Successful project managers have expertise and skills in leadership/interpersonal areas, project management/administration areas, and technical areas. The understanding of policies, operating procedures, and regulations of external stakeholder organizations is representative of project management/administrative skills. [Executing]

Verma 1995, 27

173. c. Vertical or horizontal

Requested changes are an output of the direct and manage project execution process and may change project scope, modify policies or procedures, modify the project cost or budget, or revise the project schedule. [Executing]

PMI®, *PMBOK*® *Guide*, 2008, 87

174. c. Prepare a staff release plan

The staff release plan determines the method and timing of releasing team members. Morale is improved if there are smooth transitions for the staff to upcoming projects. This staff release plan also helps to mitigate human resource risks that may occur. It is part of the staffing management plan, which is part of the human resource plan. [Planning]

PMI®, *PMBOK*® *Guide*, 2008, 224

175. d. Identify each stakeholder's impact or support and classify them

The second step in the stakeholder analysis process is to identify the potential impact or support each stakeholder could generate and then to classify the stakeholders to define an approach or strategy. [Initiating]

PMI®, *PMBOK*® *Guide*, 2008, 248–249

176. a. Culture shock

Project managers should focus on execution and not on convincing others of their own values or work styles. Project managers need to be aware of possible culture shock so they can recognize its effects during negotiations. [Professional and Social Responsibility]

Verma 1996, 150

177. d. Withdrawal

Confronting is considered to be the most effective resolution style, followed in order by compromising, smoothing, forcing or competing, and withdrawal. Forcing is detrimental because it leads to win-lose outcomes and creates hard feelings. Withdrawing tends to minimize conflict; however, it fails to resolve the conflict, which only causes further problems in the future. [Executing]

Adams et al. 1997, 181–189; Verma 1996, 139

178. b. A power/influence grid

Although a number of classification models are available to help prioritize the key stakeholders, the power/influence grid groups stakeholders based on their level of authority or power and their active involvement or interest in the project. [Initiating]

PMI®, *PMBOK® Guide*, 2008, 249

179. b. Checklists for risk identification

Checklists are a tool and a technique of the identify risks process and include risks encountered on similar, previous projects identified through the lessons learned process. The project team should review the checklist as part of the identify risks process as well as during closeout, adding to the list as necessary, based on its experience, to help others in the future. [Planning]

PMI®, *PMBOK® Guide*, 2008, 287

180. d. The ISO, proprietary, and nonproprietary methods

Project quality management is intended to be compatible with other existing quality methods, and PMI® recognizes modern quality management methods are compatible completely with project management. [Executing]

PMI®, *PMBOK® Guide*, 2008, 190

181. b. All potential sellers are given equal standing

Bidders conferences are conducted to ensure all prospective sellers have a clear and common understanding of the requirements. They are not used to prequalify vendors. Thus, all vendors are treated equally. [Executing]

PMI®, *PMBOK® Guide*, 2008, 331

182. b. Building trust

Building trust helps to build the foundation of the relationship and helps with the delivery of both good and bad news to stakeholders. [Executing]

PMI®, *PMBOK® Guide*, 2008, 264

183. d. Avoidance

Risk avoidance is taking an action to eliminate the threat posed by an adverse risk. [Planning]

PMI®, *PMBOK® Guide*, 2008, 303–305

184. a. Terminate procurements

Termination is a word used to define a contract ending through mutual agreement or breach. [Closing]

PMI®, *PMBOK® Guide*, 2008, 342

185. d. Conduct a procurement audit

The procurement audit attempts to identify successes and failures relative to the procurement process. Uncovering and reporting both successes and failures can contribute to the project management knowledge base and improve the quality of project management services. A procurement audit should be conducted as part of the close procurements process. [Closing]

PMI®, *PMBOK® Guide*, 2008, 343

186. c. Perform qualitative risk analysis

Risks that may occur in the near-term need urgent attention. The purpose of the risk urgency assessment is to identify those risks that have a high likelihood of happening sooner rather than later. [Planning]

PMI®, *PMBOK® Guide*, 2008, 293

187. d. Brainstorming

Brainstorming is a frequently used information-gathering technique for risk identification because it enables the project team to develop a list of potential risks relatively quickly. Project team members, or invited experts, participate in the session. Risks are easily categorized for follow-on analysis. [Planning]

PMI®, *PMBOK® Guide*, 2008, 286

188. a. Conduct a procurement audit

A procurement audit is a tool and technique for the close procurements process. It is conducted to identify the strengths and weaknesses of all aspects of the contract. As such, knowledge gained from the process can be used in other contracts. [Closing]

PMI®, *PMBOK® Guide*, 2008, 343

189. d. To establish minimum requirements of performance for one or more of the evaluation criteria

Weighting systems are developed and used to help select the best vendor. By assigning a numerical weight to each evaluation criteria, the buyer can emphasize one area as being more important than another. It is a tool and technique in the conduct procurements process. [Executing]

PMI®, *PMBOK® Guide*, 2008, 329 and 331

190. b. Material culture

Material culture refers to tangible elements such as the physical objects or technologies created by people and often involves tools, skills, work habits, and work attitudes. Knowledge of material culture is especially helpful to project managers as they plan for negotiations with international partners. [Professional and Social Responsibility]

Verma 1996, 150

191. c. Cost-plus-a-percentage-of-cost

This contract type reimburses an allowable cost of services performed plus an agreed-upon percentage of the estimated cost as profit. It provides the least risk to the seller. [Planning]

PMI®, *PMBOK® Guide*, 2008, 322–324

192. d. Verification that the work and deliverables were transferred and accepted

The processes of closing a contract and closing out a project or project phase both involve verifying and documenting that the results are accepted as satisfactory. Archiving relevant documents is also an important element in both processes. [Closing]

PMI®, *PMBOK® Guide*, 2008, 100 and 342

193. b. Administer procurements process

During administer procurements, seller performance is assessed and documented. Such information can be used by the buyer to determine whether the seller should be used on another contract. [Executing]

PMI®, *PMBOK® Guide*, 2008, 340

194. a. Open items list

Issues or an open item list are examples of inputs if contract negotiation is an independent process. Outputs are documented decisions. While contract negotiations may need to be a separate process for complex procurements, for simple procurement items, the terms and conditions of the contract can be fixed and nonnegotiable. [Executing]

PMI®, *PMBOK® Guide*, 2008, 333

195. a. Plan procurements

Enterprise environmental factors, which include marketplace conditions that the team needs to be aware of as it develops its plans for purchases and acquisition, are an input to the plan procurements process. [Planning]

PMI®, *PMBOK® Guide*, 2008, 320

196. b. Portfolio manager or the portfolio review board

Portfolio managers are the people responsible for the high-level governance of the projects and programs in the organization. The portfolio review board is composed of executives who are responsible for selecting projects to implement and for determining whether or not projects should be continued. As part of the review process, the return on investment, value, risks, and other attributes of each project is considered. [Initiating]

PMI®, *PMBOK® Guide*, 2008, 25

197. c. Expert judgment and some form of evaluation criteria

Expert judgment is a tool and technique used in the conduct procurements process. It, along with some form of evaluation criteria as developed during the plan procurements process, is used to rate and score proposals. This does not preclude the use of other tools and techniques, but these tools and techniques are used in all evaluations. [Executing]

PMI®, *PMBOK® Guide*, 2008, 331–332

198. a. Sender-receiver models

Sender-receiver models help with identifying the feedback loops as well as the barriers to communication and the filters that change the interpretation of the message. [Executing]

PMI®, *PMBOK® Guide*, 2008, 258

199. a. 7 percent

Albert Meharabian, a researcher, discovered that words alone account for just 7 percent of any message's impact. Vocal tones account for 38 percent of the impact and facial expressions account for 55 percent of the message. Thus, project managers should use nonverbal ingredients to complement verbal message ingredients whenever possible and should recognize that nonverbal factors generally have more influence on the total impact of a message than verbal factors. The lack of nonverbal cues makes project communications in a virtual environment more challenging. [Executing]

Verma 1996, 19

200. a. Cultural differences

Certain words, terms, or gestures have different meanings and interpretations in different cultures. When working in a multicultural environment, sensitivity to differing interpretations of words, terms, or gestures is important to promote good communication. [Professional and Social Responsibility]

Verma 1996, 24–25

APPENDIX
STUDY MATRIX

Overview

In 2000, the Project Management Institute (PMI®) published *the Project Management Professional (PMP®) Role Delineation Study (RDS)*. This study serves as the foundation for the PMP® certification examination. The study also serves as the foundation for our 200-question practice test.

The role delineation study identified six broad performance domains and determined how the 175 questions on the PMP® exam would be distributed according to these domains*. The distribution is as follows:

I	Initiating	11%
II	Planning	23%
III	Executing	27%
IV	Monitoring and Controlling	21%
V	Closing	9%
VI	Professional and Social Responsibility	9%

The matrix beginning on page 359 identifies each practice test question according to its performance domain and its knowledge area in the *PMBOK® Guide*.

The matrix is designed to help you—

- Assess your strengths and weaknesses in each of the performance domains

- Identify those areas in which you need additional study before you take the PMP® exam

Here is an easy way to use the matrix:

---

* PMI® distributes 25 pretest questions across the six domains in any way that it deems appropriate for the purpose of "testing" the questions.

Step 1   Circle all the questions you missed on the practice test in Column 1.

Step 2   For each circled question, note the corresponding process or professional and social responsibility in Column 2.

Step 3   To determine whether any patterns emerge indicating weak areas, tally the information you obtained from the matrix.

Step 4   To ensure that you have a good understanding of the major management processes that define a particular knowledge area, including the input, tools and techniques, and output, refer to the appropriate knowledge area in the *PMBOK® Guide*.

The last column in the matrix is provided for your notes.

Study Matrix

Practice Test Question Number	Performance Domain (Process or Professional and Social Responsibility)	Knowledge Area	Study Notes
1	Planning	Integration	
2	Executing	Integration	
3	Professional and Social Responsibility		
4	Planning	Scope	
5	Planning	Integration	
6	Monitoring and Controlling	Procurement	
7	Executing	Integration	
8	Planning	Integration	
9	Planning	Scope	
10	Executing	Quality	
11	Professional and Social Responsibility		
12	Monitoring and Controlling	Procurement	
13	Monitoring and Controlling	Integration	
14	Planning	Procurement	
15	Monitoring and Controlling	Integration	
16	Initiating	Integration	
17	Executing	Quality	
18	Monitoring and Controlling	Integration	
19	Monitoring and Controlling	Integration	

Practice Test Question Number	Performance Domain (Process or Professional and Social Responsibility)	Knowledge Area	Study Notes
20	Monitoring and Controlling	Integration	
21	Planning	Scope	
22	Closing	Integration	
23	Monitoring and Controlling	Integration	
24	Executing	Quality	
25	Monitoring and Controlling	Scope	
26	Closing	Integration	
27	Executing	Quality	
28	Planning	Risk	
29	Planning	Scope	
30	Executing	Quality	
31	Monitoring and Controlling	Integration	
32	Initiating	Integration	
33	Executing	Human Resources	
34	Monitoring and Controlling	Time	
35	Professional and Social Responsibility		
36	Monitoring and Controlling	Time	
37	Planning	Scope	
38	Closing	Integration	
39	Planning	Scope	
40	Monitoring and Controlling	Cost	

Practice Test Question Number	Performance Domain (Process or Professional and Social Responsibility)	Knowledge Area	Study Notes
41	Executing	Human Resources	
42	Monitoring and Controlling	Cost	
43	Monitoring and Controlling	Cost	
44	Initiating	Integration	
45	Professional and Social Responsibility		
46	Professional and Social Responsibility		
47	Monitoring and Controlling	Cost	
48	Planning	Scope	
49	Executing	Communications	
50	Monitoring and Controlling	Cost	
51	Executing	Human Resources	
52	Planning	Scope	
53	Professional and Social Responsibility		
54	Planning	Risk	
55	Executing	Human Resources	
56	Monitoring and Controlling	Cost	
57	Monitoring and Controlling	Cost	
58	Initiating	Integration	
59	Closing	Integration	
60	Planning	Risk	
61	Executing	Human Resources	

Practice Test Question Number	Performance Domain (Process or Professional and Social Responsibility)	Knowledge Area	Study Notes
62	Planning	Time	
63	Monitoring and Controlling	Cost	
64	Planning	Time	
65	Executing	Human Resources	
66	Planning	Time	
67	Monitoring and Controlling	Human Resources	
68	Monitoring and Controlling	Integration	
69	Planning	Time	
70	Planning	Time	
71	Planning	Time	
72	Planning	Time	
73	Monitoring and Controlling	Quality	
74	Executing	Integration	
75	Executing	Human Resources	
76	Closing	Procurement	
77	Professional and Social Responsibility		
78	Initiating	Integration	
79	Monitoring and Controlling	Quality	
80	Executing	Human Resources	
81	Monitoring and Controlling	Quality	
82	Executing	Human Resources	

Practice Test Question Number	Performance Domain (Process or Professional and Social Responsibility)	Knowledge Area	Study Notes
83	Monitoring and Controlling	Quality	
84	Monitoring and Controlling	Quality	
85	Executing	Human Resources	
86	Monitoring and Controlling	Time	
87	Professional and Social Responsibility		
88	Initiating	Integration	
89	Executing	Communications	
90	Monitoring and Controlling	Quality	
91	Monitoring and Controlling	Quality	
92	Planning	Cost	
93	Planning	Cost	
94	Executing	Human Resources	
95	Closing	Procurement	
96	Monitoring and Controlling	Quality	
97	Planning	Time	
98	Executing	Human Resources	
99	Monitoring and Controlling	Human Resources	
100	Professional and Social Responsibility		
101	Planning	Time	
102	Planning	Time	

Practice Test Question Number	Performance Domain (Process or Professional and Social Responsibility)	Knowledge Area	Study Notes
103	Monitoring and Controlling	Time	
104	Executing	Human Resources	
105	Initiating	Integration	
106	Monitoring and Controlling	Risk	
107	Initiating	Integration	
108	Closing	Integration	
109	Planning	Time	
110	Executing	Human Resources	
111	Closing	Procurement	
112	Closing	Integration	
113	Closing	Integration	
114	Initiating	Integration	
115	Executing	Human Resources	
116	Executing	Human Resources	
117	Executing	Human Resources	
118	Professional and Social Responsibility		
119	Initiating	Integration	
120	Monitoring and Controlling	Risk	
121	Initiating	Integration	
122	Monitoring and Controlling	Risk	
123	Monitoring and Controlling	Risk	

Practice Test Question Number	Performance Domain (Process or Professional and Social Responsibility)	Knowledge Area	Study Notes
124	Monitoring and Controlling	Procurement	
125	Monitoring and Controlling	Procurement	
126	Planning	Time	
127	Initiating	Integration	
128	Executing	Human Resources	
129	Executing	Human Resources	
130	Initiating	Integration	
131	Professional and Social Responsibility		
132	Executing	Human Resources	
133	Planning	Time	
134	Executing	Human Resources	
135	Initiating	Integration	
136	Closing	Integration	
137	Planning	Cost	
138	Closing	Integration	
139	Executing	Human Resources	
140	Monitoring and Controlling	Time	
141	Monitoring and Controlling	Scope	
142	Executing	Human Resources	
143	Executing	Communications	
144	Initiating	Communications	
145	Executing	Communications	

Practice Test Question Number	Performance Domain (Process or Professional and Social Responsibility)	Knowledge Area	Study Notes
146	Executing	Communications	
147	Initiating	Communications	
148	Executing	Quality	
149	Planning	Cost	
150	Professional and Social Responsibility		
151	Closing	Integration	
152	Monitoring and Controlling	Scope	
153	Professional and Social Responsibility		
154	Initiating	Communications	
155	Initiating	Communications	
156	Executing	Integration	
157	Planning	Time	
158	Professional and Social Responsibility		
159	Initiating	Communications	
160	Planning	Quality	
161	Planning	Quality	
162	Planning	Quality	
163	Executing	Procurement	
164	Executing	Procurement	
165	Executing	Procurement	
166	Professional and Social Responsibility		
167	Planning	Human Resources	

Practice Test Question Number	Performance Domain (Process or Professional and Social Responsibility)	Knowledge Area	Study Notes
168	Planning	Human Resources	
169	Planning	Human Resources	
170	Executing	Integration	
171	Closing	Procurement	
172	Executing	Communications	
173	Executing	Integration	
174	Planning	Time	
175	Initiating	Communications	
176	Professional and Social Responsibility		
177	Executing	Communications	
178	Initiating	Communications	
179	Planning	Risk	
180	Executing	Quality	
181	Executing	Procurement	
182	Executing	Communications	
183	Planning	Risk	
184	Closing	Procurement	
185	Closing	Procurement	
186	Planning	Risk	
187	Planning	Risk	
188	Closing	Procurement	
189	Executing	Procurement	
190	Professional and Social Responsibility		
191	Planning	Procurement	

Practice Test Question Number	Performance Domain (Process or Professional and Social Responsibility)	Knowledge Area	Study Notes
192	Closing	Integration	
193	Executing	Procurement	
194	Executing	Procurement	
195	Planning	Procurement	
196	Initiating	Communications	
197	Executing	Procurement	
198	Executing	Communications	
199	Executing	Communications	
200	Professional and Social Responsibility		

REFERENCES

Acker, David D. *Skill in Communication: A Vital Element in Effective Management.* 2nd ed. Ft. Belvoir, Va.: Defense Systems Management College, 1992.

Adams, John R., and Bryan W. Campbell. *Roles and Responsibilities of the Project Manager.* Upper Darby, Penn.: Project Management Institute, 1982.

Adams John R., et al. *Principles of Project Management.* Newton Square, Penn.: Project Management Institute, 1997.

AGCA (*see* The Associated General Contractors of America).

The Associated General Contractors of America. *Construction Planning and Scheduling.* Washington, D.C.: The Associated General Contractors of America, 1994.

Bell, Chip R. *Managing as Mentors: Building Partnerships for Learning.* San Francisco: Berrett-Koehler, 1996.

Bicheno, John. *The Quality 50.* Melbourne, Australia: Nestadt Consulting Party, 1994.

Bockrath, Joseph T. *Contracts, Specifications, and Law for Engineers.* 4th ed. New York: McGraw-Hill, 1986.

Brake, Terence, Danielle Medina Walker, and Thomas (Tim) Walker. *Doing Business Internationally: The Guide to Cross-Cultural Success.* 2nd ed. Boston: McGraw-Hill, 2002.

Cable, Dwayne, and John R. Adams. *Organizing for Project Management.* Upper Darby, Penn.: Project Management Institute, 1982.

Carter, Bruce, Tony Hancock, Jean-Marc Morin, and Ned Robins. *Introducing RISKMAN Methodology: The European Project Risk Management Methodology.* Oxford, England: NCC Blackwell, 1994.

Cavendish, Penny, and Martin D. Martin. *Negotiating and Contracting for Project Management.* Upper Darby, Penn.: Project Management Institute, 1987.

Cibinic, John, Jr., and Ralph C. Nash, Jr. *Cost-Reimbursement Contracting.* 2nd ed. Washington, D.C.: The George Washington University, National Law Center, Government Contracts Program, 1993.

Cleland, David I., and Lewis R. Ireland. *Project Management: Strategic Design and Implementation*. 5th ed. New York: McGraw-Hill, 2007.

Cohen, Dennis J., and Robert J. Graham. *The Project Manager's MBA: How to Translate Project Decisions into Business Success*. San Francisco: Jossey-Bass, 2001.

Corbin, Arthur L. *Corbin on Contracts*. St. Paul, Minn.: West Publishing, 1952.

Covey, Stephen R. *The Seven Habits of Highly Effective People: Powerful Lessons in Personal Change*. New York: Free Press, 2004.

Crosby, Philip B. *Quality Is Free: The Art of Making Quality Certain*. New York: McGraw-Hill, 1979.

_____. *Quality Without Tears: The Art of Hassle-Free Management*. New York: McGraw-Hill, 1984; reprint, New York: Penguin Books, 1985.

Defense Systems Management College. *Risk Management: Concepts and Guidance*. Ft. Belvoir, Va.: Defense Systems Management College, 1989.

DeMarco, Tom, and Timothy Lister. *Peopleware: Productive Projects and Teams*. New York: Dorset House Publishing, 1987.

Dinsmore, Paul C. *Human Factors in Project Management*. Rev. ed. New York, NY: American Management Association, 1990.

Dinsmore, Paul C., and Manuel M. Benitez. "Challenges in Managing International Projects." *AMA Handbook of Project Management,* edited by Paul C. Dinsmore. New York: AMACOM Books, 1993, 463–464.

Dinsmore, Paul C., M. Dean Martin, and Gary T. Huettel. *The Project Manager's Work Environment: Coping with Time and Stress*. Upper Darby, Penn.: Project Management Institute, 1985.

Dobler, Donald W., and David N. Burt. *Purchasing and Supply Management: Text and Cases*. 6th ed. New York: McGraw-Hill, 1996.

Dreger, J. Brian. *Project Management: Effective Scheduling*. New York: Van Nostrand Reinhold, 1992.

Evans, James R., and William M. Lindsay. *The Management and Control of Quality*. 6th ed. Mason, Ohio: South-Western, 2005.

Ferraro, Gary P. *The Cultural Dimension of International Business*. 3rd ed. Upper Saddle River, N.J.: Prentice Hall, 1998.

Filley, Alan C. *Interpersonal Conflict Resolution*. Glenview, Ill.: Scott, Foresman, and Co., 1975.

Fisher, Roger, William Ury, and Bruce Patton. *Getting to Yes: Negotiating Agreement Without Giving In*. 2nd ed. New York: Penguin Books, 1991.

Fleming, Quentin W. *Cost/Schedule Control Systems Criteria: The Management Guide to C/SCSC*. Chicago: Probus Publishing, 1988.

_____. *Project Procurement Management Contracting, Subcontracting, Teaming.* Tustin, Calif.: FMC Press, 2003.

Fleming, Quentin W., and Joel M. Koppelman. *Earned Value Project Management.* 2nd ed. Newtown Square, Penn.: Project Management Institute, 2000.

Forsberg, Kevin, Hal Mooz, and Howard Cotterman. *Visualizing Project Management.* New York: John Wiley and Sons, 1996.

Frame, J. Davidson. *Managing Projects in Organizations: How to Make the Best Use of Time, Techniques, and People.* 3rd ed. San Francisco, Calif.: Jossey-Bass, 2003.

_____. *The New Project Management: Tools for an Age of Rapid Change, Corporate Reengineering, and Other Business Realities.* 2nd ed. San Francisco, Calif.: Jossey-Bass, 2002.

Friedman, Jack P. *Dictionary of Business Terms.* 2nd ed. Hauppauge, N.Y.: Barron's Educational Series, Inc., 1994.

Garrett, Gregory A. *World-Class Contracting.* 4th ed. Riverwoods, Ill.: CCH Incorporated, 2007.

Hirsch, William J. *The Contracts Management Deskbook.* Rev. ed. New York: American Management Association, 1986.

Imai, Masaaki. *Kaizen: The Key to Japan's Competitive Success.* New York: McGraw-Hill, 1986.

Ireland, Lewis R. *Quality Management for Projects and Programs.* Drexel Hill, Penn.: Project Management Institute, 1991.

Jentz, Gaylord A., Kenneth W. Clarkson, and Roger LeRoy Miller. *West's Business Law.* 2nd ed. St. Paul, Minn.: West Publishing, 1984.

Katzenbach, Jon R., and Douglas K. Smith. *The Wisdom of Teams.* New York: HarperBusiness, 1994.

Kerzner, Harold. *Project Management: A Systems Approach to Planning, Scheduling, and Controlling.* 9th ed. New York: John Wiley & Sons, Inc., 2006.

Kirchof, Nicki S., and John R. Adams. *Conflict Management for Project Managers.* Upper Darby, Penn.: Project Management Institute, 1989.

Kostner, Jaclyn. *Knights of the Tele-Round Table: Third Millennium Leadership.* New York: Warner Books, 1994.

Levin, Ginger, and Steven Flannes. *Essential People Skills for Project Managers.* Vienna, Va.: Management Concepts Inc., 2005.

Lewis, James P. *Project Planning, Scheduling, and Control.* Chicago: Probus Publishing, 1991.

Mansir, Brian E., and Nicholas R. Schacht. *An Introduction to the Continuous Improvement Process: Principles and Practices*. Bethesda, Md.: Logistics Management Institute, 1988.

Martin, Martin D., C. Claude Teagarden, and Charles F. Lambreth. *Contract Administration for the Project Manager*. Upper Darby, Penn.: Project Management Institute, 1990.

Maslow, Abraham H. *Motivation and Personality*. New York: Harper and Row, 1954.

McGregor, Douglas. *The Human Side of Enterprise*. New York: McGraw-Hill, 1960.

Meredith, Jack R., and Samuel J. Mantel, Jr. *Project Management: A Managerial Approach*. 7th ed. New York: John Wiley and Sons, 2009.

Pennypacker, James S., ed. *Principles of Project Management: Collected Handbooks from the Project Management Institute*. Sylva, N.C.: Project Management Institute, 1997.

PMI® (*see* Project Management Institute).

Pritchard, Carl L., ed. *Risk Management: Concepts and Guidance*. 3rd ed. Arlington, Va.: ESI International, 2005.

Project Management Institute. PMI® Code of Ethics and Professional Conduct. http://www.pmi.org/

_____. PMI® Conflict of Interest Policy. http://www.pmi.org/

_____. *A Guide to the Project Management Body of Knowledge, (PMBOK® Guide)*. 4th ed. Newtown Square, Penn.: Project Management Institute, 2008.

_____. *Practice Standard for Work Breakdown Structures*, 2nd ed. Newtown Square, Penn.: Project Management Institute, 2006

_____. *Project Management Experience and Knowledge Self-Assessment Manual*. Newtown Square, Penn.: Project Management Institute, 2000.

_____. *Project Management Professional (PMP®) Certification Handbook*. http://www.pmi.org/

_____. *Project Management Professional (PMP)*SM *Credential Handbook*, 2009. http://www.pmi.org/

_____. *Project Management Professional (PMP®) Examination Specification*, Newtown Square, Penn.: Project Management Institute, 2005

_____. *Project Management Professional (PMP®) Role Delineation Study*. Newtown Square, Penn.: Project Management Institute, 2000.

Rose, Kenneth H. *Project Quality Management: Why, What and How*. Boca Raton, Fla.: J. Ross Publishing, 2005.

Rosen, Robert, Patricia Digh, Marshall Singer, and Carl Phillips. *Global Literacies: Lesson on Business Leadership and National Cultures.* New York: Simon & Schuster, 2000.

Schmauch, Charles H. *ISO 9000 for Software Developers.* Milwaukee: ASQC Quality Press, 1994.

Soin, Sarv Singh. *Total Quality Control Essentials: Key Elements, Methodologies, and Managing for Success.* New York: McGraw-Hill, 1992.

Stuckenbruck, Linn C., ed. *The Implementation of Project Management: The Professional's Handbook.* Reading, Mass.: Addison-Wesley, 1981.

Stuckenbruck, Linn C., and David Marshall. *Team Building for Project Managers.* Upper Darby, Penn.: Project Management Institute, 1985.

Thamhain, Hans J., and David L. Wilemon. "Conflict Management in Project Life Cycles." *Sloan Management Review* 16, no. 3 (Spring 1975): 31–50.

Verma, Vijay K. *Human Resource Skills for the Project Manager.* Vol. 2 of *The Human Aspects of Project Management.* Upper Darby, Penn.: Project Management Institute, 1996.

_____. *Managing the Project Team.* Vol. 3 of *The Human Aspects of Project Management.* Upper Darby, Penn.: Project Management Institute, 1997.

_____. *Organizing Projects for Success.* Vol. 1 of *The Human Aspects of Project Management.* Upper Darby, Penn.: Project Management Institute, 1995.

Verzuh, Eric. *The Fast Forward MBA in Project Management.* Hoboken, N.J.: John Wiley & Sons, 2005.

Vroom, Victor H. *Work and Motivation.* San Francisco: Jossey-Bass, 1995.

Ward, J. LeRoy. *Dictionary of Project Management Terms.* 3rd ed. Arlington, Va.: ESI International, 2008.

Wideman, R. Max, ed. *Project and Program Risk Management: A Guide to Managing Project Risks and Opportunities.* Preliminary ed. Drexel Hill, Penn.: Project Management Institute, 1992.

Willborn, Walter, and T. C. Edwin Cheng. *Global Management of Quality Assurance Systems.* New York: McGraw-Hill, 1994.

Youker, Robert. "Communication Styles Instrument: A Team Building Tool." In *The Project Management Institute 1996 Proceedings: Revolutions, Evolutions, Project Solutions*, 27th Annual Seminars and Symposium, Papers Presented October 7–9, 1996, Boston, Mass., 796–799. Upper Darby, Penn.: Project Management Institute, 1996.

A NOTE TO OUR READERS

Preparing for the PMP® exam is strenuous and time consuming. We hope this tool significantly maximizes your study time. We tried to be as accurate and complete as possible, carefully checking the text and the references. But, given the nature of this collaborative work, some of the material may have fallen short of the mark.

The true test of this book's usefulness, however, is how well it helps you get ready for the PMP® exam. So let us know how it works for you. We welcome your comments and your suggestions for making the next edition even more useful.

Send your comments to—

Vice President, Product Development
ESI International
901 North Glebe Road, Suite 200
Arlington, VA 22203
Phone: 1-888-ESI-8884
Fax: 1-703-558-3001

Also From ESI International

***CBAP® Practice Test & Study Guide.* First Edition. $39.95.**
Glenn R. Brûlé

Prepare yourself to pass the Certified Business Analysis Professional™* (CBAP®)** certification exam with the help of this invaluable study guide! This book provides study hints, a list of exam topics, and 40 multiple-choice questions for each of the six content areas covered by the International Institute of Business Analysis (IIBA®)*** CBAP® exam. Add in two 150-question practice tests that are representative of the CBAP® exam, and you have the recipe for a structured preparation approach that will validate your knowledge and experience and that will familiarize you with industry phrases and terminology—all within a focused study that might otherwise prove to be overwhelming.

CAPM® Exam Online Practice Test. $39.95.

This 150-question, Web-based practice test precisely follows the PMI® CAPM® exam blueprint. You will answer the same number of questions in each of the *PMBOK® Guide* process areas as on the actual exam, including the professional responsibility domain. After logging in, you are given exactly three hours to take the exam, and the results are automatically scored, telling you the number of right and wrong answers in each of the process areas tested. Reduce your anxiety and let ESI help you to succeed. This Web-based practice test will greatly increase your chances of passing the CAPM® exam the first time.

***Dictionary of Project Management Terms.* Third edition. 2008. 512 pages. $39.95.**
J. LeRoy Ward, PMP, PgMP

Now in its third edition, this practical, pocket-sized book is more than 200 pages longer and includes 1,400 more terms than its last edition. The *Dictionary of Project Management Terms* contains 3,400 key terms, words, and phrases used in the day-to-day practice of project management. Along with traditional project management terms, it includes broader business terms to help seasoned managers and their successors navigate more easily the ubiquitous language of project-speak. You will find that the *Dictionary of Project Management Terms* provides you with a distinct advantage on every project you face!

---

* Certified Business Analysis Professional™ is a trademark owned by International Institute of Business Analysis.
** CBAP® is a registered certification mark owned by International Institute of Business Analysis. This certification mark is used with the express permission of International Institute of Business Analysis.
*** IIBA® is a registered trademark owned by International Institute of Business Analysis. It is used with the express permission of International Institute of Business Analysis.

Project Management Tools CD, Version 4.3. $125—individual license*.

This practical CD contains more than 100 tools and templates that cover all aspects of project management. These tools and templates will assist the project manager and the team through all the project processes. Each tool was developed by ESI for use in the field.
*For organization-wide use, please contact us at **totalsolutions@esi-intl.com**.

***The Complete Project Management Office Handbook*. Second edition. 2007. 752 pages. $59.99.**
Gerard M. Hill, PMP

This handbook offers a structured approach for developing critical project management capabilities through project management office (PMO) functionality. It describes 20 PMO functions that are crucial to defining and developing an effective approach to project oversight, control, and support.

PMP® Exam Online Practice Test. $39.95.

This 200-question, Web-based practice test precisely follows the PMI® PMP® exam blueprint. You will answer the same number of questions in each of the *PMBOK® Guide* process areas as on the actual exam, including the professional responsibility domain. And the questions are just like the ones that you will see on the real exam. After logging in, you are given exactly four hours to take the exam, and the results are automatically scored, telling you the number of right and wrong answers in each of the process areas tested. Don't use the real exam as your first "practice" test: Rather, reduce your anxiety and let ESI help you succeed. Together with our other proven PMP® exam study tools, this Web-based practice test will greatly increase your chances of passing the PMP® exam

The Portable PMP® Exam Prep: Conversations on Passing the PMP® Exam. Three volumes, nine CDs. Third edition. $99.95.
Carl L. Pritchard, PMP and J. LeRoy Ward, PMP, PgMP

This three-volume set of nine CDs addresses the nine areas of the project management body of knowledge and includes a bonus session on professional responsibility. Ward and Pritchard's informative, engaging style is easy to listen to, plus you can take the CDs anywhere you go. In addition, there are sessions on preparing for the current exam and test-taking tips that ESI students have found - indispensable.

***PMP® Exam Challenge!* Fifth edition. 2009. 600 pages. $48.95.**
J. LeRoy Ward, PMP, PgMP and Ginger Levin, DPA, PMP, PgMP

This easy-to-use, flashcard-format book lets you quiz yourself on all nine of the project management knowledge areas, as well as the professional and social responsibility domain. Each of the 600 questions includes references to the five project management process groups on the PMP® certification exam.

The Project Management Drill Book: A Self-Study Guide. 2003. 197 pages. $54.95.
Carl L. Pritchard, PMP

Gear up for the PMP® certification exam! Learn project management one drill at a time. ESI's *Project Management Drill Book* provides a provocative way to challenge you with hundreds of project management practice drills. From earned value to expected value, from precedence diagrams to decision trees and from the WBS to professional responsibility, this data-packed volume builds your understanding of the language and confidence in the practice of project management. Multiple-choice, fill-in-the-blank, and true-or-false drills deepen your understanding of available project management tools and how to use them effectively.

PMessentials: An Online Reference Tool®

PMessentials® provides online, just-in-time access to the information project managers need to solve problems and successfully manage their projects. It is designed to support your organization's ESI training and increase the productivity of your project managers.

With PMessentials®, users can search from a concise, targeted database of hundreds of ESI online learning materials. Users can customize their search by four categories:
1. Key Word or Phrase
2. *PMBOK® Guide* Knowledge Areas
3. ESI Core Project Management Course Content
4. ESI Tools

The comprehensive repository contains a variety of valuable resources, including:
- Expert Tips
- Simulated Web Sites
- Printable ESI Tools
- Comprehensive Project Management Glossary of Terms
- And much more

For more about PMessentials®, including licensing information, please call either **(877) 766-3337** or **+1 (703) 558-4445** or e-mail **totalsolutions@esi-intl.com.**

Precedence Diagramming: Successful Scheduling in a Team Environment. **Second edition. 2002. 62 pages. $25.**
Carl Pritchard, PMP

The biggest challenge in project management is bringing order to the sheer volume of competing priorities. By using precedence diagrams, project managers can clearly identify the sequence and interdependence of critical activities, clarify work processes and solidify team member roles and buy-in.

This concise overview teaches you how to construct and interpret precedence diagrams—the most common model used in software programs—and apply them to strengthen team commitment and project success.

Complimentary Resources from ESI

ESI offers a number of useful, free tools and resources covering essential topics such as:

- Managing Projects and Programs
- Building Business Analysis Competencies
- Developing Critical "Soft Skills"
- Managing Vendor Relationships
- Applying Earned Value Management

White Papers

ESI offers informative, complimentary white papers on the trends and real-world issues professionals and organizations face in project management, sourcing management, business analysis and business skills. ESI's white papers are designed to give you the resources you need to take actionable, real-world approaches to solving business problems. Download a complimentary white paper today at **www.esi-intl.com/whitepaper**.

Podcasts

Download ESI podcasts to your MP3 player for free and listen to them in the office, at the gym, on a plane or anywhere else in the world. Project managers and business analysts who listen to these podcasts are eligible for Self Directed Learning (SDL) PDUs from the Project Management Institute (PMI®). Visit **www.esi-intl.com/podcast** today.

Webinars

Watch on-demand presentations online from top industry experts on the issues you deal with daily on the job. Project managers, business analysts, contract managers and program managers will find these online seminars valuable to their professional development. ESI's library of on-demand Webinars are available any time you want, as often as you want. Download a Webinar today at **www.esi-intl.com/webinar**.

ESI Horizons Newsletter

ESI Horizons is a free, monthly newsletter focusing on issues, processes and challenges in project management and business analysis. As a subscriber, you'll receive an e-mail notification each month when the newest issue is live. You'll also have access to the *Horizons* archives, where you can view past articles. Subscribe today! Americas: **www.esi-intl.com/horizons** EMEA: **www.esi-emea.com** Asia: **www.esi-intl.com.sg**

Individual and Organizational Assessments

Whether you're focusing on individual capabilities, or measuring the knowledge and skills of your organization as a whole, ESI has assessment services to help you identify strengths and areas that need improvement.

Individual Assessments

By assessing individual competencies for each employee, you can more effectively target your training efforts, set pre- and post-course benchmarks to measure success and determine areas in which training reinforcement is necessary.

Our **appraisal products** provide a snapshot of your team's grasp of best-in-class methods and techniques. This ensures that your employees are receiving the training they need and that you're getting the most from your training dollars.

ESI can also help you assess employee competency beyond technical knowledge. Our **360-degree evaluation** measures project manager's hard and soft skills and provides detailed reports of their effectiveness in these key categories:
- Organizational and industry acumen
- Process expertise
- Customer focus
- Team leadership, communications and effectiveness

Organizational Assessments

ESI's **Organizational Maturity Assessments** help assess the maturity and capability of your organization and provide recommendations on how to improve efficiency and effectiveness. By assessing organizational performance, you can ensure that you have the systems and processes in place to efficiently complete your projects on time and on budget while also identifying obstacles in the way of success.

With ESI's data-driven assessment models, you can—
- Analyze your project managers' performance within your organization
- Baseline project management capability
- Identify organizational executive-level involvement
- Develop short- and long-term improvement strategies

In addition to conducting organizational maturity assessments, ESI has a proven track record in conducting **Level 3 Training Assessments**, which can help you gain insight into how much of your employees' new knowledge is being applied back on the job after their training is complete. You'll be able to evaluate the value of your investment and identify the key catalysts for success and the key obstacles that often lead to below-par results.

For more information about ESI's individual and organizational assessments, please call **(877) 766-3337** or **+1 (703) 558-4445** or e-mail **totalsolutions@esi-intl.com.**